Posttraumatic Stress

Posttraumatic Stress Disorder: A Clinical Review

Edited by Robert S. Pynoos, M.D., M.P.H.

The Sidran Press
2328 West Joppa Road
Suite 15
Lutherville, MD 21093
(410) 825-8888

The views expressed by individual contributors in this book do not necessarily represent the policies and opinions of The Sidran Press or The Sidran Foundation for Mental Illness. Contributors' comments about therapy should not be considered medical advice. The editors and publisher of this volume recommend that readers follow the advice of a physician who is directly involved in their care or the care of a member of their family.

Copyright 1994 The Sidran Press. All rights reserved. No part of this book may be used or reproduced in any manner whatsoever without written permission except in the case of brief quotations embodied in critical articles or reviews. For information write The Sidran Press, 2328 W. Joppa Rd., Suite 15, Lutherville, MD 21093, (410) 825-8888.

Permission was granted by American Psychiatric Press, Inc. to reprint this material from *Review of Psychiatry, Volume 12, 1993*, edited by John M. Oldham, M.D., Michelle B. Riba, M.D., and Allan Tasman, M.D. First published by American Psychiatric Press, Inc., Washington, D.C. and London, England. Copyright 1993. All rights reserved.

International Standard Book Number: 0-9629164-4-7
Library of Congress Card Catalogue Number: 93-087409
Printed in the United States of America

Posttraumatic stress disorder : a clinical review / edited by Robert S. Pynoos.
   p. cm.
   Includes bibliographical references.
   Preassigned LCCN: 93-087409.
   ISBN 0-9629164-4-7

   1. Post-traumatic stress disorder.   I. Pynoos, Robert S., 1947-

RC552.P67P67 1994   616.85'21
                               QBI93-22527

Posttraumatic Stress Disorder: A Clinical Review

Contents

Introduction	vii
Preface	ix
Robert S. Pynoos, M.D., M.P.H., Editor	

Chapter 1 — 1
Issues in the Diagnosis of Posttraumatic Stress Disorder
Jonathan Davidson, M.D.

What Characterizes an Event as Traumatic?	1
Singular or Plural: Traumatic Stress Disorder or Traumatic Stress Disorders?	6
Cohesiveness of PTSD	10
Pretrauma and Interactive Risks for PTSD	12
Conclusion	13
References	14

Chapter 2 — 17
Ethnocultural Aspects of Posttraumatic Stress Disorder
Anthony J. Marsella, Ph.D., Matthew J. Friedman, M.D., Ph.D., and E. Huland Spain, Ph.D.

Overview of the Research and Clinical Literature	19
Basic Considerations in Conducting Ethnocultural Research on PTSD	29
Conducting Cross-Cultural Studies of PTSD	33
Closing Thoughts and Conclusions	34
References	36

Chapter 3 — 43
Neurobiology of Posttraumatic Stress Disorder
J. Douglas Bremner, M.D., Michael Davis, Ph.D., Steven M. Southwick, M.D., John H. Krystal, M.D., and Dennis S. Charney, M.D.

Noradrenergic Brain Systems	44
Corticotropin-Releasing Factor-Hypothalamic-Pituitary-Adrenal Axis System	48
Dopaminergic Brain Systems	50
Benzodiazepine Brain Systems	51
Endogenous Opiate Systems	52
Neural Mechanisms of Learning and Memory: Relevance to the Re-experiencing of PTSD Symptoms	53

Neural Mechanisms of Extinction: Relevance to the Chronicity of PTSD Symptoms	55
Neural Mechanisms of Behavioral Sensitization in PTSD	55
Deficits in Short-Term Memory in PTSD	56
Concluding Comments	58
References	61

Chapter 4   65
Traumatic Stress and Developmental Psychopathology in Children and Adolescents
Robert S. Pynoos, M.D., M.P.H.

Traumatic Stress	66
Resistance and Vulnerability to the Traumatic Experience(s)	74
Distress	76
Complex of Proximal Stress-Related Pathology	79
Potential Effects of Traumatic Stress on Proximal Development	80
Resilience and Adjustment	84
Effects on Emerging Personality and Distal Development	88
Complex of Distal Posttraumatic Stress-Related Pathology	91
Conclusion	93
References	93

Chapter 5   99
An Integrated Approach for Treating Posttraumatic Stress
Charles R. Marmar, M.D., David Foy, Ph.D., Bruce Kagan, M.D., Ph.D., and Robert S. Pynoos, M.D., M.P.H.

Factors Influencing the Response to Trauma	99
Dynamic Psychotherapy of PTSD	105
Cognitive-Behavior Treatment of PTSD	111
Psychopharmacologic Treatment of PTSD	117
Common Goals and Change Mechanisms	126
References	130

Chapter 6   133
Posttraumatic Stress Disorder and Rape
Edna B. Foa, Ph.D. and David S. Riggs, Ph.D.

Postrape Psychopathology	134
Etiology of PTSD: An Information-Processing Perspective	135
Development of PTSD: Empirical Studies	144
Treatment of Rape-Related PTSD	153
Conclusion	157
References	158

Afterword	165
Robert S. Pynoos, M.D., M.P.H., Editor	
Contributors	169
About the Sidran Foundation	171

Posttraumatic Stress Disorder
Introduction

Early in 1993, the Sidran Press published *Dissociative Disorders: A Clinical Review*, a volume that originally was part of the American Psychiatric Association's *Review of Psychiatry, Volume 10, 1991*. This book has been very well-received by professionals in a range of disciplines, as well as interested patients and family members. We are pleased that American Psychiatric Press has granted us permission to reprint the section concerning posttraumatic stress disorders (PTSD)—originally a part of the *Review of Psychiatry, Volume 12, 1993*—in an inexpensive paperback edition.

While trauma and its aftereffects have been around for centuries, it is only in the past several decades that they have been paid significant attention by the psychotherapeutic community. In this volume a variety of distinguished mental health professionals—writing primarily for other professionals, but in language that is accessible to educated lay readers—consider issues of diagnosis, ethnic and cultural variations in the incidence and distribution of PTSD, neurobiology (the effects of stress on the body and its systems), PTSD in children and adolescents, and treatment approaches. In addition, the final chapter focuses on rape and its traumatic aftereffects.

This book is intended to shed light on posttraumatic stress and its resulting symptoms, bringing state-of-the-art information about the disorder to a broader audience, thus helping trauma victims in the process of healing.

Esther Giller
The Sidran Foundation

Posttraumatic Stress Disorder
Preface

by Robert S. Pynoos, M.D. M.P.H., Editor

It has been just over a decade since the inclusion of posttraumatic stress disorder (PTSD) in DSM-III (American Psychiatric Association 1980), and 5 years since DSM-III-R (American Psychiatric Association 1987) made specific mention of the clinical presentation in children. During this period there has been a rapid growth of interest in this diagnosis among clinicians and researchers. However, the diagnosis remains controversial. In great measure, this is due to the special place PTSD occupies within psychiatric nosology, where the diagnostic gateway is the occurrence of a specific personal experience. In a dramatic fashion, PTSD reopened the psychiatric door to the serious vicissitudes of life, and there has been tremendous clinical pressure to push through this opening an enormous backlog of human experience that otherwise seems to have no place in an "etiologically free" classification system. If this opportunity is not to be lost, great care and discipline are needed to ensure that we proceed on a sound scientific and clinical course.

In Chapter 1, "Issues in the Diagnosis of Posttraumatic Stress Disorder," Dr. Davidson presents an up-to-date review of current issues in the diagnosis of PTSD and other related disorders. The discussion concerns what characterizes an event as being traumatic, how well the diagnosis of PTSD accounts for trauma-related psychopathological states, how cohesive is the symptomatology of PTSD across different types of traumatic stresses, and what is the role of premorbid risk factors and their interactions with the event and the severity and course of PTSD. Dr. Davidson summarizes the growing clinical consensus that the symptoms seen in victims of repeated or prolonged interpersonal brutality and abuse are not totally captured by the diagnostic criteria for PTSD.

In Chapter 2, "Ethnocultural Aspects of Posttraumatic Stress Disorder," Drs. Marsella, Friedman, and Spain present a comprehensive overview of ethnocultural aspects of PTSD. The authors include discussion of epidemiological and clinical studies of PTSD among refugees (both adults and children), victims of natural disasters, victims of political and interpersonal violence, and military veterans. Traumatic experiences are deeply embedded in a cultural context that permeates the experience, meaning, and assimilation of traumatic stresses; symptom presentation; expectations in regard to recovery; and family, community, and societal responsiveness. The authors make research and clinical recommendations to achieve cultural sensitivity in assessment procedures and to improve the ethnocultural applicability of intervention strategies, including psychotherapy and psychopharmacology.

One of the most active areas of current research is the topic of Chapter 3, "Neurobiology of Posttraumatic Stress Disorder." Drs. Bremner, Davis, Southwick, Krystal, and Charney summarize the scientific evidence that extreme threat constitutes a major biological challenge that results in long-term changes in behavior and neurobiological systems. The authors focus on the interrelatedness of neurohormonal responses, neurophysiological pathways, and neurocommunication processes, both regional and global, that constitute a biological substrate to PTSD. They also describe the self-preservative functions of these complicated neuromechanisms in enhancing memory, attention, and vigilance, which can induce long-term alterations in brain memory systems. They argue that these chronic changes underlie a number of core symptoms of PTSD, including memory disturbances, and, in many respects, reflect a biological response that persists long after its utility for the individual.

Nowhere is the effort to elucidate the rightful place of traumatic experiences in the framework of psychopathology more important than in considering children and adolescents. As PTSD has become a more accepted diagnosis, there appears to have been a trend for this concept to be reified, and to lose the intimate union of traumatic stress and human development. In **Chapter 4,** "Traumatic Stress and Developmental Psychopathology in Children and Adolescents," Dr. Pynoos offers an expanded conceptual scheme to characterize the complex interactions of child development with traumatic stress and its sequelae. A developmental psychopathology perspective suggests important areas of clinical assessment and intervention, and new avenues for future research. This perspective includes the use of more rigorous descriptive typologies of traumatic exposures, reminders, and secondary stresses as these relate to proximal and distal risks of stress-related psychopathology, developmental disturbances, and maladaptive adjustment.

In Chapter 5, "An Integrated Approach for Treating Posttraumatic Stress," Drs. Marmar, Foy, Kagan, and Pynoos present an integrated approach for treating PTSD. Until recently, different therapeutic modalities were being pursued in research and clinical practice in relative isolation from one another. However, the field of traumatic stress studies has progressed to the point where there is a healthy trend toward rapprochement among those oriented to psychodynamic, cognitive-behavioral, and psychopharmacologic approaches. Within each modality, there is accumulating empirical evidence to provide a basis for rational clinical decision making, including indications for varying treatment strategies, depending on where a patient rests along the continuum of normative reactions or acute or chronic PTSD. The three modalities provide complementary perspectives in addressing the attribution of meaning, acquisition of new fears, reactivity to external and internal reminders, and disturbances in the stability of self-concepts and biological systems.

Unlike the other chapters in this section, which focus on general themes in the area of PTSD, Drs. Foa and Riggs focus on a single type of trauma in Chapter 6, "Posttraumatic Stress Disorder and Rape." Rape stands at the forefront of civilian traumatic experiences, both in its incidence and its powerful etiological role in the onset of PTSD. The authors provide an in-depth analysis of the rape experience and its sequelae, utilizing a sophisticated information-processing framework to account for the psychological processes that lead to and maintain PTSD. This model focuses on the generation of perceptions of the world as dangerous and uncontrollable and the acquisition or reactivation of negative self-schemata, including guilt. The authors emphasize a cognitive-behavior treatment approach that addresses both the organization of the trauma memory and the impact on self-schema.

REFERENCES

American Psychiatric Association: Diagnostic and Statistical Manual of Mental Disorders, 3rd Edition. Washington, DC, American Psychiatric Association, 1980

American Psychiatric Association: Diagnostic and Statistical Manual of Mental Disorders, 3rd Edition, Revised. Washington, DC, American Psychiatric Association, 1987

Chapter 1

Issues in the Diagnosis of Posttraumatic Stress Disorder

Jonathan Davidson, M.D.

Few psychiatric disorders are defined on the basis of etiology; most are phenomenologically defined symptoms. Of the few etiologically defined disorders in the *Diagnostic and Statistical Manual of Mental Disorders,* 3rd Edition, Revised (DSM-III-R) (American Psychiatric Association 1987), posttraumatic stress disorder (PTSD) has perhaps generated the greatest attention over the last few years. It also serves as a touchstone for a number of general questions about the nature of psychiatric illness. These questions include the etiology of psychiatric disorder, the nature of stress, the relationship between stress and onset of illness, the interrelationship between stress and individual risk factors, and the placement of individual psychiatric disorders within a nomenclature system.

In this chapter, I focus on four questions: What characterizes an event as being traumatic? How well does PTSD account for the universe of trauma-induced psychopathological states? How cohesive is the symptomatology of PTSD across groups? What are the premorbid risk factors for PTSD and their interactions with the event? To begin with, the current DSM-III-R criteria for PTSD are described (Table 1–1).

WHAT CHARACTERIZES AN EVENT AS TRAUMATIC?

One event may have widely differing effects on two people. Taking aerial combat as an example, Bond (1952) noted that chance factors could determine whether a traumatic event induced psychiatric symptoms. Such factors as position in the flying formation, individual perceptions of a wounded or parachuting man, personal acquaintance with the wounded individual, the expression on a wounded man's face, and degree of injury all influenced the "traumatogenicity" of an event. There may be little uniformity about traumatic events, and the above description makes it clear that specific details need to be understood about each experience, including characteristics of the event itself and the perceptions, affects, and interpretations on the part of the victim. These are addressed in the following paragraphs.

The foregoing considerations remind us that a comprehensive assessment of the traumatic event, and the victim's reactions to it, is an essential part of the diagnostic workup. Furthermore, as trauma evaluations become more detailed, our understanding of trauma becomes more complex. Differences in evaluation techniques can also account, in part, for some of the inconsistencies and disagreements in the literature.

Table 1-1. DSM-III-R diagnostic criteria for posttraumatic stress disorder

A. The person has experienced an event that is outside the range of usual human experience and that would be markedly distressing to almost anyone.

B. The traumatic event is persistently reexperienced in at least one of the following ways:
  (1) recurrent and intrusive distressing recollections of the event
  (2) recurrent distressing dreams of the event
  (3) sudden acting or feeling as if the traumatic event were recurring
  (4) intense psychological distress at exposure to events that symbolize or resemble an aspect of the traumatic event, including anniversaries of the trauma

C. Persistent avoidance of stimuli associated with the trauma or numbing of general responsiveness (not present before the trauma), as indicated by at least three of the following:
  (1) efforts to avoid thoughts or feelings associated with the trauma
  (2) efforts to avoid activities or situations that arouse recollections of the trauma
  (3) inability to recall an important aspect of the trauma
  (4) markedly diminished interest in significant activities
  (5) feeling of detachment or estrangement from others
  (6) restricted range of affect
  (7) sense of a foreshortened future

D. Persistent symptoms of increased arousal (not present before the trauma), as indicated by at least two of the following:
  (1) difficulty falling or staying asleep
  (2) irritability or outbursts of anger
  (3) difficulty concentrating
  (4) hypervigilance
  (5) exaggerated startle response
  (6) physiologic reactivity upon exposure to events that symbolize or resemble an aspect of the traumatic event

E. Duration of the disturbance (symptoms in B, C, and D) of at least 1 month.

Source. Modified from American Psychiatric Association: *Diagnostic and Statistical Manual of Mental Disorders,* 3rd Edition, Revised. Washington, DC, American Psychiatric Association, 1987, pp. 250–251. Used with permission.

Characteristics of the Event

Originally, in DSM-III (American Psychiatric Association 1980, p. 238), PTSD could be diagnosed only in the wake of a "recognizable stressor that would evoke symptoms of significant distress in almost everyone." This definition was broadened in DSM-III-R to include those events that were "outside the range of usual human experience and that would be markedly distressing to almost anyone" (p. 250).

The major purpose of such a definition was to distinguish unusual stresses, with which people are unprepared to deal, from the everyday stresses, which can be expected to affect everybody at one time or another. The origins of this distinction lay in the well-established tradition that a special phenomenological, and probably etiological, link existed between the symptom picture now known as PTSD and untoward stresses. Belief in this unique connection has received epidemiological validation (Davidson and Fairbank 1993). A second reason was to give due recognition to the needs of a special group of people: those who had undergone exceptional privation, suffering, or loss. Hitherto, no category of psychiatric disorder had adequately represented this phenomenon, although certain parts of it no doubt could be spoken for by one or another disorder.

Despite the obvious advance made by defining a traumatic event and its linkage to the PTSD symptom picture, at least two problems became apparent.

First, it was by no means certain how well people might agree on the two parameters of trauma: the degree of unusualness and the universally distressing nature of the event. As we have increasingly recognized, a number of traumatic events, such as incest, rape, and criminal assault, are far from being rare (Herman 1993; Kilpatrick and Resnick 1993; Norris 1992). Does this then invalidate such events as being traumatic? Obviously, the answer is that it does not. The second part of the definition, marked distress in almost everyone, presupposes that most people can agree on the difference between moderate and marked distress, for which no guidelines have ever been given.

The second problem relates to the incomplete way in which DSM-III-R addressed the importance of the subjective perception and appraisal in response to an event. As we have seen, this is very likely to be important, perhaps of equal importance as the event itself. The DSM-III-R text acknowledges this in stating that the stressor is usually experienced with intense fear, terror, and helplessness. All three affects are assumed to result, but data have not been provided to support this.

In examining the matter of how one might define the trauma (i.e., criterion A of the PTSD diagnostic criteria), the DSM-IV PTSD work group made a number of observations and suggestions, summarized below, after a review of pertinent literature in this area.

Trauma Intensity

March (1993) reviewed the literature on what makes a stressor traumatic. In the great majority of studies reviewed, a linear relationship emerged between stressor magnitude and risk of developing PTSD. If one divides stressors into low- and high-magnitude types, using admittedly arbitrary distinctions, then it appears that low-magnitude events (e.g., divorce, loss of job, uncomplicated bereavement) are rarely associated with PTSD. Unfortunately, no real conclusions can be drawn yet, since few studies have carefully controlled in a prospective fashion for stressor magnitude.

A twin study by Goldberg et al. (1990) found a positive relationship between intensity of combat exposure and risk of PTSD in monozygotic twins. When genetic variance is controlled, the risk of PTSD rises with exposure intensity from 1.7% under noncombat conditions to 3.0%, 5.3%, and 9.2%, respectively, for low, medium, and high levels of combat. This study speaks especially clearly to the influence of trauma intensity because it controls, as no other study has done, for the provable effects of genetic variability.

Risk Factors in the Event

Kilpatrick and Resnick (1993) demonstrated a relationship between certain event characteristics and risk of PTSD in crime victims. In those who experienced neither life-threat nor injury, the prevalence rates ranged from 9.1% to 14.7%. With life-threat, they increased to 34.5%–38.6%; with injury, they increased further to 42.9%. When life-threat and injury were both present, prevalence rates increased to 59.2%–65.9%. Similar findings occurred in all three PTSD symptom categories.

In a report by Davidson and Smith (1990), the risk of PTSD following trauma was associated with physical injury, seeing a physician after the event (for nonpsychiatric reasons), and being hospitalized (for nonpsychiatric reasons). Blank (1993) suggested that an event is traumatic if it involves a personal experience or witnessing of death, threat of death, or injury.

Subjective Appraisal

A number of subjective factors are likely to influence the response to a traumatic event or to create the perception of traumatogenicity. These include unpreparedness (Davidson and Smith 1990), extreme fear, terror (American Psychiatric Association 1987; March 1993), denial and avoidance (Green et al. 1985; Solomon et al. 1988), and lack of controllability (Frye and Stockton 1982).

This review poses an important and, as yet, unanswered question: To what extent are the PTSD symptoms related to intensity of, characteristics of, and subjective response to the trauma? Previous studies of PTSD have always linked the trauma (criterion A) to symptoms of intrusion, avoidance or numbing, and hyperarousal (B, C, D criteria, respectively). No serious attempt has previously been made to examine criterion A in relation to these criteria. The ongoing DSM-IV field trials are now doing so, and their results will be forthcoming.

Proposed Definitions of Criterion A

The matter of defining criterion A is crucial because the remaining symptoms or criteria of PTSD depend for their diagnostic existence on being linked to the stressor criterion. As an example, by slightly varying the way in which criterion A is defined, prevalence rates of PTSD can vary from 1.8% to 12.0% in a veteran population (Snow et al. 1988).

A number of definitions have been proposed for criterion A—all of which are being considered for inclusion in DSM-IV. These definitions are as follows:

- DSM-III-R. "The person has experienced an event that is outside the range of usual human experience and that would be markedly distressing to almost anyone, e.g., serious threat to one's life or physical integrity; serious threat or harm to one's children, spouse, or other close relatives and friends; sudden destruction of one's home or community; or seeing another person who has recently been, or is being, seriously injured or killed as the result of an accident or physical violence" (p. 250).
- ICD-10 (World Health Organization 1992). Exposure to an exceptional mental or physical stressor, either brief or prolonged.
- DSM-IV (Proposal 1). The person has experienced, witnessed, or been confronted with an event or events that involve actual or threatened death or injury, or a threat to the physical integrity of oneself or others.
- DSM-IV (Proposal 2). The person has been exposed to a traumatic event in which both of the following have been present:

   A. The person has experienced, witnessed, or been confronted with an event or events that involve actual or threatened death or injury, or a threat to the physical integrity of oneself or others.
   B. The person's response involved intense fear, helplessness, or horror.

The second of the two proposed definitions will probably be adopted in DSM-IV, but there will be continuing debate and further study of this very important question that may one day illuminate the nature and effects of stress, and the host organism's response as mediated by protective or vulnerability factors.

A related question arises as to the specificity of the relationship between trauma as defined in, say, DSM-III or DSM-III-R, and the diagnosis of PTSD. Is there any evidence to support the view that high-magnitude stress gives rise to PTSD more often than other disorders? Or is it merely a nonspecific, yet extreme, stress that can provoke a wide range of psychopathology?

Two epidemiological studies showed that PTSD in the community increased in association with a volcanic eruption (Shore et al. 1986) and sexual assault (Winfield et al. 1990). Shore et al. demonstrated that only 3 of 13 possible psychiatric disorders increased in the year after Mount Saint Helens in Washington erupted—all 3 disorders were heavily colored with PTSD symptomatology (PTSD, first episode depression, generalized anxiety disorder). Winfield et al., although unable to identify age at onset of PTSD, showed that PTSD was one of only a few psychiatric disorders to increase in association with sexual assault. Disorders ongoing after the trauma were major depression and alcohol and substance abuse. PTSD also increased in frequency, but age of onset was not determined. Thus, the epidemiological literature provides some construct validity in support of the traditional clinical beliefs embodied in DSM-III and DSM-III-R regarding PTSD.

SINGULAR OR PLURAL: TRAUMATIC STRESS DISORDER OR TRAUMATIC STRESS DISORDERS?

Nosological recognition of PTSD authenticates the notion of trauma-related psychiatric disorder. However, it is now widely recognized that PTSD as the only "official" trauma-induced disorder does scant justice to the full panoply of trauma-associated disturbances; many other states must surely exist. I first consider those conditions that are already recognized in DSM-III-R as an outcome of trauma, some of which are rarely used; certainly their use in a medicolegal context is unusual. Then I review proposed trauma-related disorders, currently unrepresented in DSM-III-R. These disorders could ultimately form the basis of an expanded category of psychological disorders related to trauma (perhaps in DSM-V).

Recognized Trauma-Related Disorders

Brief reactive psychosis. This disorder is of sudden onset and of no more than 1 month's duration, with full return of premorbid function. The psychotic symptoms appear shortly after one or more events that, singly or together, would be markedly stressful to almost anyone in similar circumstances in that person's culture. This is really a variant of acute PTSD, which would probably have been labeled as such in DSM-I (American Psychiatric Association 1952).

Multiple personality disorder. In this disorder, at least two distinct personalities or personality states exist within the person. Such changes occur suddenly. In nearly all cases, multiple personality disorder has been preceded by abuse or other form of severe emotional trauma in childhood.

Dissociative fugue. Dissociative fugue results in sudden, unexpected disappearance from home or work, usually with the assumption of a new identity and inability to recall the previous identity. Like brief reactive psychosis, it is of short duration. It usually follows severe psychosocial stress, such as marital quarrels, personal rejection, military conflict, or a natural disaster.

Dissociative amnesia. Dissociative amnesia can refer both to the diagnosis and to a characteristic dissociative symptom of PTSD. A diagnosis is given in the presence of sudden inability to recall important personal information beyond a degree that could be put down to ordinary forgetfulness. It follows severe psychosocial stress, often involving a threat of physical injury or death or abandonment. Other stresses can include unacceptable impulses or acts.

Conversion disorder. Extreme psychosocial stress (e.g., warfare or recent death of a significant figure) can predispose to this disorder of altered physical functioning, which is usually of sudden onset and offset.

Depersonalization disorder. Severe stress, such as military combat or an auto accident, may result in this disorder, which is one of altered experience of the self. It is usually of rapid onset and gradual offset.

Dream anxiety disorder. This infrequently described disorder consists of repeated awakenings from sleep with detailed recall of frightening dreams. About 60% of cases describe a prior major life stress. Sleep disturbance in general, either as a primary problem or as symptomatic of some other disorder (e.g., depression, substance abuse or withdrawal), can often serve as the herald of a traumatically induced disorder.

Somatization disorder. This disorder of chronic or recurrent, multiple, somatic complaints, beginning prior to age 30 and carrying a dramatic quality, is probably a long-term outcome of early abuse in many instances.

Borderline personality disorder. This disorder is characterized by pervasive instability of self-image, mood, and interpersonal relationships. Among its constituents are many with a history of early childhood trauma.

Antisocial personality disorder. This condition of irresponsible antisocial behavior, beginning in childhood or adolescence, can sometimes arise from predisposing abuse as a child.

Postulated Trauma-Related Disorders

Acute traumatic stress. There is a strong tradition to support the existence of acute disorganizational states in the immediate aftermath of trauma. These states may include dissociative or psychotic behavior, psychomotor agitation or retardation, insomnia, and extreme emotional lability. The relation between such reactions and brief reactive psychosis needs further clarification. The inclusion of such an entity in DSM-IV remains under consideration. ICD-10 has proposed an acute stress reaction, defined as occurring within 1 hour of exposure to trauma and being of short duration.

Disorders of extreme stress not otherwise specified. It is believed that the symptom criteria for PTSD do not adequately reflect, nor do they represent, the clinical phenomena found in victims of repeated or prolonged trauma that has been brought about by brutal or abusive treatment at the hands of others. Such traumata might include incest, repeated abuse in childhood, spouse abuse, captivity, or torture.

Herman (1993) outlined the essential features of a syndrome that is believed to be sufficiently different from PTSD that it should warrant a separate diagnosis. No name has yet received general acceptance, but the terms *victimization disorder* and *disorder of extreme stress not otherwise specified* (DESNOS) have been advanced. Whether or not the official nomenclature adopts such a condition, it is important that experienced clinicians seem to agree broadly on its existence and its features. To describe these can be useful, not only as a way of informing, but also because knowledge of the concept may help with clinical management.

There appear to be three ways in which the phenomena of DESNOS transcend those of PTSD. These relate to symptoms, character (personality), and repeated harm-seeking behaviors.

SYMPTOMS

Symptoms of DESNOS are generally more severe and polymorphic than in other disorders. Specific symptoms include

- *Somatization.* Headache, abdominal, back or pelvic pain, nausea,

choking, and gastrointestinal disturbances may occur. It is likely that these symptoms represent somatic expression of earlier trauma, and it is of interest that in Briquet's (1859) original description of somatization disorder, more than 40% had been the victim of childhood abuse.
- *Dissociation.* There is much evidence to suggest increased rates of dissociative symptoms in those who are held captive and in survivors of childhood abuse. These are particularly evident among individuals with multiple personality disorder. An association has been found between severity of childhood abuse and extent of dissociative symptoms in patients with borderline personality disorder (Herman et al. 1989).
- *Affective symptoms.* The losses, humiliation, and betrayal of trust, which are the result of abusive trauma, can give rise to persistent and often profound depression. Chronic suicidality may also supervene. This form of traumatic depression is often misread by therapists, who see in such a patient merely the depression but miss its underlying traumatic origin.

PERSONALITY CHANGES
- *Pathological relationships.* Perpetrators of violence and abuse can be expected to establish relationships with their victims characterized by control, isolation, and intimidation. A victim may therefore develop extreme dependency on the abuser ("traumatic bonding"), avoidance of relationships with others, passivity, a sense of powerlessness, and fear of abandonment. Melges and Swartz (1989) described the oscillations between extreme submissiveness and rebelliousness in traumatized individuals with a diagnosis of borderline personality disorder.
- *Changes in identity.* Altered sense of self can range from occasional feelings of not being one's self, to the fragmented self of multiple personality, all the way through to losing the sense of self altogether. Any of these may be found in victims of chronic abuse or brutality. Belief of the self as evil may also be found.

HARM SEEKING AND REVICTIMIZATION
Self-injurious or suicidal behavior, already referred to, may be found frequently in victims of chronic child abuse, but is rare after single traumatization. Reexposure to adult traumatization occurs, as exemplified by rape and battery. Previously abused children can also turn into child or spouse abusers themselves once they reach adulthood (Herman 1993).

In summary, the literature and clinical experience of many traumatologists suggest that serious consideration needs to be given to the concept of a DESNOS-like entity. It is currently being tested in field trials, in which it is hoped to determine if it meets acceptable reliability and validity. DESNOS may conceptually be related to a proposed entity in DSM-IV referred to as *personality change disorders*. One of the proposed disorders in this category, termed *personality change resulting from catastrophic experience*, bears a number of similarities to DESNOS, but it also differs in important ways. Unlike DESNOS, this proposed condition explicitly describes clinically significant personality change following severe stressors in individuals without preexisting vulnerability; that is, the absence of pretraumatic maladaptive personality features must have been established.

Posttraumatic depression. The enmeshing of clinical depression with DESNOS has been described above. It appears that yet another form of depression may emerge following single-episode traumata in adulthood. After the eruption of Mount Saint Helens volcano, increases were noted in PTSD, generalized anxiety disorder, and depression over the next year. Of interest was the fact that those with depression had no previous history of depression (i.e., may have had lower risk for the illness in the absence of extreme stress), and that several of the key PTSD manifestations were also present. Biological findings tend to support the existence of a form of depression following trauma that is distinct from primary major depression (e.g., Yehuda et al. 1990).

In reviewing the various syndromes that may develop following trauma, it is important to note that several of them may coexist or follow one another in various sequences. For example, a trauma victim may have PTSD, borderline personality disorder, and acute episodes of conversion disorder. The patterning and combining of these entities is often multidetermined, but in many cases of early or chronic victimization, personality development and self-image are adversely affected such that enduring and pathological personality traits appear. This is in part captured by the DESNOS criteria. DESNOS addresses primarily the phenomena that may follow repeated early traumatization; ICD-10 proposes a category of enduring personality changes after catastrophic experience, which applies to adult victims of later trauma.

COHESIVENESS OF PTSD

Establishment of a diagnosis requires the demonstration that its criteria are invariant with respect to the population. Thus little difference should be observed among victim groups. To a large extent, this appears to be the case.

In adult victims of crime, Kilpatrick and Resnick (1993) showed that all PTSD symptoms in DSM-III-R occurred frequently and with a high degree of correct classification in community subjects. They also addressed the question of avoidance symptoms, finding that a number of distressed traumatized individuals failed to exhibit the required three avoidance symptoms. They raised the question as to whether the threshold was set too high with respect to this criterion and suggested that a minimum of two avoidant symptoms be required. Analysis of data showed that by reducing the minimum number of criteria from three to two, the prevalence rate of PTSD rose by 15%–16%.

In veterans and in disaster victims, the 15 DSM-III-R PTSD symptoms show good internal cohesiveness as a group, with high intercorrelations (Green 1993; Keane 1993).

A principal components analysis of DSM-III-R PTSD symptoms in Vietnam veterans affirmed the tripartite division of symptoms into intrusive, avoidant, and hyperarousal groups. Of special interest was a finding that PTSD avoidant symptoms (the C criteria in Table 1–1) loaded on two separate factors: PTSD avoidance and general loss of interest or detachment. Careful inspection of the seven C criteria reveals that items 1 and 2 refer to phobic avoidance pertaining to the trauma (i.e., avoidance of thoughts or actions). Item 3 refers to avoidance in memory of the trauma. These three items, then, can be distinguished from the remaining four items, which are nonspecific to PTSD (being found in other states such as depression) and which, moreover, can be evaluated at times only with imprecision in PTSD. These items are loss of interest for things (which was not present before the trauma), emotional constriction, numbing, and failure to see a future ("foreshortened future"). In studying, or applying, the loss of interest criterion, it may be hard, or at times impossible, to evaluate whether loss of interest was present or absent before the trauma, when the trauma may have been prolonged abuse in childhood or combat that took place 30–40 years previously.

PTSD symptoms in childhood have been reviewed by McNally (1993) and Pynoos et al. (1987). McNally's review showed that, broadly speaking, the same symptoms are found in children, although data are sparse with respect to frequencies of flashbacks, irritability, amnesia, and sense of foreshortened future. A factor analysis by Pynoos et al. showed three factors, each with high internal consistency. These factors were 1) intrusive/avoidant symptoms/anhedonia, 2) fear/general anxiety, and 3) poor sleep/concentration/nightmares. Impairment of concentration was also found as a factor by Davidson et al. (1989).

Thus, on the basis of multivariate and frequency studies in four different United States populations, the DSM-III-R symptom criteria for PTSD appear to bear out the constructs, traditions, and clinical wisdom embodied in the description. There is a need, however, for further studies in other populations (e.g., studies of chronic abuse victims and of transcultural comparisons).

PRETRAUMA AND INTERACTIVE RISKS FOR PTSD

Not every traumatized individual develops PTSD; not everyone is at equal risk for traumatization. Risks for developing PTSD relate to the trauma, to preexisting vulnerability factors, and to an interaction between the two.

The epidemiological literature is especially informative as to this topic. Indeed, we should pay particular attention to epidemiological studies because of their ability to garner large samples and to reach beyond the constraints imposed by studies that are limited only to the small minority of subjects with PTSD who seek treatment: a minority that may be as small as 5% (McFarlane 1988).

Pretrauma vulnerability factors for PTSD include positive history of psychiatric illness among first-degree relatives (Breslau et al. 1991; Davidson et al. 1989, 1991; Kulka et al. 1990), early sexual or other childhood trauma (Davidson et al. 1991), parental poverty (Davidson et al. 1991), behavior disorder in childhood or adolescence (Helzer et al. 1987), early separation or divorce of parents before the subject was 10 years old (Davidson et al. 1991), high neuroticism (Breslau et al. 1991; McFarlane 1989), introversion (McFarlane 1989), prior psychiatric disorder (Breslau et al. 1991; McFarlane 1989), poor self-confidence before age 15 (Card 1987), life stress before and after the trauma (McFarlane 1989), and being female (Breslau et al. 1991; Davidson et al. 1991; Shore et al. 1986).

Certain factors also independently increase the risk of experiencing trauma. These include extroversion and neuroticism, lack of a college education, early conduct disorder, family psychiatric history, and being male (Breslau et al. 1991; Helzer et al. 1987).

It is likely that interactive effects occur between the event and the host that either increase or decrease risk of PTSD. In the context of extreme trauma, host factors may diminish in importance, whereas in milder trauma, vulnerability factors may be of greater importance. Such a position is consistent with data from Shore et al. (1986) in their studies of a volcanic eruption.

McFarlane (1989) examined risk factor patterns over time after trauma. He concluded that extreme adversity played a central precipitating role in the onset of morbidity, but that other factors grew in importance, while importance of the trauma diminished with the passage of time. The extent to which this important observation may generalize to samples other than firefighters exposed to a discrete one-time event needs to be assessed. However, it is consistent with the early theorizing of DSM-I about PTSD.

Kulka et al. (1990) concluded that, among veterans of Vietnam, both background and trauma factors exerted independent effects on risk for

PTSD, and one might conclude that their view differs somewhat from that of McFarlane (1989). However, McFarlane's report was unique in looking at the effect of time since trauma on risk.

Differential accuracy of memory may play a role in explaining the findings of such studies. McFarlane (1989) found that subjects without PTSD differed from subjects with PTSD in their recall of events, which raises the possibility that some observed differences may be spurious, or at least inaccurate.

CONCLUSION

Of many issues relating to the diagnosis of PTSD, I selected in this chapter the critical questions of what constitutes a trauma, the possible existence of a group of trauma-related disorders, and cohesiveness of the symptomatology.

With regard to the event itself, there are problems relying on universal standards of statistical "normality" and "marked distress" with respect to events. Trauma intensity, trauma characteristics (loss, death, injury or witnessing thereof, to self or others), and subjective response (intensity of affect or negative appraisal) are all probably important.

The second point, concerning a possible category of trauma-related illnesses, is far from being settled. However, even in DSM-III-R, it is acknowledged that there are 12 different states that, to varying degrees, are related to traumatic (or "exceptional") stress. Presumably this view is based on the sound clinical option of pundits. The next step, therefore, would be to examine prospectively the exact relationship between trauma and each disorder, looking at types of trauma, whether they were antecedent to the disorder, and the frequency of such a relationship. A comparison across disorders would also be of interest, and a control group of supposedly "nontraumatic" conditions would be needed.

Evaluation of symptom frequency, cohesiveness, and factor structure in four different victim groups supports in broad terms the present conceptualization of PTSD, leaving open the question that other nonrepresented disorders such as DESNOS may extend the diagnostic net to include other traumatic states.

Clearly, there are several important and reasonably well-established premorbid vulnerability risk factors for PTSD. In their presence, an event may assume greater traumatogenicity. The extent and characteristics of ways in which these two factors interact need to be studied further. At least we should pay attention to the degree to which such risk factors are present when we evaluate individuals in the aftermath of trauma.

REFERENCES

American Psychiatric Association: Diagnostic and Statistical Manual: Mental Disorders. Washington, DC, American Psychiatric Association, 1952

American Psychiatric Association: Diagnostic and Statistical Manual of Mental Disorders, 3rd Edition. Washington, DC, American Psychiatric Association, 1980

American Psychiatric Association: Diagnostic and Statistical Manual of Mental Disorders, 3rd Edition, Revised. Washington, DC, American Psychiatric Association, 1987

Blank AS Jr: The longitudinal course of posttraumatic stress disorder, in Posttraumatic Stress Disorder: DSM-IV and Beyond. Edited by Davidson JRT, Foa EB. Washington, DC, American Psychiatric Press, 1993, pp 3–22

Bond DD: The Love and Fear of Flying. New York, International Universities Press, 1952

Breslau N, Davis GC, Andreski P: Traumatic events and posttraumatic stress disorder in an urban population of young adults. Arch Gen Psychiatry 48:216–222, 1991

Briquet P: Traité de L'Hysterie. Paris, Bailliere et Fils, 1859

Card JJ: Epidemiology of PTSD in a national cohort of Vietnam veterans. J Clin Psychol 43:6–17, 1987

Davidson JRT, Fairbank JA: The epidemiology of posttraumatic stress disorder, in Posttraumatic Stress Disorder: DSM-IV and Beyond. Edited by Davidson JRT, Foa EB. Washington, DC, American Psychiatric Press, 1993, pp 147–169

Davidson JRT, Smith RD: Traumatic experience in psychiatric outpatients. Journal of Traumatic Stress 3:459–476, 1990

Davidson JRT, Smith RD, Kudler HS: Validity and reliability of the DSM-III criteria for posttraumatic stress disorder: experience with a structured interview. J Nerv Ment Dis 177:336–341, 1989

Davidson JRT, Hughes DL, Blazer DG, et al: Posttraumatic stress disorder in the community: an epidemiological study. Psychol Med 21:713–721, 1991

Frye S, Stockton R: Discriminant analysis of posttraumatic stress disorder among a group of Vietnam veterans. Am J Psychiatry 139:52–56, 1982

Goldberg J, True WR, Eisen SA, et al: A twin study of the effects of the Vietnam war on posttraumatic stress disorder. JAMA 263:1227–1232, 1990

Green BL: Disasters and posttraumatic stress disorder, in Posttraumatic Stress Disorder: DSM-IV and Beyond. Edited by Davidson JRT, Foa EB. Washington, DC, American Psychiatric Press, 1993, pp 75–97

Green BL, Grace MC, Glesen CG: Identifying survivors at risk: long-term impairment following the Beverly Hills Supper Club Fire. J Consult Clin Psychol 53:672–678, 1985

Helzer JE, Robins LN, McEvoy L: Posttraumatic stress disorder in the general population. N Engl J Med 317:1630–1634, 1987

Herman JL: Sequelae of prolonged and repeated trauma: evidence for a complex posttraumatic syndrome (DESNOS), in Posttraumatic Stress Disorder: DSM-IV and Beyond. Edited by Davidson JRT, Foa EB. Washington, DC, American Psychiatric Press, 1993, pp 213–228

Herman JL, Perry BC, van der Kolk BA: Childhood trauma in borderline personality disorder. Am J Psychiatry 146:490–495, 1989

Keane TM: Symptomatology of Vietnam veterans with posttraumatic stress disorder, in Posttraumatic Stress Disorder: DSM-IV and Beyond. Edited by Davidson JRT, Foa EB. Washington, DC, American Psychiatric Press, 1993, pp 99–111

Kilpatrick DG, Resnick HS: Posttraumatic stress disorder associated with exposure to criminal victimization in clinical and community populations, in Posttraumatic Stress Disorder: DSM-IV and Beyond. Edited by Davidson JRT, Foa EB. Washington, DC, American Psychiatric Press, 1993, pp 113–143

Kulka RA, Schlenger WE, Fairbank JA, et al: Trauma and the Vietnam War Generation. New York, Brunner/Mazel, 1990

March JS: What constitutes a stressor? the criterion A issue, in Posttraumatic Stress Disorder: DSM-IV and Beyond. Edited by Davidson JRT, Foa EB. Washington DC, American Psychiatric Press, 1993, pp 37–54

McFarlane AC: The phenomenology of post traumatic stress disorders following a natural disaster. J Nerv Ment Dis 176:22–29, 1988

McFarlane AC: The aetiology of post-traumatic stress morbidity: predisposing, precipitating and perpetuating factors. Br J Psychiatry 154:221–228, 1989

McNally RJ: Stressors that produce posttraumatic stress disorder in children, in Posttraumatic Stress Disorder: DSM-IV and Beyond. Edited by Davidson JRT, Foa EB. Washington, DC, American Psychiatric Press, 1993, pp 57–74

Melges FT, Swartz MS: Oscillations of attachment in borderline personality disorder. Am J Psychiatry 146:1115–1120, 1989

Norris FH: Sex, race and age differences in the frequency and impact of traumatic life events. J Consult Clin Psychol 60:409–418, 1992

Pynoos RS, Frederick C, Nader K, et al: Life threat and posttraumatic stress in school-age children. Arch Gen Psychiatry 44:1057–1063, 1987

Shore JH, Tatum E, Vollmer WM: Psychiatric reactions to disaster: the Mount Saint Helen's experience. Am J Psychiatry 143:590–595, 1986

Snow B, Stellman J, Stellman S, et al: Posttraumatic stress disorder among American Legionnaires in relation to combat experience in Vietnam. Environ Res 47:175–192, 1988

Solomon Z, Mikulincer M, Flum H: Negative life event, coping resources, and combat-related psychopathology: a prospective study. J Abnorm Psychiatry 97:302–307, 1988

Winfield I, George LK, Swartz MS, et al: Sexual assault and psychiatric disorders among women in a community population. Am J Psychiatry 147:335–341, 1990

World Health Organization: The ICD-10 Classification of Mental and Behavioural Disorders: Clinical Descriptions and Diagnostic Guidelines. Geneva, World Health Organization, 1992

Yehuda R, Southwick SM, Perry BD, et al: Interactions of the hypothalamopituitary-adrenal axis and the catecholaminergic system in posttraumatic stress disorder, in Biological Assessment and Treatment of Posttraumatic Stress Disorder. Edited by Giller EL Jr. Washington, DC, American Psychiatric Press, 1990, pp 115–134

Chapter 2

Ethnocultural Aspects of Posttraumatic Stress Disorder

Anthony J. Marsella, Ph.D.,
Matthew J. Friedman, M.D., Ph.D.,
and E. Huland Spain, Ph.D.

Within the last two decades, there has been an increased interest in the study of ethnocultural aspects of posttraumatic stress disorder (PTSD). This interest has manifested itself via the publication of numerous books, technical reports, and journal articles on a spectrum of ethnic populations and ethnic aspects of PTSD. However, during this time period, there have been few literature reviews on the topic, and those literature reviews that have been published have been limited to specific topics (e.g., assessment), specific traumata (e.g., refugee status), or specific ethnic groups (e.g., the Indo-Chinese). Penk and Allen (1991) summarized the research literature on clinical assessment among ethnic minority Vietnam War veterans. De Girolamo (1992) summarized the literature on the treatment and prevention of PTSD among victims of natural disasters in different countries. Friedman and Jaranson (in press) summarized the literature on PTSD among refugees. Marsella et al. (1992) offered a brief overview of the topic with an accompanying annotated bibliography.

One reason for the limited number of literature reviews on ethnocultural aspects of PTSD is that the information on the topic is distributed across hundreds of publications that focus on different 1) ethnocultural groups (e.g., African Americans, American Indians, Asian Americans, Cambodians, Hispanics); 2) victim populations (e.g., war veterans, refugees, torture victims, prisoners-of-war, rape and

---

Preparation of this manuscript was partially supported by Public Law 101-507, directing the National Center for PTSD to conduct research on ethnocultural aspects of PTSD among selected ethnic minority Vietnam War veterans. M.J.F. is the principal investigator of this contract; A.J.M. is chief scientific adviser to the contract; and E.H.S. is a research scientist on the project.

Appreciation is extended to Michael Boschaert, Edward Kubany, Richard Rohde, and Catherine Sorensen of the Honolulu Veterans Administration office for their bibliographic assistance.

The opinions expressed in this manuscript are those of the authors and do not necessarily reflect those of the Department of Veterans Affairs or any of its affiliated agencies or programs.

other crime victims, victims of natural and human-caused disasters), 3) traumatic events (e.g., Vietnam War, Afghan War, Northern Ireland conflict, Buffalo Creek disaster, Chernobyl, Three Mile Island, San Ysidro massacre, refugee camp internment, rapes and other criminal assaults); and 4) clinical topics (e.g., epidemiology of PTSD, measurement of PTSD, clinical diagnosis, alternative therapies).

The diversity and scope of publications on ethnocultural aspects of PTSD resist the imposition of a simple organizational format. The books alone that have been published within the last decade could occupy a special review, because there have been more than 18 published that contain ethnocultural, racial, or other ethnic material on PTSD.

In addition to the problematic nature of surveying, organizing, and critically reviewing such a sizable research and clinical literature, there is the issue of research quality. Quite simply, there are considerable variations in the quality of the published reports. Many of the publications concerned with ethnocultural topics have not used scientifically acceptable methodologies for conducting cross-cultural research. This raises serious questions regarding the validity of their findings because of insensitivities to ethnocultural aspects of psychopathology, assessment, and treatment.

For example, the majority of ethnocultural studies on PTSD have assumed that by studying one or more racial or ethnocultural groups, they were in fact accounting for the variance associated with ethnocultural factors. However, as is pointed out in detail later, a comparison of different races or ethnic groups in the absence of a priori criteria for defining meaningful group divisions limits our understanding of any group differences found.

What does it mean when whites, African Americans, and Hispanics are found to differ in rates of PTSD if the samples studied also differ in educational level, social class, exposure to trauma, regional background (e.g., Hispanics from Cuba, Puerto Rico, Mexico), urban-rural residence, and so forth? Using broad categories of ethnocultural group membership as the basis for research studies may in fact create more problems than it resolves. It is essential that clinical studies that attribute differences in PTSD rates, expression, and treatment responsivity to ethnocultural variables control for, or at least account for, these and other possible sources of variance.

In addition, there are many within-group ethnocultural differences among African Americans, Hispanics, Asian Americans, and whites, and these differences must be considered in valid cross-cultural research. For example, there is no single African American subculture. There are a variety of black experiences, and these differ from one another in dramatic ways. Consider the contrasts among African American groups such as Haitians, Cuban blacks, Jamaicans, Ethiopians, Southern rural blacks, Northern urban blacks, wealthy professional blacks, and impoverished blacks. PTSD among these different groups may not have similar causes, expressions, or experiential and social implications because these groups are in fact different from one another in numerous ways.

Despite the many publications addressing ethnocultural aspects of PTSD, relatively little is yet known about the relationship between ethnocultural factors and the etiology, epidemiology, onset, diagnosis, course, outcome, and assessment and treatment of PTSD. In this chapter, we have three major purposes: 1) to summarize and review critically the existing cross-cultural PTSD literature, especially as it pertains to veterans and refugees; 2) to discuss some of the major conceptual and methodological issues involved in understanding the relationship between culture and PTSD; and 3) to recommend conceptual and research approaches for studying ethnocultural aspects of PTSD. Although we have made every effort to review the numerous articles on the topic, we wish to point out that this review should be considered comprehensive but not exhaustive. We do not review the published ethnocultural literature on children; the interested reader is referred to Pynoos (Chapter 4).

Although a universal neurobiological response to traumatic events most likely does exist, there is room for considerable ethnocultural variation in the expressive and phenomenological dimensions of the experience, especially among comorbidity patterns and associated somatic, hysterical, and paranoid symptoms and experiences. The extensive research literature on ethnocultural variations in psychopathology points to the importance of our understanding the pathoplastic aspects of severe psychopathology and other forms of mental disorder. If more sensitive cross-cultural research and clinical methods are used in the study of PTSD, ethnocultural variations may emerge with greater regularity and clarity. Friedman and Jaranson (in press) and Marsella et al. (1992) noted some of the major issues that must be considered in ethnocultural studies of PTSD. Therefore, at this time, it appears that a number of research questions remain to be answered regarding the relationship between ethnocultural factors and the etiology, rates, expression, experience, and treatment of PTSD. We examine some of these questions.

OVERVIEW OF THE RESEARCH AND CLINICAL LITERATURE

Epidemiological and Clinical Studies of PTSD Among Refugees

To date, there have been no published literature reviews on ethnocultural variations in the epidemiology of PTSD. However, several review publications have examined mental disorders among populations that are considered to be at high risk for PTSD (e.g., refugees, immigrants, veterans, concentration camp survivors) that can shed partial light on possible relationships between traumata and the rates and clinical manifestations of PTSD in different ethnocultural populations (e.g., Arthur 1982; Beiser 1990; Friedman and Jaranson, in press; Garcia-Peltoniemi 1992a, 1992b; Mollica 1988; Weisaeth and Eitenger 1991). In addition, the *National Center for PTSD Research Quarterly* (National Center for PTSD 1991) compiled a bibliography of traumatic reactions among European refugee, concentration camp, and veteran populations. Garcia-Peltoniemi's (1992a, 1992b) recent reviews of psychopathology among refugees, although not specific to PTSD, support the view of a direct relationship between traumatic experiences and a spectrum of neurotic and psychotic disorders.

A German neurologist, Oppenheim (1889), was the first to use the term *traumatic neurosis*. Subsequent interest in traumatic neuroses continued in the work of Janet and Freud. By the end of World War I, there was strong interest in Europe in the relationship between trauma and psychiatric functioning (e.g., Myers 1940; Salmon 1917). This interest continued into the World War II period, as scientists and clinicians noted the effects of traumata such as war, concentration camp internment, torture, and refugee status on psychiatric adjustment.

However, it has only been within recent years that attention has been focused on PTSD as a distinct response to these traumata. For much of the past 50 years, European researchers have given primary attention to depression, suicide, anxiety, paranoid states, somatization, and reactive psychoses among these high-risk populations (see Eitenger 1964; Garcia-Peltoniemi 1992b; Strom 1968). It is likely that much of what was diagnosed in these categories was in fact PTSD; however, there is no way to verify this conclusion.

In an older study of traumatic neuroses and reactive depressions, Pfister-Ammende (1955) found that World War II refugees in Switzerland showed twice the rates of these disorders compared with the general Swiss population. In a study of World War II refugees resettled in England, Murphy (1955) reported a direct relationship between the extent of trauma experienced and the severity of mental illness among this group. He also noted that certain aspects of the resettlement experience, including friendliness of the host society and assimilation, were related to rates of mental disorder.

In studies of refugees resettled in Norway, Eitenger (1960, 1964) and Eitenger and Grunfeld (1966) reported high rates of reactive psychoses among disabled and physically ill World War II refugees and Hungarian refugees of the ill-fated 1956 Hungarian Revolution. The Hungarian refugees demonstrated significantly higher rates of psychoses, suggesting an interaction between exposure to trauma and refugee status.

Other demonstrations of the effects of trauma on psychiatric disorders are available in a study by Krupinski et al. (1973), which examined psychiatric disorders among Jewish concentration camp survivors who migrated to Australia. Among these survivors, there was a distinct syndrome that was termed the *concentration camp* or *KZ* (German *Konzentrationslager*) *syndrome* (see Becker 1963; Chodoff 1963; Ostwald and Bittner 1968), consisting of sleep disturbances, recurrent nightmares, chronic anxiety and depression, impaired memory and concentration, anergia, and feelings of guilt. This cluster closely resembles what today is called PTSD. Thus, although the formal diagnosis of PTSD is a recent nosological convention, the human response to trauma has long been recognized to include a psychiatric syndrome. In addition to the concentration camp syndrome, the refugee syndrome, the prisoner of war and war trauma (e.g., combat fatigue) syndrome, there were also lesser known syndromes such as the war sailor syndrome reported by Askevold (1976, 1980) to describe the symptom complex found in many Norwegian sailors whose boats were sunk during World War II.

More recent studies of PTSD among Indo-Chinese refugees continue to support the close relationship between the traumata associated with refugee status and PTSD and related anxiety and depressive disorders (e.g., Beiser et al. 1989; Boehnlein 1987a; Boehnlein et al. 1985; de Girolamo et al. 1989; Friedman and Jaranson, in press; Goldfeld et al. 1988; Kinzie et al. 1984, 1990; Kroll et al. 1989; E. Lin et al. 1985; Mollica et al. 1987; Moore and Boehnlein 1991; Nicassio 1985). Westermeyer and his colleagues (e.g., Westermeyer 1988; Westermeyer et al. 1992; Williams and Westermeyer 1986) edited and authored a number of books on the specific topic of refugee mental health that contain extensive material on the diagnosis and treatment of PTSD among Indo-Chinese refugees and other groups. Rozee and Van Boemel (1989) looked at the effect of war trauma on older Cambodian women.

An example of the extensive studies on PTSD among Indo-Chinese refugees is provided by Kinzie et al. (1984), who surveyed 322 patients at a psychiatric clinic for Indo-Chinese refugees to determine the presence of PTSD. They found that 226 patients met the criteria for a current diagnosis of PTSD, and an additional 15 met the criteria for a past diagnosis. The Mein (Laotian hill people) had the highest rate of PTSD (93%), and the Vietnamese had the lowest (54%). They concluded that PTSD is a common disorder among Indo-Chinese refugees, but the diagnosis is often difficult to make because of communication difficulties that complicate the diagnostic process.

Cervantes et al. (1989) investigated self-reported symptoms of depression, anxiety, somatization, generalized distress, and PTSD in a community sample of 258 immigrants from Central America and Mexico and 329 native-born Mexican Americans and white Americans. Research instruments included the Symptom Checklist 90—Revised (SCL-90-R; Derogatis 1983) and the Center for Epidemiologic Studies Depression Scale (CES-D) (Radloff 1977). They found that immigrants had higher levels of generalized distress than native-born Americans. They also found that 52% of Central American immigrants who migrated as a result of war or political unrest reported symptoms consistent with a diagnosis of PTSD, compared with 49% of Central Americans who migrated for other reasons and 25% of Mexican immigrants. Other studies have been published that involve Hispanic PTSD refugee victims (Lopez et al. 1988; Summerfield and Toser 1991; Urrutia 1986).

Clinical and Epidemiological Studies of International Natural Disasters and Political and Family Traumata

Perry (1986), de Girolamo (1992), and de Girolamo and Orley (1992) summarized much of the literature on the relationship between natural disasters and PTSD across national boundaries. They concluded that natural disasters are an important source of psychiatric adjustment difficulties among survivors regardless of the country in which the disaster occurred. One example of PTSD following a natural disaster was reported by de la Fuente (1990), who evaluated emotional reactions in 573 people (ages 18–64 years) associated with the Mexican earthquakes and found that 32% of the victims displayed PTSD, 19% had generalized anxiety, and 13% had depression. In the same study, he found that of 208 women housed in shelters, 72.3% showed no psychopathological symptoms, 18% displayed some signs of decompensation, and 9.5% suffered severe decompensation.

Holen (1990), Malt (1988), Malt et al. (1989), and Weisaeth (1989) studied the effects of industrial disasters and civilian accidents among Scandinavian populations. Weisaeth (1989) found a direct relationship between the severity of trauma exposure and PTSD symptoms among survivors of a paint factory explosion in Norway. Immediate PTSD reactions were reported by 80% of the high-stressor exposure group, whereas only 5% showed a delayed PTSD response. The 7-month point prevalence of PTSD was 37% among the high-stressor exposure group but only 4% among the low-stressor exposure group. The direct relationship between stressor exposure and PTSD among this cultural population is consistent with reports of others around the world and suggests a possible universal relationship between extent of trauma and risk of PTSD symptomatology.

Holen (1990) and Malt and his colleagues (Malt 1988, Malt et al. 1989) found PTSD responses among victims of industrial disasters and civilian accidents in Scandinavian countries. Kim (1987) discussed

PTSD-like symptoms among battered housewives in Korea. K. Solomon (1989) discussed the dynamics of PTSD in South African political detainees. Lima et al. (1991) evaluated 102 victims of the Armero volcanic eruption and mud slide disaster and found that the majority of the victims met DSM-III-R (American Psychiatric Association 1987) criteria for PTSD and depression.

Epidemiological and Clinical Studies of American Military Veterans

There have also been numerous publications on ethnocultural variations in the rates and clinical phenomenology of PTSD among American military veterans. Studies of PTSD among American Vietnam War veterans have reported conflicting results with regard to rates of PTSD. Some studies suggested African Americans have higher rates of PTSD than whites or Hispanics (e.g., Allen 1986; Green et al. 1990; Laufer et al. 1984; Parson 1984; Penk et al. 1989).

Parson (1985) proposed a "tripartite adaptational dilemma" among ethnocultural minority Vietnam War veterans in which the veterans must resolve the triple effects of a bicultural identity, institutional racism, and residual stress from trauma in dealing with the war. As a result, he suggested an increased risk of PTSD and other psychiatric disorders for ethnocultural minority veterans. Penk and Allen (1991), in commenting on possible differences in the rates of PTSD among different ethnic groups, stated:

> Research has consistently demonstrated that effects of the Vietnam war are more pronounced among the American minorities who served. That is, studies of treatment seeking and non-treatment seeking samples concur in showing higher rates of maladjustment among non-whites than whites.... Readjustment needs of any veteran are complex but those of the American minority veteran are compounded by the traditional ethnic minority problems of other stresses produced by prejudice in a segregated and racist society. Racism adds stresses to traumatic experiences.... But many clinicians have not comprehended the additional complications experienced by many American minority Vietnam veterans whose stress reactions are increased by their experiences of not being majority culture members. (p. 45)

Marsella et al. (1990) suggested that ethnocultural minority Vietnam veterans might have an increased risk for developing PTSD because of a number of factors. First, ethnocultural minority soldiers were subjected to increased stress because of racial stereotypes, ridicule, and inequitable treatment. Second, they were subjected to increased stress because they were asked to fight against nonwhite people on behalf of a country that many considered to be racist. Third, the Vietnamese reminded many of the veterans of family, friends, and other minority groups, thus making them unable to "dehumanize" the Vietnamese. Fourth, their personality and interpersonal style did not fit in with military preferences. In brief, ethnocultural minority veterans may have had increased levels of stress and reduced coping resources available to them, resulting in a higher risk of PTSD.

However, issues have been raised about the confounding effects of substance abuse problems (e.g., Carter 1982) and early life stressors (e.g., Breslau et al. 1991), more severe combat stressors among African Americans. Green et al. (1990) were surprised to find high lifetime PTSD diagnosis probabilities of 42% for whites and 72% for African Americans, and current PTSD probabilities of 30% for whites and 47% for African Americans. Linking these differences to the Vietnam War experience, however, was problematic because of confounds that arise as a result of status and historical differences between the two groups.

Some studies have suggested that Hispanics were also at increased risk for PTSD (e.g., Becerra 1982; Escobar et al. 1983). Escobar et al. noted that PTSD was rarely seen as a discrete entity among Hispanics, but rather was mixed in with other DSM-III (American Psychiatric Association 1980) categories. Pina (1985) also noted both increased risks and diagnostic variations in PTSD among Hispanic veterans.

The National Vietnam Veterans Readjustment Study (NVVRS) of PTSD rates was a comprehensive national epidemiological survey of current and lifetime prevalence rates of PTSD conducted under contract from the Department of Veterans Affairs (see Kulka et al. 1990). This study offered a comparison of PTSD among white, African American, and Hispanic male and female populations. Other ethnocultural groups were considered too small in number to provide comparative data. The NVVRS study found that Hispanic populations suffered higher current rates of PTSD (28%) than African Americans (19%) or whites (14%). However, it should be pointed out that when data were controlled for war zone trauma exposure, white versus African American prevalence rate differences disappeared, and white versus Hispanic prevalence rates became much smaller. In another analysis of NVVRS data, Jordan et al. (1991) reported that Hispanics were at an increased risk for alcohol or substance abuse and general anxiety disorder, and African Americans for antisocial personality disorder.

Both of these studies are good examples of the importance of accounting for nonethnocultural factors in ethnocultural research. However, the NVVRS made no effort to use culturally sensitive assessment materials in the determination of cases. Further, the study did not sample American Indian, Asian American, or Pacific Island veterans in sufficient sizes to reach conclusions about the prevalence of PTSD among these groups. As a result, the United States Congress directed the National Center for PTSD of the Department of Veterans Affairs to study rates of PTSD among ethnocultural groups not included in the study and to develop culturally sensitive instruments for the detection and differentiation of PTSD among these groups. This study is currently in progress (see Friedman et al. 1992).

There have been few studies of PTSD among American Indian or Asian American veterans of the Vietnam War. However, several authors have suggested that minority status stress, racial prejudice, and identification with the Vietnamese people and culture may have increased the risk of PTSD among American Indians (e.g., Barse 1984; Holm 1982, 1989; Silver 1984) and Asian Americans (e.g., Hamada et al. 1988; Marsella et al. 1990). It is noteworthy that Parson (1984) and Allen (1986) stated that the risk of PTSD was enhanced among African American veterans because of their identification with the Vietnamese people.

Epidemiological and Clinical Studies of Non-American Military Veterans

There have been numerous studies of PTSD among veterans from other nations, including Australia (e.g., Streimer et al. 1985; Tennant et al. 1990), Canada (e.g., Stretch 1990, 1991), Israel (e.g., Z. Solomon 1989; Z. Solomon and Mikulincer 1987; Z. Solomon et al. 1986, 1987), and Sweden (Kettner 1972)). These studies are not methodologically comparable to the American veteran studies of PTSD so comparisons of data are difficult. However, they do provide additional demonstrations of the linkage between PTSD and combat experiences.

Tennant et al. (1990) reported that 19% of the Australian Vietnam War veterans suffered from PTSD. However, limitations in sampling and assessment confounded the results. Stretch (1991) reported a prevalence rate of 65% among self-selected Canadian (and some American) Vietnam War veterans using PTSD symptomatology as the case index rather than clinical diagnoses. He attributed this exceptionally high rate to a lack of recognition, a lack of PTSD services, and isolation of veterans in Canada. Z. Solomon and her colleagues (e.g., Z. Solomon et al. 1987) reported that 59% of a sample of Israeli soldiers who fought in the 1982 Lebanese conflict had PTSD 1 year after the end of the war. The variations in these rates are a result of different case criteria and research methodologies. However, as a group, they point to the fact that combat experience is closely linked to PTSD. It should be noted that Solomon and her colleagues published a score of studies on PTSD among Israeli soldiers. The magnitude of her work exceeds the present chapter's space mandates for review. However, interested readers should be aware of her numerous publications.

Assessment Studies and Issues

There are only a few published ethnocultural studies of PTSD concerned with assessment issues, despite the fact that cultural sensitivity in assessment procedures may be a major factor in the determination of PTSD rates and clinical features (e.g., Penk and Allen 1991; Penk et al. 1989). Allodi (1991) reviewed some of the assessment methods used with international victims of torture; he reported no efforts to accommodate methods to specific ethnocultural populations. Westermeyer and Wahmemholm (1989) commented on the difficulties of assessing the traumatized combat and refugee patient. Mollica et al. (1992) attempted to develop a questionnaire for measuring trauma, torture, and PTSD among Indo-Chinese refugees using refugee experiences rather than Western standards. However, most studies of nonwhite PTSD populations have tended to use standard clinical methods. As a result, questions arise about the validity of the conclusions reached since many of these instruments were constructed and normalized with white populations. Nevertheless, it is important to note that consistent symptomatology has been reported with the use of a variety of popular Western psychiatric instruments—for example, the SCL-90-R, the Diagnostic Interview Schedule (Robins et al. 1981), the Minnesota Multiphasic Personality Inventory (Hathaway and McKinley 1970), and the CES-D—across a variety of different ethnocultural groups. An unpublished article by J. Jaranson and N. Shiota ("Refugee Mental Health: Psychiatric Interviewing of Refugee Patients," University of Minnesota, Minneapolis, 1989) is noteworthy because they developed an interview assessment package for specific use with Indo-Chinese refugee PTSD victims.

Therapy Studies

Psychotherapy studies. There have been no systematic comparisons of therapy outcomes or processes among PTSD victims from different cultures using accepted experimental design procedures (e.g., control groups, alternative therapies, multiple outcome measures). However, there have been a number of reports on various therapy experiences with different ethnocultural groups. Some of these indicate the importance of adjusting therapies to the patient's ethnocultural background.

For example, Parson (1990) discussed a special form of PTSD therapy that he used for African American veterans. He called his therapy approach "post-traumatic psychocultural therapy." In contrast to other therapies, Parson integrated the Vietnam sector, the African slavery sector, the Eurocentric sector, and the post-Vietnam sector of the African American veterans' experiential world. He cited 10 basic principles that distinguished this therapy from other psychotherapies. Baumgartner (1986) reported success with African American veterans using sociodrama, a form of group therapy that encourages catharsis. However, he did not specify procedures that would be therapeutically unique to different ethnic groups, nor did he discuss the biases and problems associated with this method among other populations. Allen (1986) noted that therapy with African American veterans is complicated by a variety of factors, including the tendency to misdiagnose African American patients, the varied manifestations of PTSD in this group, and the frequent alcohol and drug abuse and medical, legal, personality, and vocational problems of African American patients. Allen acknowledged that these factors make it difficult to treat African American veterans using traditional therapeutic approaches.

Krippner and Colodzin (1989) cited the success of using indigenous healers (American Indian, Asian American) in treating PTSD among Vietnam War veterans from these groups. They noted that the traditional practitioners used therapies that helped veterans "regain power," "cleanse themselves," and "decrease shame, guilt, and rage." Among American Indians, sweat lodge, vision quests, and other indigenous practices have been used successfully with veterans. Holm (1982) and Silver and Wilson (1990) reported success with a variety of American Indian "purification and healing" practices.

Lee and Lu (1989) called attention to the importance of considering ethnocultural factors in the treatment of Asian American populations. In their article, they discussed functional and dysfunctional coping strategies of Asian American immigrants and refugees and offered some principles for the psychiatric assessment of Asian immigrants and refugees who may have PTSD. Culturally specific treatment strategies are discussed, including crisis intervention; supportive, behavioral, and psychopharmacological approaches; Amytal (amobarbital) and hypnosis; and folk healing. Niem (1989) also noted some of the problems and possibilities associated with the use of Western psychiatric therapies among Vietnamese refugee populations.

Boehnlein (1987a, 1987b) noted the importance of considering cultural factors in PTSD therapy with Cambodian women who were concentration camp survivors. He noted that attention to cultural factors helped provide more comprehensive and valid diagnostic and treatment formulations. Kinzie and Fleck (1987) described their therapy experiences with four severely traumatized refugees from different Indo-Chinese countries. They noted that therapeutic problems include the setting in which therapy takes place, reactivation of PTSD, lack of objectivity by the therapist, and the failure of the therapist to provide effective assistance with the immediate social and urgent financial needs of the refugees.

Jaranson (1990), Kinzie (1985, 1989), Kinzie and Fleck (1987), Kinzie et al. (1980), Mollica and Lavelle (1988), Rosser (1986), and Westermeyer (1989) all noted that counseling and psychotherapy adjusted for the ethnocultural traditions of Indo-Chinese refugees can be helpful in reducing traumatic stress. They urged increased sensitivity to cultural factors in treatment procedures.

Dobkin de Rios and Friedman (1987) used a culturally sensitive hypnotherapeutic intervention for Hispanic burn patients with symptoms of PTSD because of the difficulties that recent monolingual Mexican migrants experience in responding to psychological interventions that are culturally insensitive. A combination of the hypnotherapeutic interventions, systematic desensitization, and other culturally sensitive therapeutic activities helped the effective rehabilitation of Hispanic burn patients. Arredondo et al. (1989) discussed the value of family therapy in treating Central American war refugees who have suffered traumata.

Although many countries have torture rehabilitation centers that are heavily concerned with PTSD, there are no comparative reports of the therapeutic effectiveness of different approaches (e.g., psychoanalysis versus behavior modification) as a function of ethnocultural variables. Research on this topic should be encouraged because of the ready opportunity for well-designed comparative cultural studies.

Psychopharmacology studies. It is noteworthy that interest in ethnopharmacology has grown considerably in the last decade. Much of the current research on the topic has been generated by K. Lin and his colleagues at the research project on ethnopharmacology funded by the National Institute of Mental Health and based at the University of California at Los Angeles (see K. Lin and Finder 1983; K. Lin and Shen 1991; K. Lin et al. 1986). Kinzie et al. (1987) and Kroll et al. (1989) discussed the use of antidepressants in Southeast Asian patients. Jaranson (1991) offered a summary of his medication experiences with refugee populations. However, there have no been no carefully controlled experimental studies of psychoactive treatments of trauma victims from different ethnocultural backgrounds.

One of the few clinical studies on the topic was an open trial of clonidine and imipramine in Cambodian PTSD patients conducted by Kinzie and Leung (1989). They reported that 68 severely traumatized Cambodian refugee patients who suffered from chronic PTSD and major depression improved symptomatically when treated with a combination of clonidine, an α_2-adrenergic agonist, and imipramine, a tricyclic antidepressant. In addition, a prospective study of 9 Cambodian PTSD patients (ages 31–64 years) using this combination resulted in improved symptoms of depression among 6 patients, 5 of whom improved to the point that DSM-III-R diagnoses were no longer applicable. Kinzie and Leung concluded that clonidine and imipramine reduced, but did not eliminate, hyperarousal symptoms, intrusive thoughts, nightmares, and startle reactions in their Cambodian patients. They felt that the imipramine plus clonidine combination was well tolerated and should be explored further in treating severely depressed and traumatized patients. Freimer et al. (1989) reported the use of amobarbital interviews with a 23-year-old male Laotian refugee veteran whose symptoms and clinical course fit DSM-III-R criteria for combat-related disorder and PTSD. They noted that the patient was more responsive following three amobarbital interviews, and this provided diagnostic information that helped treatment through expanded use of suggestion and abreaction.

Summary of therapy. With the exception of the Parson (1990) report, there have been no systematic efforts to develop alternative forms of psychotherapy that are applicable to distinct ethnocultural groups of PTSD victims. The use of indigenous methods holds some promise for future treatment; however, it will be necessary to conduct rigorous experimental studies (e.g., studies with control groups) to test the efficacy of these methods. Most reports of psychotherapy with PTSD victims from different ethnocultural groups have explored Western methods, making adjustments for certain ethnocultural traditions. Much the same can be said of the psychopharmacology reports on PTSD among different ethnocultural groups. What is needed now are experimental studies with double-blind, crossover designs to test the effects of psychoactive medications on different ethnocultural groups with PTSD. There are no current publications that offer information on differential treatments (e.g., dosage, medications, side effects, titration levels). The use of indigenous therapies (e.g., sweat lodges, vision quests) presents some interesting options, but should be studied systematically to determine their effectiveness.

BASIC CONSIDERATIONS IN CONDUCTING ETHNOCULTURAL RESEARCH ON PTSD

Ethnocentricity

The study of ethnocultural aspects of PTSD can provide insight into a number of important dimensions of the problem, including the role of ethnocultural variables in the etiology, epidemiology, diagnosis, expression, treatment, and prevention of PTSD. However, it is critical that the insidious risks of ethnocentricity be closely monitored in cross-cultural studies of PTSD. Like many other psychiatric disorders, virtually all of the theory, research, and measurement on PTSD has been generated by North American, European, Israeli, and Australian researchers and professionals. When this knowledge is applied to members of these cultural traditions, issues of cross-cultural validity and reliability are not as serious a problem because the concepts and approaches are consistent with Western cultural traditions. However, when these concepts and approaches are applied "indiscriminately" to members of non-Western cultural traditions, including ethnic minority members who still practice or are identified with these cultural traditions, there are serious risks of "ethnocentric" bias.

Ethnocentricity can be defined in this context as "the tendency to view one's own way of thinking or behaving as the right, correct, or moral way, and to reject all others as incorrect or of limited accuracy or value." As a result of ethnocentric bias, concepts and methods of measurement of PTSD may have only limited cross-cultural relevancy and utility because they do not encompass or consider the experience of non-Western people, particularly with regard to their notions of health, illness, personhood, and normality, as well as their expressions of symptomatology and phenomenological experiences of disorders such as PTSD.

In the last few decades, cross-cultural researchers have raised numerous questions about the ethics and consequences of applying ethnocentric concepts and methods, especially when these concepts and methods serve to distort the nature of phenomena from the viewpoint of indigenous people. Numerous journals (e.g., *Culture Medicine and Psychiatry, Journal of Cross-Cultural Psychology, Journal of Hispanic Psychology, Medical Anthropology, Social Science and Medicine, Transcultural Psychiatric Research Review*) and books (e.g., see Comas-Diaz and Griffith 1988; Gaw 1992; Kleinman and Good 1986; Leff 1988; Marsella and White 1982; Pedersen et al. 1984; Simons and Hughes 1985; Sue and Sue 1990; Triandis and Draguns 1980) have been devoted to the study of cross-cultural variations in psychopathology and psychotherapy.

In general, these publications have suggested that ethnocultural factors are a critical determinant of virtually all aspects of psychiatric disorders, including etiology, epidemiology, clinical phenomenology, and treatment. Although this fact has often been ignored in favor of putative universalistic viewpoints, careful cross-cultural research has continuously revealed cultural variation in depression, anxiety, schizophrenia, and other psychiatric problems related to PTSD (e.g., Kirmayer 1989; Kleinman and Good 1986; Marsella 1988; Neal and Turner 1991).

Definition of Culture

Kluckhohn and Murray (1957) stated: "Every man is like all other men, like some other men, and like no other man." The wisdom of these words is obvious. All human beings share a common biological heritage that makes them all "similar." But, it is also true that human beings belong to thousands of different ethnocultural groups, each of which shapes both the content and process of their acquired learning. It is also true that each human being is unique because of the specific interactions of their biological, psychological, and cultural natures. Thus, in the process of dealing with PTSD and other psychiatric disorders, we are dealing with at least three different dimensions of human nature—universal, cultural, and personal uniqueness.

Marsella and Kameoka (1989, p. 233) defined culture as

> Shared learned behavior which is transmitted from one generation to another to promote individual and group adjustment and adaptation. Culture is represented externally as artifacts, roles, and institutions, and is represented internally as values, beliefs, attitudes, cognitive styles, epistemologies, and consciousness patterns.

Ethnocultural Identity

Within the last decade, increased interest and support for the concept of diversity and cultural pluralism has resulted in a greater use of ethnocultural identity as the principal independent variable in cross-cultural research. Marsella (1990) defined ethnocultural identity as

> The extent to which an individual or group is committed to both endorsing and practicing a set of values, beliefs, and behaviors which are associated with a particular ethnocultural tradition.

Among ethnocultural minorities, the variations in behavior within a given ethnocultural group are dramatic and profound, and any effort to group people together for research on the basis of the largest possible ethnocultural dimension (e.g., Arab, Asian American, African American, American Indian, Hispanic) contributes excessive error variance to the design. Even within these larger categories, the shared culture may be minimal because of geographic, genetic, and psychocultural variation. In brief, we must emphasize the variations and patterns within an ethnocultural tradition and heritage and not simply use the general category when conducting cross-cultural research. For example, we should not group data according to large variables such as Japanese, but should rather break the group down into subgroups according to the extent to which they embrace or endorse traditional practices and behaviors.

The emergence of highly diverse and pluralistic cultures has led to discontent with older views of ethnocultural identity, which posited linear notions of acculturation and assimilation (i.e., each new generation becomes progressively more American). These views considered the dominant ethnocultural majority as being the end point toward which all ethnocultural minorities were striving. Today we recognize that there are a number of social statuses for minorities who fail to acculturate to the majority culture, including "acculturated," "bicultural," "marginal," "anomic," "deviant," and "multicultural." In addition, emphasis is now placed on multiculturalism, including multiple identities that emerge in response to situation demands and prerequisites.

If research on ethnocultural identity is to progress and replace or complement our current reliance on broader ethnic categories (e.g., Arab, Asian American, African American, American Indian, Hispanic), it is critical that efforts be made to develop valid and reliable methods for assessing ethnocultural identity. There are a number of different ways for assessing ethnocultural identity (e.g., Marsella 1990).

Equivalency in Assessment

If measurement concepts and methods are to be valid when applied across cultures, it is necessary to meet certain requirements regarding equivalency in language, concepts, scales, and norms. By equivalency, we are referring to the extent to which these topics are similar or equivalent for the different cultural groups under study. There are four types of equivalency that are important in psychiatric assessment: linguistic, conceptual, scale, and normative equivalence (Marsella and Kameoka 1989). If measures are not equivalent, validity is questionable.

Ethnosemantic Methods

If the measures being employed in a study do not meet the equivalency challenges, a researcher may want to consider developing instruments for the culture under study. This can be done through the use of ethnosemantic methods, a series of techniques that have long been established in anthropology to reduce ethnocentricity and bias. Marsella (1987) outlined the ethnosemantic procedures and steps for the measurement of depressive affect and experience. However, the procedures and steps are relevant to the study of any concept (e.g., PTSD, emotion, health). The value of this approach is that it begins with the subjective experience of the respondent rather than the assumptions of the researcher. This helps reduce ethnocentricity and bias resulting from the use of culturally insensitive and inappropriate materials and procedures. For example, it cannot be assumed that "anxiety," as we define and measure it in the Western world, is applicable to the world of the African tribal member. It is not simply a question of translation, it is a question of worldview, and the implications that different worldviews may have for understanding human behavior.

CONDUCTING CROSS-CULTURAL STUDIES OF PTSD

Epidemiology

In assessing the incidence and the prevalence of PTSD and related psychiatric disorders, it is important to consider ethnocultural variations in the definition and expression of the disorders. If standard psychiatric definitions such as those of DSM-III-R and ICD-10 (World Health Organization 1992) are to be used for case inclusion, it is possible that false positives and false negatives will enter into the rates, resulting in erroneous and potentially pernicious conclusions. For example, if researchers are studying traditional American Indian populations living on reservations, and they are using DSM-III-R standards, they may misdiagnose cases. It will be necessary to use idioms of distress and indigenous concepts to determine an accurate rate of the disorder. Several publications have addressed the problems associated with cross-cultural epidemiology (e.g., Marsella 1978; Marsella et al. 1986). These publications offer detailed suggestions for conducting cross-cultural epidemiology studies.

Recommended Clinical Studies of PTSD

There are a number of research strategies that can be used to conduct clinical research studies of PTSD and related disorders across ethnic and racial groups, including (for discussion, see Marsella 1979)

- *Symptom frequency*—exploring symptom frequencies of standard psychiatric and indigenous symptoms among cohorts or samples from different ethnocultural groups.
- *Matched diagnosis*—exploring symptom profiles among populations from different ethnocultural groups who share a common diagnosis of PTSD or a related disorder.
- *International survey*—conducting surveys of symptomatology and other clinical parameters of patients with PTSD from different countries.
- *Matched samples*—exploring symptom profiles and other clinical phenomenology of PTSD by comparing its presence in matched samples from different ethnocultural groups. In this instance, the emphasis is placed on matching for age, gender, education, social class, and so forth to reduce the variance associated with these variables in general population studies.
- *Indigenous symptom expressions and folk disorders*—studying the symptomatological expressions in non-Western populations via investigations of culture-specific disorders, such as latah, koro, and

susto, and folk expressions and symptom metaphors, such as heavy heart, soul loss, shaking stomach, and brain fag.
- *Factor analytic approaches*—using factor analysis to derive empirically the structure of symptom patterns among different ethnocultural groups. Rather than accept existing Western notions about symptom clusters, researchers can administer symptom checklists to different ethnocultural groups and then submit the responses to factor analyses for each of the groups studied. The factorial structures or symptom clusters can then be compared using factor comparison methods to determine the degree of similarity. Thus this method offers the chance to determine ethnocultural variations in symptom patterns empirically rather than accepting a priori notions based on Western assumptions and experiences.

CLOSING THOUGHTS AND CONCLUSIONS

Ethnocultural studies of PTSD offer an opportunity to identify the universal and the culture-specific aspects of the PTSD experience by comparing ethnocultural group differences in the distribution, expression, and treatment of PTSD. Identifying these differences can help clinicians adjust their practices and procedures to accommodate to the shared and the unique aspects of the PTSD experience.

There have been numerous studies of PTSD that have examined ethnocultural aspects of PTSD rates, expressions, and treatment regimens. These studies have investigated different ethnocultural groups (e.g., African Americans, the Indo-Chinese), victim populations (e.g., refugees, veterans, victims of natural disaster), traumatic events (e.g., Vietnam War, rapes and other crimes), and clinical topics (e.g., epidemiology, expression patterns, alternative therapies).

The results of these studies are generally consistent with the results of existing biological research, which suggests that there is a universal biological response to traumatic events that involves psychophysiological activation and dysregulation of the adrenergic, opioid, and hypothalamic-pituitary-adrenal axis systems, with attendant clinical symptomatology. It has also been speculated that there are permanent changes in the structure and neurochemical response patterns of the locus coeruleus. However, although the response to a traumatic event may share some universal features, especially as the trauma becomes more severe, ethnocultural factors may play an important role in the individual's vulnerability to PTSD, the expression of PTSD, and the treatment responsivity of PTSD.

In one of the most thorough studies of PTSD among Vietnam War veterans (i.e., the NVVRS), sizable differences in the prevalence of

PTSD among African Americans, Hispanics, and whites were reported; these differences were reduced when combat-exposure was controlled. However, even this study did not incorporate culturally sensitive research strategies (e.g., degree of ethnic identity or acculturation of the veterans, indigenous symptom scales, ethnic minority interviewers). Thus, questions still remain about differential PTSD rates across ethnocultural groups.

Limitations in the cross-cultural sensitivity of much of the existing ethnocultural research constrain our knowledge about culture-specific aspects of PTSD. Some researchers have suggested that although intrusive thoughts and memories of a traumatic event may transcend cultural experiences, the avoidance-numbing and hyperarousal symptomatology may be highly determined by ethnocultural affiliation. In addition, ethnocultural factors may be important determinants of vulnerability to trauma (by shaping concepts of what constitutes a trauma), personal and social resources for dealing with traumata, early childhood experiences, exposure to multiple trauma, premorbid personality, disease profiles (e.g., substance abuse, alcoholism), and treatment options that successfully contain and control the trauma experience.

The measurement of PTSD remains a serious problem because the existing instruments often do not include indigenous idioms of distress and causal conceptions of PTSD and related disorders. For example, it is widely known that many non-Western ethnic groups present symptoms somatically rather than psychologically or existentially. Since somatization symptoms are not broadly sampled in many of the PTSD measurement instruments, it is possible that important ethnocultural variations are not being considered. In addition, of course, there are problems of norms, scale formats, translation of materials, and the appropriateness of concepts.

Therapeutic approaches to PTSD have taken a variety of psychotherapeutic and psychopharmacological forms. Although these have generated some interesting hypotheses and some avenues for further exploration, there has been a dearth of well-controlled therapy studies that would enable us to reach scientific conclusions about the treatment of PTSD in different ethnocultural groups. A promising area of inquiry appears to be the use of indigenous healing ceremonies for treating traumata.

Existing studies provide an opportunity for generating and testing critical hypotheses about the role of ethnocultural factors in PTSD. With the careful application of accepted cross-cultural research methods and the use of more experimentally controlled studies, future research will enable us to understand the role of ethnocultural factors in the etiology, expression, and treatment of PTSD.

Not all victims of trauma develop PTSD. Further, some develop it immediately, whereas others develop a delayed syndrome. There is a need for more research among ethnocultural minority populations to identify the sources of strength and resiliency that somehow mediate the onset, course, and outcome of PTSD. One wonders if there are certain philosophical or religious beliefs, social interaction patterns, or personal dispositions and personality orientations that may be critical mediators of PTSD among certain ethnocultural groups.

Clearly, exposure to an extreme and brutalizing traumatic event seems to override ethnocultural variations. But there are people exposed to the same traumatic event who do not develop PTSD in any of its forms. Is there something that these people have learned—something within their ethnocultural experience—that can provide an inoculating effect? More and better research on ethnocultural aspects of PTSD is needed.

REFERENCES

Allen I: Post-traumatic stress disorders among Black Vietnam veterans. Hosp Community Psychiatry 37:55–61, 1986

Allodi F: Assessment and treatment of torture victims: a critical review. J Nerv Ment Dis 179:4–11, 1991

American Psychiatric Association: Diagnostic and Statistical Manual of Mental Disorders, 3rd Edition. Washington, DC, American Psychiatric Association, 1980

American Psychiatric Association: Diagnostic and Statistical Manual of Mental Disorders, 3rd Edition, Revised. Washington, DC, American Psychiatric Association, 1987

Arredondo P, Orjucla E, Moore L: Family therapy with Central American war refugee families. Journal of Strategic and Systematic Therapies 8:28–35, 1989

Arthur R: Psychiatric syndromes in prisoners of war and concentration camp survivors, in Extraordinary Disasters and Human Behavior. Edited by Fiemann C, Faquet R. New York, Plenum, 1982

Askevold F: War sailor syndrome. Psychother Psychosom 27:133–138, 1976

Askevold F: The war sailor syndrome. Dan Med Bull 27:222–223, 1980

Barse H: Post traumatic stress disorder and the American Indian Vietnam veteran. Stars and Stripes, April 19, 1984, p. 1

Baumgartner D: Sociodrama and the Vietnam combat veteran: a therapeutic release for a wartime experience. Journal of Group Psychotherapy, Psychodrama, and Sociometry 39:31–39, 1986

Becerra R: The Hispanic Vietnam veterans: mental health issues and therapeutic approaches, in Mental Health and Hispanic-Americans. Edited by Becerra R, Escobar K. New York, Grune & Stratton, 1982, pp 169–180

Becker M: Extermination camp syndrome. N Engl J Med 269:1145, 1963

Beiser M: Mental health of refugees in resettlement countries, in Mental Health of Immigrants and Refugees. Edited by Holtzman WH, Bornemann TH. Austin, TX, Hogg Foundation, 1990, pp 51–65

Beiser M, Turner R, Ganesan S: Catastrophic stress and factors affecting its consequences among Southeast Asian refugees. Soc Sci Med 28:183–189, 1989

Boehnlein J: Clinical relevance of grief and mourning among Cambodian refugees. Soc Sci Med 25:765–772, 1987a

Boehnlein J: Culture and society in post-traumatic stress disorder: implications for psychotherapy. Am J Psychother 41:519–530, 1987b

Boehnlein J, Kinzie D, Rath B, et al: One year follow-up study of post-traumatic stress disorder among survivors of Cambodian concentration camps. Am J Psychiatry 142:958–968, 1985

Breslau N, Davis G, Andreski P, et al: Traumatic events and post-traumatic stress disorder in an urban population of young adults. Arch Gen Psychiatry 48:216–222, 1991

Carter J: Alcoholism in Black Vietnam veterans: symptoms of post-traumatic stress disorder. J Natl Med Assoc 74: 655–660, 1982

Cervantes R, Salgado de Snyder V, Padilla A: Posttraumatic stress in immigrants from Central America and Mexico. Hosp Community Psychiatry 40:615–619, 1989

Chodoff P: Late effects of the concentration camp syndrome. Arch Gen Psychiatry 8:323–333, 1963

Comas-Diaz L, Griffith EE (eds): Clinical Guidelines in Cross-Cultural Mental Health. New York, Wiley, 1988

de Girolamo G: International perspectives on the treatment and prevention of post traumatic stress, in International Handbook of Traumatic Stress Syndromes. Edited by Wilson J, Raphael B. New York, Plenum, 1992

de Girolamo G, Orley J: Psychosocial Consequences of Disasters: Prevention and Management. Geneva, Switzerland, Division of Mental Health, World Health Organization, 1992

de Girolamo G, Diekstra R, Williams C: Report of a Visit to Border Encampments on the Kampuchea-Thai Border. Geneva, Switzerland, World Health Organization, 1989

de la Fuente R: The mental health consequences of the 1985 earthquakes in Mexico. International Journal of Mental Health 19:21–29, 1990

Derogatis L: SCL-90-R Manual II. Towson, MD, Clinical Psychometric Research, 1983

Dobkin de Rios M, Friedman J: Hypnotherapy with Hispanic burn patients. Int J Clin Exp Hypn 35:87–94, 1987

Eitenger L: The symptomatology of mental disease among refugees in Norway. Journal of Mental Science 106:947–966, 1960

Eitenger L: Concentration Camp Survivors in Norway and Israel. London, Allen & Unwin, 1964

Eitenger L, Grunfeld B: Psychoses among refugees in Norway. Acta Psychiatr Scand 42:315–328, 1966

Escobar J, Randolph E, Puente G, et al: Post-traumatic stress disorders in Hispanic Vietnam vets: clinical phenomenology and sociocultural characteristics. J Consult Clin Psychol 52:79–87, 1983

Freimer N, Lu F, Chen J: Post-traumatic stress and conversion disorders in a Laotian refugee veteran: use of amobarbital interviews. J Nerv Ment Dis 177:432–433, 1989

Friedman M, Jaranson J: PTSD among refugees, in Amidst Peril and Pain: The Mental Health and Social Wellbeing of the World's Refugees. Edited by Marsella A, Borneman T, Ekblad S, et al. Washington, DC, American Psychological Association (in press)

Friedman M, Marsella A, Ashcraft M, et al: The Matsunaga Study: Clinical and Epidemiological Studies of American Indian, Native Hawaiian, and Japanese American Vietnam War Veterans (project technical report 1). White River Junction, VT, National Center for PTSD, VA ROMC, 1992

Garcia-Peltoniemi R: Clinical manifestations of psychopathology in refugees, in Refugee Mental Health and Social Adjustment: A Guide to Clinical and Preventive Services. Edited by Westermeyer J, Williams C, Nguyen N. Washington, DC, U.S. Government Printing Office, 1992a, pp 42–55

Garcia-Peltoniemi R: Epidemiological perspectives, in Refugee Mental Health and Social Adjustment: A Guide to Clinical and Preventive Services. Edited by Westermeyer J, Williams C, Nguyen N. Washington, DC, U.S. Government Printing Office, 1992b, pp 24–41

Gaw A: Culture, Ethnicity, and Mental Illness. Washington, DC, American Psychiatric Press, 1992

Goldfeld A, Mollica R, Pesavento R, et al: The physical and psychological sequelae of torture. JAMA 259:2725–2729, 1988

Green B, Grace M, Lindy J, et al: Race differences in response to combat stress. Journal of Traumatic Stress 3:379–393, 1990

Hamada R, Chemtob C, Sautner R, et al: Ethnic identity and Vietnam: a Japanese-American Vietnam veteran with PTSD. Hawaii Med J 47:100–109, 1988

Hathaway SR, McKinley JC: Minnesota Multiphasic Personality Inventory—2. Minneapolis, MN, University of Minnesota, 1970

Holen A: A Long Term Outcome Study of Survivors from a Disaster. Oslo, Norway, University of Oslo, 1990

Holm T: Indian veterans of the Vietnam War: restoring harmony through tribal ceremony. Four Winds 3:34–37, 1982

Holm T: Warriors All: 170 American Indian Vietnam Era veterans. Tucson, AZ, University of Arizona, 1989

Jaranson J: Mental health treatment of refugees and immigrants, in Mental Health of Immigrants and Refugees. Edited by Holtzman WH, Bornemann TH. Austin, TX, Hogg Foundation, 1990, pp 207–215

Jaranson J: Psychotherapeutic medication, in Mental Health Services for Refugees. Washington, DC, U.S. Department of Health and Human Services, 1991, pp 132–145

Jordan K, Schlenger W, Hough R, et al: Lifetime and current prevalence of specific psychiatric disorders among Vietnam veterans and controls. Arch Gen Psychiatry 48:207–215, 1991

Kettner B: Combat strain and subsequent mental health: a follow-up of Swedish soldiers serving in the United Nations armed forces in 1961–62. Acta Psychiatr Scand Suppl 230:1–112, 1972

Kim K: Severely battered wives: clinical manifestations and problems in Korea. International Journal of Family Psychiatry 8:387–414, 1987

Kinzie D: Cultural aspects of psychiatric treatment with Indochinese patients. American Journal of Social Psychiatry 1:47–53, 1985

Kinzie D: Therapeutic approaches to traumatized Cambodian refugees. Journal of Traumatic Stress 2:75–91, 1989

Kinzie D, Fleck J: Psychotherapy with severely traumatized Cambodian refugees. Am J Psychother 41:82–94, 1987

Kinzie D, Leung P: Clonidine in Cambodian patients with PTSD. J Nerv Ment Dis 177:546–550, 1989

Kinzie D, Tran K, Breckenridge A, et al: An Indochinese refugee clinic: culturally accepted treatment approaches. Am J Psychiatry 137:1429–1432, 1980

Kinzie D, Frederickson R, Rath B, et al: Post-traumatic stress disorder among survivors of Cambodian concentration camps. Am J Psychiatry 141:645–650, 1984

Kinzie D, Leung P, Boehnlein J, et al: Tricyclic antidepressant blood levels in Southeast Asians: clinical and cultural implications. J Nerv Ment Dis 175:480–485, 1987

Kinzie D, Boehnlein J, Leung P, et al: The prevalence of PTSD and its clinical significance among Southeast Asian refugees. Am J Psychiatry 147:913–917, 1990

Kirmayer L: Cultural variations in the response to psychiatric disorders and emotional distress. Soc Sci Med 29:327–339, 1989

Kleinman A, Good B (eds): Culture and Depression. Los Angeles, CA, University of California Press, 1986

Kluckhohn C, Murray H: Personality in Nature, Culture and Society. New York, Basic Books, 1957

Krippner S, Colodzin B: Multicultural methods of treating Vietnam veterans with PTSD. Int J Psychosom 36:79–85, 1989

Kroll J, Habenicht M, MacKenzie T, et al: Depression and post-traumatic stress disorders in Southeast Asians. Am J Psychiatry 146:1592–1597, 1989

Krupinski J, Stoller A, Wallace L: Psychiatric disorders of Eastern European refugees in Australia. Soc Sci Med 7:31–49, 1973

Kulka R, Schlenger W, Fairbank J, et al: Trauma and the Vietnam War Generation. New York, Brunner/Mazel, 1990

Laufer R, Gallops M, Frey-Wouters E: War stress and trauma: the Vietnam veterans experience. J Health Soc Behav 18:236–244, 1984

Lee E, Lu F: Assessment and treatment of Asian-American survivors of mass violence. Journal of Traumatic Stress 2:93–120, 1989

Leff J: Psychiatry Around the Globe. Washington, DC, American Psychiatric Press, 1988

Lima B, Pai S, Santacruz H, et al: Psychiatric disorders among poor victims following a major disaster: Armero, Columbia. J Nerv Ment Dis 179:420–427, 1991

Lin E, Ilhe L, Tazuma L: Depression among Vietnamese refugees in a primary care clinic. Am J Med 78:41–44, 1985

Lin K, Finder K: Neuroleptic dosages for Asians. Am J Psychiatry 140:480–491, 1983

Lin K, Shen W: Pharmacotherapy for Southeast Asian psychiatric patients. J Nerv Ment Dis 179:346–350, 1991

Lin K, Poland R, Lesser M: Ethnicity and psychopharmacology. Cult Med Psychiatry 10:151–165, 1986

Lopez A, Boccellari A, Hall K: Post-traumatic stress disorder in a Central American refugee. Hosp Community Psychiatry 39:1309–1311, 1988

Malt U: The long term psychiatric consequences of accidental injuries: a longitudinal study of 107 adults. Br J Psychiatry 153:810–818, 1988

Malt U, Blikra G, Hoivik B: The three year biopsychosocial outcome of 551 hospitalized accidentally injured adults. Acta Psychiatr Scand Suppl 355:84–93, 1989

Marsella AJ: Thoughts on cross-cultural studies on the epidemiology of depression. Cult Med Psychiatry 2:343–357, 1978

Marsella AJ: Cross-cultural studies of mental disorders, in Perspectives on Cross-Cultural Psychology. Edited by Marsella AJ, Tharp R, Ciborowski T. New York, Academic Press, 1979, pp 233–264

Marsella AJ: The measurement of depressive experience and disorder across cultures, in The Measurement of Depression. Edited by Marsella AJ, Hirschfeld R, Katz M. New York, Guilford, 1987, pp 376–398

Marsella AJ: Cross-cultural research on severe mental disorders: issues and findings. Acta Psychiatr Scand Suppl 344:7–22, 1988

Marsella AJ: Ethnocultural identity: the "new" independent variable in cross-cultural research. Focus: Newsletter of The American Psychological Association Minority Division 3:7–8, 1990

Marsella AJ, Kameoka VA: Ethnocultural issues in the assessment of psychopathology, in Measuring Mental Illness: Psychometric Assessment for Clinicians. Edited by Wetzler S. Washington, DC, American Psychiatric Press, 1989, pp 229–256

Marsella AJ, White G: Cultural conceptions of mental health and therapy. Boston, MA, G Reidel, 1982

Marsella AJ, Sartorius N, Jablensky A, et al: Cross-cultural studies of depression: an overview, in Culture and Depression. Edited by Kleinman A, Good B. Los Angeles, CA, University of California Press, 1986

Marsella A, Chemtob C, Hamada R: Ethnocultural aspects of PTSD in Vietnam War veterans. National Center for Post-Traumatic Stress Disorder Clinical Newsletter 1:1–3, 1990

Marsella AJ, Friedman M, Spain H: A selective review of the literature on ethnocultural aspects of PTSD. PTSD Research Quarterly 2:1–7, 1992

Mollica R: The trauma story: the psychiatric care of refugee survivors of violence and torture, in Post-traumatic Therapy and Victims of Violence. Edited by Ochburg F. New York, Brunner/Mazel, 1988, pp 295–314

Mollica R, Lavelle J: The trauma of mass violence and torture: an overview of psychiatric care of the Southeast Asian refugee, in Clinical Guidelines in Cross-Cultural Mental Health. Edited by Comas-Diaz L, Griffith EE. New York, Wiley, 1988, pp 262–304

Mollica R, Wyshak G, Lavelle J: The psychosocial impact of war trauma and torture on Southeast Asian refugees. Am J Psychiatry 144:1567–1572, 1987

Mollica R, Caspi-Yavin Y, Bollini P, et al: The Harvard Trauma Questionnaire: validating a cross-cultural instrument for measuring torture, trauma, and PTSD in Indochinese refugees. J Nerv Ment Dis 180:111–116, 1992

Moore L, Boehnlein J: Post-traumatic stress disorder, depression, and somatic symptoms in U.S. Mien patients. J Nerv Ment Dis 179:728–733, 1991

Murphy H: Refugee psychoses in Great Britain: admissions to mental hospitals, in Flight and Resettlement. Edited by Murphy H. Paris, UNESCO, 1955, pp 173–194

Myers C: Shell Shock in France, 1914–1918. Cambridge, England, Cambridge University Press, 1940

National Center for PTSD: Selected abstracts of European PTSD literature. National Center for PTSD Research Quarterly 2:1–7, 1991

Neal A, Turner S: Anxiety disorders research with African Americans: current status. Psychol Bull 109:400–410, 1991

Nicassio P: The psychosocial adjustment of the Southeast Asian refugee. Journal of Cross-Cultural Psychology 16:153–173, 1985

Niem T: Treating Oriental patients with Western psychiatry: a 12 year experience with Vietnamese refugee psychiatric patients. Psychiatric Annals 19:648–652, 1989

Oppenheim H: Die Traumatischen Neurosen: Nach den in Nervenklinik der Charite in den Letzten 5 Jahren Gesammelten Beobachtungen. Berlin, Hirschwald, 1889

Ostwald P, Bittner E: Life adjustment after severe persecution. Am J Psychiatry 124:1393–1400, 1968

Parson E: The "gook" identification and post-traumatic stress disorders in Black Vietnam veterans. Black Psychiatrists of America Quarterly 11:14–18, 1984

Parson E: Ethnicity and traumatic stress: the intersecting point in psychotherapy, in Trauma and Its Wake: The Study and Treatment of PTSD. Edited by Figley C. New York, Brunner/Mazel, 1985, pp 314–337

Parson E: Post-traumatic psychocultural therapy (PTpsyCT): integration of trauma and shattering social labels of the self. Journal of Contemporary Psychotherapy 20:237–258, 1990

Pedersen P, Sartorius N, Marsella AJ: Mental Health Services: The Cross-Cultural Context. Beverly Hills, CA, Sage, 1984

Penk W, Allen I: Clinical assessment of post-traumatic stress disorder (PTSD) among American minorities who served in Vietnam. Journal of Traumatic Stress 4:41–66, 1991

Penk W, Robinowitz R, Dorsett D, et al: Post-traumatic stress disorder: psychometric assessment and race, in Stressful Life Events. Edited by Miller T. Madison, CT, International Universities Press, 1989, pp 525–552

Perry R: Minority Citizens and Disasters. Athens, University of Georgia Press, 1986

Pfister-Ammende M: The symptomatology, treatment, and prognosis of mentally ill refugees and repatriates in Switzerland, in Flight and Resettlement. Edited by Murphy H. Paris, UNESCO, 1955, pp 147–172

Pina G: Diagnosis and treatment of PTSD among Hispanic Vietnam veterans, in The Trauma of War: Stress and Recovery in Vietnam Veterans. Edited by Sonneberg SM, Blank AS Jr, Talbott JA. Washington, DC, American Psychiatric Press, 1985, pp 389–402

Radloff LS: The CES-D Scale: a self-report depression scale for research in the general population. Applied Psychology Measurements 1:385–401, 1977

Robins LN, Helzer JE, Croughan J, et al: National Institute of Mental Health Diagnostic Interview Schedule: its history, characteristics, and validity. Arch Gen Psychiatry 38:381–389, 1981

Rosser R: Reality therapy with the Khmer refugees resettled in the United States. Journal of Reality Therapy 6:21–29, 1986

Rozee P, Van Boemel G: The psychological effect of war trauma and abuse on older Cambodian women. Women and Therapy 8:23–50, 1989

Salmon T: The care and treatment of mental disorders and war neuroses ("shell shock") in the British Army. New York, War Work Committee of the National Committee for Mental Hygiene, 1917

Silver S: Worth of the Warrior Project. Washington, DC, Readjustment Counseling Service, Veterans Administration Central Office, 1984

Silver S, Wilson J: Native American healing and purification rituals for war stress, in Human Adaptation to Stress: From the Holocaust to Vietnam. Edited by Wilson J, Harel Z, Kahanal B. New York, Plenum, 1990

Simons R, Hughes C: The Culture Bound Syndromes: Folk Illnesses of Psychiatric and Anthropological Interest. Boston, MA, D Reidel, 1985

Solomon K: The dynamics of post-traumatic stress disorder in South African political detainees. Am J Psychother 43:208–217, 1989

Solomon Z: Psychological sequelae of war: a three year prospective study of Israeli combat stress reaction casualties. J Nerv Ment Dis 177:342–346, 1989

Solomon Z, Mikulincer M: Combat stress reactions, PTSD, and social adjustment: a study of Israel veterans. J Nerv Ment Dis 175:277–285, 1987

Solomon Z, Oppenheimer B, Noy S: Subsequent military adjustment of combat stress reaction casualties: a nine year follow-up study. Mil Med 151:8–11, 1986

Solomon Z, Weisenberg M, Schwarzwald J, et al: PTSD among frontline soldiers with combat stress reaction: the 1982 Israeli experience. Am J Psychiatry 144:448–453, 1987

Streimer J, Cosstick J, Tennant C: The psychosocial adjustment of Australian Vietnam veterans. Am J Psychiatry 142:616–618, 1985

Stretch R: Post traumatic stress disorder and the Canadian Vietnam veteran. Journal of Traumatic Stress 3:239–254, 1990

Stretch R: Psychosocial readjustment of Canadian Vietnam veterans. J Consult Clin Psychol 59:188–189, 1991

Strom A (ed): Norwegian Concentration Camp Survivors. New York, Humanities Press, 1968

Sue DW, Sue D: Counseling the Culturally Different: Theory and Practice. New York, Wiley, 1990

Summerfield D, Toser L: "Low intensity" war and mental trauma in Nicaragua: a study in a rural community. Med War 7:84–89, 1991

Tennant C, Streimer J, Temperly H: Memories of Vietnam: post-traumatic stress disorders in Australian veterans. Aust N Z J Psychiatry 24:29–39, 1990

Triandis H, Draguns J: The Handbook of Cross-Cultural Psychology, Vol 6: Psychopathology. Boston, MA, Allyn & Bacon, 1980

Urrutia G: Mental health problems of encamped refugees: Guatemalan refugees in Mexican camps. Bull Menninger Clin 51:170–185, 1986

Weisaeth L: The stressors and the post-traumatic stress syndrome after an industrial disaster. Acta Psychiatr Scand Suppl 355:25–37, 1989

Weisaeth L, Eitenger L: Research on PTSD and other post-traumatic reactions: European literature. National Center for PTSD Research Quarterly 2:1–7, 1991

Westermeyer J: Mental Health for Refugees and Other Migrants. Chicago, IL, Charles C Thomas, 1988

Westermeyer J: Cross-cultural care of PTSD: research, training, and service needs for the future. Journal of Traumatic Stress 2:515–536, 1989

Westermeyer J, Wahmemholm K: Assessing the victimized psychiatric patient: special issues regarding violence, combat, terror and refuge seeking. Hosp Community Psychiatry 3:245–249, 1989

Westermeyer J, Williams C, Nguyen N (eds): Refugee Mental Health and Social Adjustment: A Guide to Clinical and Preventive Services. Washington, DC, U.S. Government Printing Office, 1992

Williams C, Westermeyer J (eds): Refugee Mental Health in Resettlement Countries. Washington, DC, Hemisphere Publishing, 1986

World Health Organization: The ICD-10 Classification of Mental and Behavioural Disorders: Clinical Descriptions and Diagnostic Guidelines. Geneva, World Health Organization, 1992

Chapter 3

Neurobiology of Posttraumatic Stress Disorder

J. Douglas Bremner, M.D., Michael Davis, Ph.D., Steven M. Southwick, M.D., John H. Krystal, M.D., and Dennis S. Charney, M.D.

Because of the fact that posttraumatic stress disorder (PTSD) has been accepted as a valid diagnosis for only the past decade, research on neurobiological mechanisms of PTSD has only recently been initiated (Pynoos et al. 1987). PTSD has been shown to be highly prevalent, affecting, for example, approximately 15% of veterans of the Vietnam War; it extracts a high cost in morbidity and loss of productivity (Kulka et al. 1990). These patients suffer from nightmares, sleep disturbance, abnormal startle reaction, physiological hyperresponsiveness to reminders of the original trauma, avoidance reactions, guilt, and intrusive memories and dissociative flashbacks over which they have little or no control.

Although few clinical studies have investigated neurobiological alterations associated with PTSD, there has been a strong tradition of research on the effects of stress on animals in the laboratory. Laboratory scientists have only recently been made aware of the direct applications of their research to individuals with stress-induced psychiatric disorders such as PTSD. Moreover, numerous clinical researchers have now turned their attention to PTSD, and they have been quick to take note of the applicability of studies of stress in animals to the study of the neurobiology of PTSD (Charney et al., in press; Krystal et al. 1989). Extreme threat to the organism, whether a laboratory animal or an individual exposed to extreme stress, may result in long-term changes in behavior and neurobiological systems.

In this chapter, we focus on the role of brain norepinephrine systems, the corticotropin-releasing factor (CRF)–hypothalamic-pituitary-adrenal (HPA) axis system, and other brain systems in the acute and chronic responses to stress (Table 3–1). Clinical examples are utilized to show how responses to stress that are initially adaptive may lead to long-term pathological changes in memory and brain neurotransmitter and neuropeptide systems.

NORADRENERGIC BRAIN SYSTEMS

Noradrenergic brain systems appear to play a role in anxiety and fear (Charney et al. 1987; Redmond and Huang 1979) as well as in vigilance and selective attention (Aston-Jones and Bloom 1981). Studies in nonhuman primates show that the locus coeruleus, located in the pons, is the site of the majority of the noradrenergic neurons in the brain and has projections to limbic brain structures involved in learning and

Table 3–1. Changes in brain neurotransmitter and neurohormonal systems with stress

Neurotransmitter	Acute stress	Chronic stress	Brain regions involved	PTSD symptoms
Norepinephrine	Increased turnover	Increased responsiveness of LC neurons	Hipp, Hypo, LC, Cor, Amyg	Anxiety, fear, hypervigilance, hyperarousal, irritability, encoding of traumatic memories
CRF–HPA axis				
Brain CRF	Increase	Increase/decrease	Hipp, Hypo, Cor, LC, Amyg	Anxiety and fear, memory alterations, hyperarousal
Peripheral ACTH	Increase	Increase/decrease		
Peripheral cortisol	Increase	Increase/decrease		
Dopamine	Increased release	Increase	PFC, NA	Hypervigilance, paranoia, alterations in memory
Benzodiazepines	Increased release	Decrease[a]	Hipp, Hypo, Cor, Stria, MB	Anxiety
Endogenous opiates	Increased release	Decrease[a]	MB, Hipp	Analgesia, emotional blunting, encoding of traumatic memories

Note. LC = locus coeruleus. Hipp = hippocampus. Hypo = hypothalamus. Cor = cerebral cortex. Amyg = amygdala. CRF = corticotropin-releasing factor. HPA = hypothalamic-pituitary-adrenal axis. ACTH = adrenocorticotropic hormone. PFC = prefrontal cortex. NA = nucleus accumbens. Stria = striatum. MB = midbrain.
[a]Decrease in receptor binding measured by B_{max}.

memory, including the temporal lobe, hippocampus, hypothalamus, amygdala, nucleus accumbens, and prefrontal cortex (reviewed in Redmond and Huang 1979). Increases in heart rate, blood pressure, and alerting behaviors essential for the response to life-threatening situations are mediated by noradrenergic brain systems. In addition, stimulation of the locus coeruleus in nonhuman primates results in behaviors that resemble those associated with human anxiety (reviewed in Redmond and Huang 1979). An increase in firing from noradrenergic neurons in the locus coeruleus of freely moving cats is seen following exposure to stressors, including 15 minutes of 100 dB white noise, seeing a dog, and restraint stress. Behaviorally activating but nonstressful stimuli, such as seeing a mouse, do not result in activation of these neurons (Abercrombie and Jacobs 1987; Levine et al. 1990).

Activation of limbic and cortical areas such as the hippocampus, amygdala, and prefrontal cortex involved in learning and memory is an important part of the stress response (Foote et al. 1983). Acute stress results in an increased release of norepinephrine in the hippocampus, hypothalamus, locus coeruleus, and other brain areas. The hippocampus and amygdala, in turn, are involved in mediating the emotional, cognitive, and alerting responses to stress (reviewed in Charney et al., in press).

Animals exposed to extreme stress develop long-term changes in noradrenergic brain systems. In 1967 Seligman and Maier first noted that beagles exposed to electric shock without the chance to escape developed specific behavioral impairments not seen in beagles who did have the chance to escape. Beagles previously exposed to inescapable shock would sit passively and not attempt to escape when they were subsequently shocked in circumstances where there was a chance to escape. The animal model of inescapable stress has since been applied widely to the study of the neurobiology of stress (reviewed in Krystal et al. 1989). Inescapable stress—such as electric shocks to the feet of rats from which they cannot escape, or being forced to swim in cold water without being able to get out—results in a massive output of norepinephrine in specific parts of the brain that are associated with learned helplessness behaviors, such as a decrease in motor activity and a lack of propensity to remove themselves from subsequent electric shocks, compared with rats exposed to escapable shocks (Weiss et al. 1981). Animals exposed to chronic stress have been shown to have an increased responsiveness of locus coeruleus neurons and increased release of extracellular norepinephrine in the hippocampus and other brain regions in response to acute stressors compared with animals without a history of exposure to chronic stress (reviewed in Simson and Weiss 1988). Evidence accumulated to date suggests that with repeated exposure to inescapable stress there is an initial increase in norepinephrine release that is associated with an increase in synthesis. It may be that with repeated stress, synthesis cannot keep pace with utilization in brain structures such as the hypothalamus, hippocampus, amygdala, locus coeruleus, and cerebral cortex, although further research is needed to clarify this area (Weiss et al. 1981).

Interventions at the level of noradrenergic brain systems can prevent the acquisition of learned helplessness in response to inescapable stress. Prevention of the depletion of norepinephrine by preadministration of the α_2-noradrenergic receptor agonist clonidine has been shown to block the development of learned helplessness following exposure to inescapable stress (Anisman et al. 1980). Release of norepinephrine from the locus coeruleus and amygdala following exposure to uncontrollable stress is also attenuated with preadministration of opiates, ethanol, and benzodiazepines, providing a rational explanation for the preference for these substances among PTSD patients (Drugan et al. 1984). The effects of administration of clonidine and benzodiazepines also suggest a possible intervention that may prevent the development of long-term changes in noradrenergic system function associated with stress. For instance, administration of these agents to individuals immediately after exposure to extreme trauma may be beneficial in the prevention of pathology associated with stress.

Clinical studies suggest alterations in noradrenergic function in patients with PTSD. Consistent with findings from preclinical studies of an acute increase in norepinephrine associated with stress, an increase in urinary norepinephrine levels has been found in PTSD patients compared with patients with major depressive disorder, bipolar (manic) disorder, paranoid schizophrenia, and undifferentiated schizophrenia (Kosten et al. 1987). In addition, an increase in urinary epinephrine levels has been noted in PTSD patients compared with patients with major depressive, paranoid schizophrenia, and undifferentiated schizophrenia, but not with bipolar patients (Kosten et al. 1987). An increase in the ratio of norepinephrine to cortisol has been found to differentiate more specifically patients with PTSD from these other patient groups (Mason et al. 1988). Other investigators, however, have not replicated these results for norepinephrine or cortisol levels in patients with PTSD compared with Vietnam veterans without PTSD (Pitman and Orr 1990). These studies are limited by the fact that assessments are based on peripheral measures of noradrenergic function. The relationship between these measures and central measures of noradrenergic function is not clear.

Studies of peripheral noradrenergic receptor function have also shown alterations in patients with PTSD. A decrease in platelet α_2-adrenergic receptor number as measured by total binding sites for the α_2 antagonist [^{3}H]rauwolscine has been noted in PTSD patients compared with control subjects (Perry et al. 1987). A significantly greater reduction in number of platelet α_2 receptors after exposure to agonist (epinephrine) has also been observed in PTSD patients compared with healthy control subjects (Perry et al. 1990). A decrease in basal adenosine 3′,5′-monophosphate (AMP) signal transduction as well as isoproterenol- and forskolin-stimulated cyclic adenosine 3′,5′-monophosphate (cAMP) signal transduction was noted in PTSD patients compared with healthy control subjects (Lerer et al. 1987). In addition, a decrease in platelet monoamine oxidase activity has been found in 23 PTSD patients compared with 19 age-matched control subjects (Davidson et al. 1985). A study of 8 female patients with noncombat-related PTSD utilizing the desipramine-growth hormone test as a probe of postsynaptic α_2-adrenoceptor function found no difference in growth hormone response between patients and matched control subjects (Dinan et al. 1990). One possible explanation for these findings is an increase in presynaptic release of norepinephrine and increased exposure of receptors to norepinephrine, which results in a down-regulation of α_2 receptors and a decrease in β-adrenergic receptor responsiveness.

Several studies have examined response to the α_2-noradrenergic receptor antagonist yohimbine, which stimulates brain norepinephrine release and has been proposed as a probe for noradrenergic correlates of anxiety (Charney et al. 1984, 1987, in press). Administration of yohimbine to patients with combat-related PTSD results in flashbacks in 40% of patients and panic attacks in 70%, an increase in intrusive memories, and increased 3-methoxy-4-hydroxyphenylglycol (MHPG), blood pressure, and heart rate response compared with control subjects (Southwick et al. 1991). Patients with generalized anxiety disorder, major depression, schizophrenia, and obsessive-compulsive disorder have not been shown to have abnormal responses to yohimbine administration (reviewed in Charney et al., in press). However, patients with panic disorder have increased MHPG and cardiovascular responses and frequently experience panic attacks following yohimbine (Charney et al. 1984, 1987). These studies suggest that common alterations in noradrenergic function may occur in PTSD and in panic disorder.

Other studies have used administration of sodium lactate to study the neurobiology of PTSD. Lactate administration has been previously shown to produce panic attacks in patients with panic disorder. Of seven patients with PTSD and comorbid panic disorder, panic attacks were seen in six patients following administration of lactate and flashbacks in all patients following administration of lactate compared with no flashbacks or panic attacks in control subjects (Rainey et al. 1987). Only two of the seven patients had flashbacks following administration of isoproterenol, and one with placebo. It is not known what the mechanism of action is of lactate in the provocation of specific symptoms in patients with panic disorder and PTSD, although a relationship between lactate's mechanism of provocation of panic attacks and noradrenergic brain systems has been hypothesized. In any case, these studies are supportive of a common neurobiological mechanism involved in the symptomatology of patients with panic disorder and with PTSD.

Preclinical and clinical studies suggest a role for alterations in noradrenergic brain systems in stress and PTSD. We hypothesize that PTSD is associated with an increased responsiveness of locus coeruleus neurons and an increased release of extracellular norepinephrine in the hippocampus and other brain regions receiving innervation from the locus coeruleus in response to stressful stimuli. We also hypothesize that PTSD is associated with a decreased sensitivity of the presynaptic α_2-noradrenergic autoreceptor, which also has the effect of increasing norepinephrine release. Our findings of increased MHPG, heart rate, and blood pressure response to yohimbine, in addition to other preclinical and clinical findings reviewed above, are consistent with this hypothesis. However, direct evidence of noradrenergic brain system function in patients with PTSD is needed to test this hypothesis more definitively.

CORTICOTROPIN-RELEASING FACTOR–HYPOTHALAMIC-PITUITARY-ADRENAL AXIS SYSTEM

The CRF–HPA axis system plays an important role in the stress response (reviewed in Nemeroff and Schatzberg 1988). CRF is distributed in several brain areas that have been implicated in the behavioral and physiological responses to stress, including the central nucleus of the amygdala, hippocampus, prefrontal and cingulate cortices, locus coeruleus, thalamus, periaqueductal gray, and cerebellum. Intraventricular injection of CRF results in a series of physiological and behavioral responses that are adaptive during stress and that are considered to be characteristic of anxiety responses. These behaviors include increased locomotion and grooming in an open field environment and a decrease in punished responding and time spent on an elevated platform. CRF injected into the central nucleus of the amygdala results in an increase in the magnitude of the startle response and significantly improves retention of the inhibitory avoidance response, a measure of learning and memory (reviewed in Dunn and Berridge 1990).

The CRF–HPA axis system appears to stimulate brain norepinephrine systems, and, conversely, brain norepinephrine systems appear to stimulate the CRF–HPA axis system. CRF-containing neurons from the paraventricular nucleus of the hypothalamus project to the locus coeruleus, and noradrenergic neurons from the locus coeruleus project to the paraventricular nucleus. Intraventricular administration of CRF results in an increase in discharge rate of locus coeruleus neurons. Administration of norepinephrine, in turn, stimulates release of CRF (reviewed in Dunn and Berridge 1990).

Exposure to acute stress results in an increase in glucocorticoids in laboratory animals, which is probably mediated by CRF and adrenocorticotropic hormone (ACTH) (reviewed in McEwen et al. 1986). Glucocorticoids are important in effecting many of the expressions of the stress response, such as increased gluconeogenesis, inhibition of growth and reproductive systems, and containment of inflammatory responses. Different effects result from exposure to chronic stress. Chronic stress has been shown to result in a decrease in glucocorticoid levels in some studies; other studies have shown an increase. Animals with a history of prior exposure to stress respond to subsequent stressors with a delay in the return of glucocorticoids to baseline following exposure to the stressor (reviewed in Nemeroff and Schatzberg 1988).

Several clinical studies suggest that alterations in HPA axis function may be associated with PTSD. A decrease in urinary cortisol levels has been found in Vietnam veterans with chronic PTSD compared with control subjects and patients with major depression, bipolar disorder (manic), paranoid schizophrenia, and undifferentiated schizophrenia (Mason et al. 1986). PTSD patients have been shown to suppress with the standard 1-mg dexamethasone suppression test (DST) in a comparable fashion to healthy control subjects (Dinan et al. 1990; Kosten et al. 1990; Kudler et al. 1987). Studies utilizing lower doses of dexamethasone (0.5 mg) suggest that PTSD may be associated with a supersuppression of the cortisol response compared with control subjects (Yehuda et al., in press), which appears to be the opposite of patients with major depression, who are nonsuppressors with the standard 1-mg DST. PTSD patients have also been found to have a significantly lower ACTH response to CRF than control subjects, suggesting a blunted ACTH response to CRF (Smith et al. 1989) and an increase in lymphocyte glucocorticoid receptors compared with control subjects (Yehuda et al. 1991). These studies suggest that alterations in cortisol and HPA axis function may be associated with PTSD.

One possible explanation of clinical findings to date is an increase in central glucocorticoid receptor responsiveness. An increase in glucocorticoid responsiveness in brain structures such as the hippocampus may lead to a heightened negative feedback system, with the net result of a decrease in peripheral cortisol, and a heightened suppression of cortisol compared with control subjects. It is important to note, however, that there are inconsistencies in findings from preclinical and clinical studies on CRF–HPA axis changes associated with stress that prevent the formulation of a single hypothesis that can explain all of the findings. Clearly further studies are required in this important area.

DOPAMINERGIC BRAIN SYSTEMS

Accumulating evidence suggests that dopaminergic brain systems are involved in the neurobiological response to stress. Mild and brief stress in the form of footshock results in a selective activation of the dopaminergic neurons of the medial prefrontal cortex (Deutch et al. 1985). Daily treatments of inescapable footshocks to rats result in increased levels of the dopamine metabolites 3,4-dihydroxyphenylacetic acid (DOPAC) in the prefrontal cortex and homovanillic acid in the nucleus accumbens (Kalivas and Duffy 1989). The dopamine innervation of the medial prefrontal cortex appears to be particularly vulnerable to stress. However, stress can enhance dopamine metabolism and release in other areas receiving dopamine innervation, such as the nucleus accumbens, providing that greater intensity or longer duration stress is used (Roth et al. 1988). Following lesions of the prefrontal cortex, footshock results in significant increases in dopamine levels in the nucleus accumbens (Deutch et al. 1990). Preadministration of the dopamine agonist apomorphine to rats prevents the acquisition of deficits in learning maze escape behaviors associated with exposure to inescapable stress (Anisman et al. 1980). These studies suggest that stress results in a preferential increase in mesoprefrontal cortical dopamine release.

Stress-induced increases in mesoprefrontal cortical dopamine release are susceptible to modulation by several neurotransmitter systems. *N*-methyl-D-aspartate (NMDA) and opiate receptor blockade in the ventral tegmental area prevent stress-induced activation of the cortical dopamine system (Kalivas and Abhold 1987). In addition, preadministration of benzodiazepines prevents attenuation of stress-induced activation of dopamine neurotransmission (Roth et al. 1988). These studies suggest that dopamine is involved in an interregulatory process with other chemical mediators of the stress response.

No studies have directly examined dopaminergic brain systems in patients with PTSD. The prefrontal cortex has been suggested to play a role in "working memory" in conjunction with other brain areas such as the hippocampus. Clinical studies have provided evidence consistent with alterations in attention and memory in PTSD patients (Bremner et al. 1992b; Sutker et al. 1991). One possible system that may be involved in alterations in working memory in patients with PTSD is the mesocortical dopaminergic system. In addition, administration of cocaine and amphetamine, which both stimulate endogenous dopamine release, results in an increase in paranoid and vigilance behaviors. One could speculate that alterations in dopamine systems may play a role in the pathophysiology of these particular symptoms in patients with PTSD.

BENZODIAZEPINE BRAIN SYSTEMS

Benzodiazepine brain systems have been hypothesized to play a role in the neurobiology of stress and anxiety (Guidotti et al. 1990). Central benzodiazepine receptors and receptors of the inhibitory neurotransmitter system, γ-aminobutyric acid (GABA) type A, are part of the same macromolecular complex. These receptors have distinct binding sites, although they are functionally coupled and regulate each other in an allosteric manner. Benzodiazepines potentiate and prolong the synaptic actions of the inhibitory neurotransmitter GABA (reviewed in Guidotti et al. 1990).

Animals exposed to inescapable stress develop approximately a 30% decrease in benzodiazepine receptor binding (B_{max}) in cortical brain tissue and other specific brain regions. These brain regions include hippocampus, hypothalamus, midbrain, and striatum, which are associated with alterations in memory manifested by deficits in maze escape behaviors (Drugan et al. 1989; Weizman et al. 1989). Changes in benzodiazepine receptor function appear to be specific to uncontrollable stress, as opposed to controllable stress, and are prevented by preadministration of benzodiazepines (Drugan et al. 1984). In addition, animals exposed to inescapable stress exhibit decreases in binding of the benzodiazepine antagonist flumazenil (Ro 15-1788) in hippocampus, hypothalamus, cerebral cortex, and striatum, but not in cerebellum or pons, which are associated with deficits in various types of learning (Drugan et al. 1989; Weizman et al. 1989). Preadministration of benzodiazepines in animals block the sequelae of exposure to inescapable stress in rats, including analgesia to pain, deficits in learning and memory manifested by deficits in shuttle escape behaviors (Drugan et al. 1984), and increased turnover of norepinephrine in the hypothalamus, amygdala, hippocampus, cortex, and locus coeruleus (reviewed in Charney et al., in press). A decrease in benzodiazepine receptor binding (B_{max}) has been demonstrated in the so-called Maudsley genetically fearful strain of rats compared with nonfearful rats in several brain structures, including the hippocampus (Robertson et al. 1978). These findings suggest the possibility that there may be genetically determined individual variations in benzodiazepine receptors that could translate into varying degrees of risk for the development of pathology following exposure to extreme stress.

No studies have examined benzodiazepine receptors in clinical populations of patients with PTSD. However, the fact that these patients appear to have an obvious preference for benzodiazepine medications that may diminish many symptoms, including startle and hyperarousal, suggests that alterations in benzodiazepine receptors may play a role in the symptomatology of PTSD. Findings from preclinical studies provide a rationale for the therapeutic administration of benzodiazepines to patients on the battlefield with acute combat stress reaction. In addition, evidence from studies in patients with other anxiety disorders supports a role for alterations in benzodiazepine receptor function in anxiety. Patients with panic disorder have been found to have decreased sensitivity to benzodiazepine administration and alterations in saccadic eye movement velocity compared with control subjects, which are consistent with a decrease in benzodiazepine receptor sensitivity in panic disorder (Roy-Byrne et al. 1990). New advances in neuroimaging methods have made possible the assessment of central benzodiazepine receptors with single photon emission tomography (SPECT) measurement of the benzodiazepine receptor ligand iomazenil (Innis et al. 1991). Clearly, future research should examine benzodiazepine receptors in patients with PTSD.

ENDOGENOUS OPIATE SYSTEMS

Endogenous opiate systems are also involved in the stress response. Exposure to stress results in an increased release of opiate peptides and the development of an analgesia to pain known as stress-induced analgesia, which can be blocked by administration of the opiate receptor antagonist naltrexone (Maier et al. 1981). Rats exposed to inescapable stress develop decreased binding of μ opiate receptor agonists in the midbrain (Stuckey et al. 1989). In addition, preadministration of morphine to rats exposed to inescapable stress attenuates the stress-induced release of norepinephrine in the hypothalamus, hippocampus, amygdala, midbrain, and thalamus (Tanaka et al. 1983). Opiates cause a decrease in firing from the locus coeruleus; this provides an explanation for the favorable response of hyperarousal symptoms of PTSD to opiates such as heroin.

Several lines of evidence suggest that alterations in endogenous opiate systems may be associated with the clinical symptomatology of PTSD. Since World War II, surgeons working on the battlefield have noted that wounded soldiers have reduced need for opiate analgesic medication, suggesting that the stress of combat is associated with an increase in endogenous opiate release. Vietnam veterans with combat-related PTSD have been shown to have high rates of heroin abuse and dependence (Kulka et al. 1990). They appear to prefer opiates as substances of abuse to other substances, such as cocaine. Also, Vietnam veterans with PTSD have been found to have a reduced sensitivity to pain during exposure to traumatic reminders in the form of videotapes with combat-related scenes (van der Kolk et al. 1989). Pitman et al. (1990) found that this analgesia to pain is reversible with the opiate antagonist naloxone, which prompted them to point out the parallel between their finding and the stress-induced analgesia response in animals.

NEURAL MECHANISMS OF LEARNING AND MEMORY: RELEVANCE TO THE REEXPERIENCING OF PTSD SYMPTOMS

Memory systems play an integral role in the stress response. Stress is associated with an increase in attention and vigilance as well as a strengthening of memory consolidation mediated by noradrenergic inputs to brain structures involved in memory, including the hippocampus, amygdala, and prefrontal cortex (Aston-Jones and Bloom 1981). It appears that exposure to extreme stress may result in long-term alterations in brain memory systems.

Conditioned fear is an important part of the stress response. Animals exposed to a neutral stimulus in conjunction with an aversive unconditioned stimulus will exhibit a conditioned emotional reaction of fear or anxiety to the neutral stimulus alone, often for years after exposure to the original aversive stimulus (reviewed in Charney et al., in press). This acquisition of conditioned fear is associated with an increase in the amplitude of the acoustic startle reflex. Fear-potentiated startle is reduced by drugs that reduce fear or anxiety, such as benzodiazepines and opiates. Electrical stimulation of the central nucleus of the amygdala markedly increases the acoustic startle response (Davis 1986). In addition, lesions of the central nucleus block the ability of conditioned or unconditioned fear stimuli to elevate startle (Hitchcock et al. 1989).

Clinically, conditioned fear manifests itself as anxiety and fear responses to reminders of the original trauma and appears to be characteristic of patients with PTSD (Kolb 1984). An example of conditioned fear would be the fear and anxiety invoked in a rape victim on being returned to the site where the rape took place. One peculiar characteristic seen in patients with PTSD is the capacity of neutral environmental stimuli to trigger memories, which have often been previously forgotten, of traumatic events from the past. For example, one veteran reported getting onto an elevator on Ash Wednesday and seeing a woman with a spot of ash on her forehead. The patient immediately had a flashback to the memory of someone who had been shot in the head, with the bullet hole looking very similar to the spot of ash on the forehead. The patient had not thought of this event or even been able to remember it since he had been in Vietnam more than 20 years ago. This memory was accompanied by an increase in heart rate, feelings of subjective anxiety and fear, rapid respiration, sweating, and a desire to escape the situation.

Clinical investigators have long been interested in manifestations of conditioned fear in war veterans with what is described today as symptoms of PTSD. Kardiner (1941) noted the exaggerated physiological responses of heart rate and blood pressure to reminders of trauma in war veterans suffering from psychiatric disturbances as a result of their combat experiences. Kolb (1984) hypothesized that the central disturbance of PTSD consisted of the "conditioned emotional response" to the original traumatic event, which resulted in a heightened physiological response to subsequent events that were reminiscent of the original trauma. Kolb felt that many of the other symptoms of PTSD were in fact secondary to the primary conditioned emotional response. Several studies have investigated conditioned emotional responses of PTSD patients using the research paradigm of the psychophysiological laboratory.

Psychophysiology laboratories have utilized the playing back of a combat tape or other methods of inducing traumatic reminders to study responses associated with traumatic reexperiencing. PTSD patients have been shown to have an increase in resting heart rate, respiratory rate, and systolic blood pressure compared with healthy control subjects and combat veterans without PTSD (Kolb 1984). Dodds and Wilson (1960) first noted an increase in heart rate and respiratory rate and alterations in alpha rhythm (measured by electroencephalography) following exposure to combat sounds in "compensated" combat veterans compared with "decompensated" (presumably patients with psychiatric disorders) combat veterans. Other studies utilizing the psychophysiological paradigm have found increases in heart rate and systolic blood pressure following exposure to combat sounds in Vietnam veterans with combat-related PTSD compared with age-matched non-veteran healthy subjects (Blanchard et al. 1982), non-PTSD combat veterans (Blanchard et al. 1986; Malloy et al. 1983), and Vietnam veterans with other psychiatric disorders (Malloy et al. 1983). Increases in plasma epinephrine, pulse, blood pressure, and subjective distress have been reported in PTSD patients compared with healthy control subjects (McFall et al. 1990). PTSD patients have also been shown to have higher heart rate, skin conductance, and frontalis electromyogram compared with control subjects after hearing "scripts" of their own combat exposure experiences read to them (Pitman et al. 1987). These studies suggest that increased sympathetic responsivity is associated with PTSD. We hypothesize that sympathetic input to the locus coeruleus may represent the link between clinical findings from psychophysiology studies and the accumulated evidence suggesting alterations in locus coeruleus and noradrenergic function in PTSD.

Abnormally exaggerated startle responses, which are associated with conditioned fear in laboratory animals, are also seen clinically in patients with PTSD. Abnormal startle reaction is one of the diagnostic criteria for PTSD, and clinical studies have provided an empirical validation of abnormal startle response in patients with PTSD. One study used eye-blink reflex electromyographic response to measure the startle reaction in 13 Vietnam combat veterans with PTSD and 12 combat veterans without PTSD. A increase in startle amplitude was noted in the PTSD patients compared with the control subjects (Butler et al. 1990).

NEURAL MECHANISMS OF EXTINCTION: RELEVANCE TO THE CHRONICITY OF PTSD SYMPTOMS

Another phenomenon of memory function of possible relevance to the neurobiology of PTSD is the failure to extinguish memories following exposure to extreme stress. Studies in animals show that repeated exposures to the conditioned fear stimulus result in the "extinction" of the previously learned conditioned emotional response. Conditioned emotional responses in laboratory animals appear not to be abolished forever, but are capable of being retrieved with reexposure to the original aversive stimulus (reviewed in Charney et al., in press). One interesting characteristic of conditioned fear responses in PTSD patients is the fact that they do not extinguish over time and with repeated exposures to the aversive stimulus. For example, a veteran who has a conditioned fear response of becoming startled and agitated with the sound of a car backfiring, which is associated with the original aversive stimulus of gunfire in Vietnam, does not become less agitated with repeated exposures to cars backfiring.

Neurochemical modulation of memory stores may provide a clue to the pathophysiology of PTSD. Multiple neurotransmitter systems that are involved in the stress response modulate memory function (McGaugh 1989). McGaugh postulated that memories may continue to be modified after the original acquisition and has used the term "memory traces" to describe the plastic nature of memory. For example, epinephrine administered after an aversive conditioning trial enhances memory retention. Other neurotransmitters and neuropeptides, including benzodiazepines, glucocorticoids, cholecystokinin, neuropeptide Y, opiate antagonists, and acetylcholine, modulate memory formation in a similar fashion (reviewed in McGaugh 1989), whereas norepinephrine has been shown to enhance neuronal firing in the hippocampus (Madison and Nicoll 1982). It is possible that neurotransmitters and neuropeptide-mediated alterations in memory acquisition may underlie PTSD symptoms related to abnormal memory, such as intrusive memories, flashbacks, and amnesia for traumatic memories.

NEURAL MECHANISMS OF BEHAVIORAL SENSITIZATION IN PTSD

Increased sensitivity refers to an increase in response magnitude to an environmental or pharmacological stimulus. An example would be an increase in extracellular dopamine following reexposure to the stimulus of a footshock. Increased dopamine release in the forebrain (Kalivas and Duffy 1989) and norepinephrine release in multiple brain areas (Anisman and Sklar 1978) is seen following exposure to a stressor in animals with a previous history of exposure to a stressor. The laboratory phenomenon of sensitization has received increased interest recently as a potential model for the pathophysiology of PTSD.

Clinical studies provide evidence for an increased sensitivity to stress following exposure to an initial trauma. In a study of Israeli combat veterans exposed to the recurrent stressors of participation in two successive wars, soldiers with a history of acute combat stress reaction following exposure to the original conflict were more likely to develop the same reaction following exposure to the subsequent conflict (Solomon et al. 1987). In fact, soldiers who developed acute combat stress reaction after the first conflict were more likely to have a recurrence with the second conflict than new recruits with no previous combat exposure. This study suggests that soldiers with a history of adverse reaction to combat stress are at increased risk of developing psychopathology with exposure to recurrent stressors. Emerging evidence suggests that Vietnam combat veterans with a history of exposure to trauma in the form of physical abuse in childhood may have been at increased risk for the development of PTSD in response to combat stress compared with combat veterans without a history of physical abuse in childhood (Bremner et al. 1993).

DEFICITS IN SHORT-TERM MEMORY IN PTSD

Several studies suggest a relationship between the cortisol response to stress and alterations in brain systems involved in memory. The hippocampus is a major target organ in the brain for glucocorticoids (reviewed in McEwen et al. 1986). Experiments involving lesions of the hippocampus and adjacent perirhinal, entorhinal, and parahippocampal cortices in monkeys have also shown these brain structures to be involved in new learning and memory (Squire and Zola-Morgan 1991; Zola-Morgan and Squire 1990). Increases in glucocorticoids seen during acute stress may be associated with damage to hippocampal neurons.

Improper and overcrowded housing of vervet monkeys provided the opportunity to examine the effects of stress on the hippocampus. Monkeys who died spontaneously following exposure to severe stress were found on autopsy to have multiple gastric ulcers, consistent with exposure to chronic stress, and hyperplastic adrenal cortices, consistent with sustained glucocorticoid release. In addition, autopsy showed damage to the CA_2 and CA_3 subfields of the hippocampus (Uno et al. 1989). Follow-up studies suggested that hippocampal damage was associated with direct exposure of hippocampal neurons to glucocorticoids (Sapolsky et al. 1990). Studies in a variety of animal species suggest that direct glucocorticoid exposure results in alterations in cellular architecture and a loss of neurons that are steroid- and tissue-specific (Sapolsky et al. 1988). Glucocorticoids appear to exert their effect by increasing the vulnerability of hippocampal neurons to a variety of insults, including endogenously released excitatory amino acids (Virgin et al. 1991). Furthermore, reduction of glucocorticoid exposure prevents the hippocampal cell loss associated with chronic stress. These studies suggest a possible relationship between stress, cortisol, and alterations in memory.

Alterations in memory have been observed as a consequence of exposure to extreme stress in clinical populations. The forgetting of one's name or identity on the battlefield has been noted by military psychiatrists since World War I. Gaps in memory and dissociative flashbacks to the original trauma are commonly seen in patients with PTSD. For example, one Vietnam veteran with combat-related PTSD reported that he was walking down a street in Boston and the next thing he knew he was in a motel room in Texas. He said that he felt embarrassed asking people what town he was in. Many PTSD patients report difficulty in remembering appointments, grocery lists, or other pieces of trivial information.

Emerging evidence suggests that alterations in memory function in PTSD patients may be associated with structural changes in the hippocampus. In a study of 22 Vietnam combat veterans with PTSD and 20 healthy matched control subjects, a decrease in hippocampal volume measured by volumetrics based on magnetic resonance imaging (MRI) was seen in patients compared with control subjects (Bremner et al. 1992a). Korean prisoners of war have been found to have an impairment of short-term verbal memory measured by the logical memory component of the Wechsler Memory Scale compared with Korean veterans without a history of containment (Sutker et al. 1991). These alterations in memory, however, could be explained by malnutrition. We have also found deficits in short-term memory in Vietnam combat veterans with combat-related PTSD compared with healthy subjects as measured by the logical memory component of the Wechsler Memory Scale, and the visual and verbal components of the Selective Reminding Test (Bushke and Fuld 1974; Hannay and Levin 1985). There was no difference in scores on the Wechsler Adult Intelligence Scale—Revised between PTSD patients and control subjects. In addition, level of current PTSD symptomatology as measured by the Mississippi Scale for Combat-Related PTSD was correlated with degree of memory impairment as measured by the Wechsler Memory Scale (Bremner et al.

1992b). These clinical studies are consistent with studies in animals suggesting an association between exposure to extreme stress and alterations in the hippocampus and memory function. We speculate that exposure to extreme stress may be associated with alterations in the hippocampus and deficits in short-term memory, possibly through glucocorticoid-mediated neurotoxicity to hippocampal neurons. This hypothesis would predict that treatment with benzodiazepines before or soon after exposure to the stressor would decrease circulating levels of glucocorticoids, possibly preventing hippocampal damage and thus preserving memory function. Research is needed to clarify this important area.

CONCLUDING COMMENTS

Exposure to stress results in the parallel activation of brain norepinephrine and the CRF–HPA axis system. These brain systems work in concert to effect a variety of behavioral and physiological responses that serve to promote survival in the face of a threat. The net effect of the stress response is to shunt energy to the brain and muscles and to activate attentional and memory systems, all with the purpose of promoting survival. What is in the short term adaptive may in the long term result in pathology. Preclinical studies suggest that exposure to extreme stress results in long-term changes in norepinephrine, CRF–HPA axis, dopamine, benzodiazepine, and opiate brain systems (Figure 3–1). Clinical studies suggest alterations in norepinephrine and the CRF–HPA axis systems inpatients with PTSD. We have hypothesized

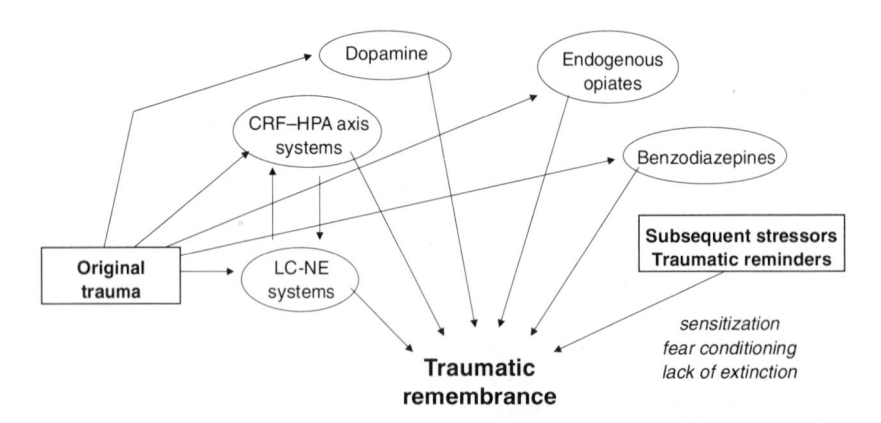

Figure 3–1. Relationship between traumatic events, changes in neurobiological systems, and establishment of chronic posttraumatic stress symptomatology. CRF = corticotropin-releasing factor. HPA = hypothalamic-pituitary-adrenal. LC = locus coeruleus. NE = norepinephrine.

that the symptoms of PTSD are a manifestation of physiological processes that began at the time of the original threat or trauma. What was of survival value in, for example, the jungle of Vietnam—an activation of noradrenergic and the CRF–HPA axis systems, the strong engraving of memory traces of the event, promotion of the startle response, and heightened attention and vigilance—may represent pathology when the veteran is sitting at the dinner table with family 20 years after the war.

An understanding of the organism's response to physical threat is important in understanding the stress response. Exposure to threat results in several rapid behavioral responses that appear to be mediated in part by the CRF–HPA axis system and brain norepinephrine systems, including alerting behaviors, increased vigilance and attention with an associated reinforcement of memory, subjective anxiety, freezing behaviors, and a suppression of appetite and reproductive behavior. Exposure to threat also results in physiological changes involving the CRF–HPA axis and brain norepinephrine systems, including shunting of oxygen and nutrients directly to the central nervous system, increased blood pressure and heart rate, increased respiratory rate, increased gluconeogenesis, inhibition of growth and reproductive systems (through CRF-mediated decreases in growth hormone and luteinizing-releasing hormone), and containment of the inflammatory-immune response (reviewed in Chrousos and Gold 1992). These behavioral and physiological changes can be seen to represent an adaptive redirecting of attention and energy to dealing with the threat.

Clinicians engaged in treatment will notice parallels between the behavioral and biological sequelae of stress and the phenomenology of PTSD symptoms in their patients. Animal models of stress such as inescapable stress parallel the experience of being pinned down in combat, or being the victim of assault. In addition, preclinical findings have direct applications to understanding the symptoms of PTSD patients. For example, increased turnover of brain norepinephrine following exposure to inescapable stress in rats parallels evidence that suggests alterations in noradrenergic systems in patients with PTSD. We have hypothesized that PTSD is associated with an increase in release of norepinephrine in the brain. Alterations in noradrenergic systems provide a potential mechanism for symptoms of physiological hyperreactivity seen clinically in patients with PTSD. Research findings are preliminary. However, some clinicians may find it helpful to consider alterations in noradrenergic function to play a potential role in the exaggerated physiological responses of their patients to traumatic reminders—for example, the veteran whose heart begins racing, whose blood pressure rises, and who becomes very agitated at the Fourth of July fireworks, which remind him of the mortar attacks in Vietnam.

In addition to being affected by stress, brain memory systems appear to mediate the organism's response to stress. Activation of the locus coeruleus with resultant activation in brain noradrenergic systems that occurs during stress facilitates selective attention, probably by means of connections with central brain structures, including the hippocampus and amygdala (Aston-Jones and Bloom 1981). It can be seen how selective attention would be beneficial in a life-threatening situation. In addition, increased release of norepinephrine in the hippocampus and amygdala with modulation of long-term potentiation, which is felt to represent the neurochemical substrate of memory, may result in a strengthening of memories acquired during stress. These strengthened memories may be ultimately adaptive in dealing with subsequent threats. However, this may result in troubling memories that are intrusive and do not fade away long after the potential danger has been removed—for example, the danger of attack from a Vietcong soldier 20 years after the war. Memory processes remain susceptible to modulating influences after information has been acquired (McGaugh 1989). Acute neurobiological responses to trauma, such as release of norepinephrine, may facilitate the encoding of traumatic memories.

Simple sensory phenomena related to the traumatic event, including sights, sounds, and smells, often result in specific intrusive memories and flashbacks. The brain regions involved in mediating these processes include the amygdala, locus coeruleus, hippocampus, and sensory cortex. The amygdala is important in fear conditioning and extinction of sensory and cognitive associations to the original trauma, as well as anxiety and fear behaviors (Squire 1991). In addition, the amygdala serves to integrate sensory and cognitive input from multiple brain areas. The hippocampus is important in the initial storing of memory and has important connections with the amygdala (Squire and Zola-Morgan 1991; Zola-Morgan and Squire 1990). In addition, both the amygdala and the hippocampus have multiple projections to cortical areas, and it appears that memories are eventually stored in the cortex (Squire 1991).

In addition to increasing our understanding of the underlying mechanisms of PTSD symptoms, studies of the neurobiology of PTSD may lead to advances in treatment (Friedman 1988). For example, the study of changes in benzodiazepine receptors in patients with PTSD may lead to medications that act at the level of the benzodiazepine receptor to alleviate the pathological anxiety that is associated with PTSD and that are nonaddictive. The development of CRF antagonists, currently used in laboratory studies, may be of benefit in the treatment of the symptomatology of PTSD. In addition, medications that act at the level of noradrenergic systems, such as clonidine, may prove to be efficacious in the treatment of PTSD. Studies in animals as well as studies of clinical populations of PTSD patients are needed to provide more information on the long-term consequences of exposure to extreme stress.

REFERENCES

Abercrombie ED, Jacobs BL: Single-unit response of noradrenergic neurons in the locus coeruleus of freely moving cats, I: acutely presented stressful and nonstressful stimuli. J Neurosci 7:2837–2843, 1987

Anisman H, Sklar LS: Catecholamine depletion upon reexposure to stress: mediation of the escape deficits produced by inescapable shock. Journal of Comparative and Physiological Psychology 93:610–625, 1978

Anisman H, Suissa A, Sklar LS: Escape deficits induced by uncontrollable stress: antagonism by dopamine and norepinephrine agonists. Behav Neural Biol 28:34–47, 1980

Aston-Jones G, Bloom FE: Norepinephrine-containing locus coeruleus neurons in behaving rats exhibit pronounced responses to non-noxious environmental stimuli. J Neurosci 1:887–900, 1981

Blanchard EB, Kolb LC, Pallmeyer TP, et al: A psychophysiological study of posttraumatic stress disorder in Vietnam veterans. Psychiatr Q 54:220–229, 1982

Blanchard EB, Kolb LC, Gerardi RJ, et al: Cardiac response to relevant stimuli as an adjunctive tool for diagnosing post-traumatic stress disorder in Vietnam veterans. Behavior Therapy 17:592–606, 1986

Bremner JD, Seibyl JP, Scott TM, et al: Decreased hippocampal volume in posttraumatic stress disorder (New Research Abstract 155). Proceedings of the 145th annual meeting of the American Psychiatric Association, Washington, DC, May 1992a

Bremner JD, Scott TM, Delaney RC, et al: Deficits in short-term memory in posttraumatic stress disorder (New Research Abstract 156). Proceedings of the 145th annual meeting of the American Psychiatric Association, Washington, DC, May 1992b

Bremner JD, Southwick SM, Johnson DR, et al: Childhood physical and sexual abuse in combat-related PTSD. Am J Psychiatry 150:235–239, 1993

Bushke H, Fuld PA: Evaluating storage, retention, and retrieval in disordered memory and learning. Neurology 24:1019–1025, 1974

Butler RW, Braff DL, Rausch JL, et al: Physiological evidence of exaggerated startle response in a subgroup of Vietnam veterans with combat-related PTSD. Am J Psychiatry 147:1308–1312, 1990

Charney DS, Heninger GR, Breier A: Noradrenergic function in panic anxiety: effects of yohimbine in healthy subjects and patients with agoraphobia and panic disorder. Arch Gen Psychiatry 41:751–763, 1984

Charney DS, Woods SW, Goodman WK, et al: Neurobiological mechanisms of panic anxiety: biochemical and behavioral correlates of yohimbine-induced panic attacks. Am J Psychiatry 144:1030–1036, 1987

Charney DS, Deutch AY, Krystal JH, et al: Psychobiological mechanisms of posttraumatic stress disorder. Arch Gen Psychiatry (in press)

Chrousos GP, Gold PW: The concepts of stress and stress system disorders. JAMA 267:1244–1252, 1992

Davidson J, Lipper S, Kilts CD, et al: Platelet MAO activity in posttraumatic stress disorder. Am J Psychiatry 142:1341–1343, 1985

Davis M: Pharmacological and anatomical analysis of fear conditioning using the fear-potentiated startle paradigm. Behav Neurosci 100:814–824, 1986

Deutch AY, Tam SY, Roth RH: Footshock and conditioned stress increase 3,4-dihydroxyphenylacetic acid (DOPAC) in the ventral tegmental area but not substantia nigra. Brain Res 333:143–146, 1985

Deutch AY, Clark WA, Roth RH: Prefrontal cortical dopamine depletion enhances the responsiveness of mesolimbic dopamine neurons to stress. Brain Res 521:311–315, 1990

Dinan TG, Barry S, Yatham LN, et al: A pilot study of a neuroendocrine test battery in posttraumatic stress disorder. Biol Psychiatry 28:665–672, 1990

Dodds D, Wilson WP: Observations on persistence of war neurosis. Diseases of the Nervous System 21:40–46, 1960

Drugan RC, Ryan SM, Minor TR, et al: Librium prevents the analgesia and shuttlebox escape deficit typically observed following inescapable shock. Pharmacol Biochem Behav 21:749–754, 1984

Drugan RC, Morrow AL, Weizman R, et al: Stress-induced behavioral depression in the rat is associated with a decrease in GABA receptor-mediated chloride ion flux and brain benzodiazepine receptor occupancy. Brain Res 487:45–51, 1989

Dunn AJ, Berridge CW: Physiological and behavioral responses to corticotropin-releasing factor administration: is CRF a mediator of anxiety or stress responses? Brain Research Review 15:71–100, 1990

Foote SL, Bloom FE, Aston-Jones G: Nucleus locus coeruleus: new evidence of anatomical and physiological specificity. Physiol Rev 63:844–914, 1983

Friedman MJ: Toward rational pharmacotherapy for posttraumatic stress disorder: an interim report. Am J Psychiatry 145:281–285, 1988

Guidotti A, Baraldi M, Leon A, et al: Benzodiazepines: a tool to explore the biochemical and neurophysiological basis of anxiety. Fed Proc 39:1039–1042, 1990

Hannay HJ, Levin HS: Selective Reminding Test: an examination of the equivalence of four forms. J Clin Exp Neuropsychol 7:251–263, 1985

Hitchcock JM, Sananes CB, Davis M: Sensitization of the startle reflex by footshock: blockade by lesions of the central nucleus of the amygdala or its efferent pathway to the brainstem. Behav Neurosci 103:509–518, 1989

Innis RB, Al-Tikriti MS, Zoghbi SS, et al: SPECT imaging of the benzodiazepine receptor: feasibility of in vivo potency measurements from stepwise displacement curves. J Nucl Med 32:1654–1761, 1991

Kalivas PW, Abhold R: Enkephalin release into the ventral tegmental area in response to stress: modulation of mesocortical dopamine. Brain Res 414:339–348, 1987

Kalivas PW, Duffy P: Similar effects of daily cocaine and stress on mesocorticolimbic dopamine neurotransmission in the rat. Biol Psychiatry 25:913–928, 1989

Kardiner A: The Traumatic Neuroses of War. Washington, DC, National Research Council, 1941

Kolb LC: The post-traumatic stress disorder of combat: a subgroup with a conditioned emotional response. Mil Med 149:237–243, 1984

Kosten TR, Mason JW, Ostroff RB, et al: Sustained urinary norepinephrine and epinephrine elevation in posttraumatic stress disorder. Psychoneuroendocrinology 12:13–20, 1987

Kosten TR, Wahby V, Giller E Jr: The dexamethasone suppression test and thyrotropin-releasing hormone stimulation test in posttraumatic stress disorder. Biol Psychiatry 28:657–664, 1990

Krystal JH, Kosten TR, Southwick SM, et al: Neurobiological aspects of PTSD: review of clinical and preclinical studies. Behavior Therapy 20:177–198, 1989

Kudler H, Davidson J, Meador K, et al: The DST and posttraumatic stress disorder. Am J Psychiatry 144:1068–1071, 1987

Kulka RA, Schlenger WE, Fairbank JA, et al: Trauma and the Vietnam War Generation: Report of Findings from the National Vietnam Veterans Readjustment Study. New York, Brunner/Mazel, 1990

Lerer B, Ebstein RP, Shestatsky M, et al: Cyclic AMP signal transduction in posttraumatic stress disorder. Am J Psychiatry 144:1324–1327, 1987

Levine ES, Litto WJ, Jacobs BL: Activity of cat locus coeruleus noradrenergic neurons during the defense reaction. Brain Res 531:189–195, 1990

Madison DV, Nicoll RA: Noradrenaline blocks accommodation of pyramidal cell discharge in the hippocampus. Nature 299:636–638, 1982

Maier SF, Davies S, Grau JW, et al: Opiate antagonists and long- term analgesic reaction induced by inescapable shock in rats. Journal of Comparative and Physiological Psychology 94:1172–1183, 1981

Malloy PF, Fairbank JA, Keane TM: Validation of a multimethod assessment of posttraumatic stress disorders in Vietnam veterans. J Consult Clin Psychol 51:488–494, 1983

Mason JW, Giller EL, Kosten TR, et al: Urinary free cortisol levels in post-traumatic stress disorder patients. J Nerv Ment Dis 174:145–149, 1986

Mason JW, Giller EL, Kosten TR, et al: Elevation of urinary norepinephrine/cortisol ratio in posttraumatic stress disorder. J Nerv Ment Dis 176:498–502, 1988

McEwen B, de Kloet E, Rostene W: Adrenal steroid receptors and actions in the nervous system. Physiol Rev 66:1121–1189, 1986

McFall ME, Murburg MM, Ko GN, et al: Autonomic responses to stress in Vietnam combat veterans with posttraumatic stress disorder. Biol Psychiatry 27:1165–1175, 1990

McGaugh JL: Involvement of hormonal and neuromodulatory systems in the regulation of memory storage: endogenous modulation of memory storage. Annu Rev Neurosci 12:255–287, 1989

Nemeroff CB, Schatzberg AF (eds): The Hypothalamic-Pituitary-Adrenal Axis: Physiology, Pathophysiology, and Psychiatric Implications. New York, Raven, 1988

Perry BD, Giller EJ, Southwick SM: Altered platelet alpha-2 adrenergic binding sites in posttraumatic stress disorder. Am J Psychiatry 144:1324–1327, 1987

Perry BD, Southwick SM, Yehuda R, et al: Adrenergic receptor regulation in posttraumatic stress disorder, in Biological Assessment and Treatment of Posttraumatic Stress Disorder. Edited by Giller EL Jr. Washington, DC, American Psychiatric Press, 1990, pp 87–114

Pitman R, Orr S: Twenty-four hour urinary cortisol and catecholamine excretion in combat-related posttraumatic stress disorder. Biol Psychiatry 27:245–247, 1990

Pitman RK, Orr SP, Forgue DF, et al: Psychophysiologic assessment of posttraumatic stress disorder imagery in Vietnam combat veterans. Arch Gen Psychiatry 44:970–975, 1987

Pitman RK, van der Kolk BA, Orr SP, et al: Naloxone-reversible analgesic response to combat-related stimuli in posttraumatic stress disorder. Arch Gen Psychiatry 47:541–544, 1990

Pynoos RS, Frederick C, Nader K, et al: Life threat and posttraumatic stress disorder in school age children. Arch Gen Psychiatry 44:1057–1063, 1987

Rainey JM, Aleem A, Ortiz A, et al: A laboratory procedure for the induction of flashbacks. Am J Psychiatry 144:1317–1319, 1987

Redmond D, Huang Y: New evidence for a locus coeruleus–norepinephrine connection with anxiety. Life Sci 25:2149–2162, 1979

Robertson HA, Martin IL, Candy JM: Differences in benzodiazepine receptor binding in Maudsley reactive and nonreactive rats. Eur J Pharmacol 50:455–457, 1978

Roth RH, Tam SY, Ida Y, et al: Stress and the mesocorticolimbic dopamine systems. Ann N Y Acad Sci 537:138–147, 1988

Roy-Byrne PP, Cowley DS, Greenblatt DJ, et al: Reduced benzodiazepine sensitivity in panic disorder. Arch Gen Psychiatry 47:534–538, 1990

Sapolsky RM, Packan DR, Vale WW: Glucocorticoid toxicity in the hippocampus: in vitro demonstration. Brain Res 453:367–371, 1988

Sapolsky RM, Uno H, Rebert CS, et al: Hippocampal damage associated with prolonged glucocorticoid exposure in primates. J Neurosci 10:2897–2902, 1990

Seligman MEP, Maier SF: Failure to escape traumatic shock. J Exp Psychol 74:1–9, 1967

Simson PE, Weiss JM: Responsiveness of locus coeruleus neurons to excitatory stimulation is uniquely regulated by alpha-2 receptors. Psychopharmacol Bull 24:349–354, 1988

Smith MA, Davidson J, Ritchie JC, et al: The corticotropin-releasing hormone test in patients with posttraumatic stress disorder. Biol Psychiatry 26:349–355, 1989

Solomon Z, Garb K, Bleich A, et al: Reactivation of combat related posttraumatic stress disorder. Am J Psychiatry 144:51–55, 1987

Southwick SM, Krystal JH, Morgan A, et al: Yohimbine and m-chlorophenylpiperazine in PTSD (New Research Abstract 348). Proceedings of the 144th annual meeting of the American Psychiatric Association, New Orleans, LA, May 1991

Squire LR, Zola-Morgan S: The medial temporal lobe memory system. Science 253:1380–1386, 1991

Stuckey J, Marra S, Minor T, et al: Changes in mu opiate receptors following inescapable shock. Brain Res 476:167–169, 1989

Sutker PB, Winstead DK, Galina ZH, et al: Cognitive deficits and psychopathology among former prisoners of war and combat veterans of the Korean conflict. Am J Psychiatry 148:67–72, 1991

Tanaka M, Kohno Y, Tsuda A, et al: Differential effects of morphine on noradrenaline release in brain regions of stressed and non-stressed rats. Brain Res 275:105–115, 1983

Uno H, Tarara R, Else JG, et al: Hippocampal damage associated with prolonged and fatal stress in primates. J Neurosci 9:1705–1711, 1989

van der Kolk BA, Greenberg MS, Orr SP, et al: Endogenous opioids, stress induced analgesia, and posttraumatic stress disorder. Psychopharmacol Bull 25:417–421, 1989

Virgin CE, Taryn PTH, Packan DR, et al: Glucocorticoids inhibit glucose transport and glutamate uptake in hippocampal astrocytes: implications for glucocorticoid neurotoxicity. J Neurochem 57:1422–1428, 1991

Weiss JM, Goodman PA, Losito BG, et al: Behavioral depression produced by an uncontrollable stressor: relationship to norepinephrine, dopamine, and serotonin levels in various regions of rat brain. Brain Research Reviews 3:167–205, 1981

Weizman R, Weizman A, Kook KA, et al: Repeated swim stress alters brain benzodiazepine receptors measured in vivo. J Pharmacol Exp Ther 249:701–707, 1989

Yehuda R, Lowry MT, Southwick SM, et al: Increased number of glucocorticoid receptors in posttraumatic stress disorder. Am J Psychiatry 148:499–504, 1991

Yehuda R, Southwick SM, Krystal JH, et al: Enhanced suppression of cortisol following dexamethasone administration in posttraumatic stress disorder. Am J Psychiatry (in press)

Zola-Morgan SM, Squire LR: The primate hippocampal formation: evidence for a time-limited role in memory storage. Science 250:288–290, 1990

Chapter 4

Traumatic Stress and Developmental Psychopathology in Children and Adolescents

Robert S. Pynoos, M.D., M.P.H.

The worldwide prevalence of children and adolescents exposed to war and disaster, intrafamilial and community violence, and sexual and physical abuse constitutes a major global public mental health concern. Although these experiences are by definition extreme, they occur with sufficient frequency to warrant clinical appreciation of their full range and potential impact. Posttraumatic stress disorder (PTSD) is now being increasingly recognized as a potentially serious disorder in children and adolescents, both as a significant source of private suffering and as an adverse influence on biological, psychological, and social development.

Childhood exposure to traumatic stress impinges on the course of proximal and distal development by shaping children's expectations about the world, the safety and security of their interpersonal life, and their sense of personal integrity. A developmental approach places knowledge about traumatic stress into an intricate matrix of a changing child and environment, and evolving familial and societal expectations, and recognizes the essential linkage between disrupted and normal development.

The pervasive interaction of trauma and development is evident in relation to the risk of exposure to various types of traumatic stresses and their duration; the perception and appraisal of traumatic events; the manifestations of posttraumatic signs and symptoms of distress and their measurement; the nature of traumatic reminders and secondary stresses; and factors related to resistance, vulnerability, resilience,

---

Many of the ideas expressed in this chapter emerged from a long-standing collaboration with Kathi Nader, D.S.W. I thank Alan Steinberg, Ph.D., and Ruth Wraith for their reviews and comments.

Support for this work was provided by the Bing Fund, David Hockney, the John D. and Catherine T. MacArthur Foundation Network on Early Childhood, and the UCLA Program in Trauma, Violence and Sudden Bereavement.

adjustment, the emerging personality, and pathology related to post-traumatic stress.

Figure 4–1 provides the conceptual framework according to which this selective review of traumatic stress in children and adolescents is organized (see Steinberg and Ritzmann 1990). The schema depicts the complex interactions of development with various key aspects of traumatic stress and its sequelae. It also suggests new avenues of investigation to integrate the study of childhood PTSD into a wider developmental framework.

TRAUMATIC STRESS

In the discussion of childhood trauma, clinical and research reports vary in their emphasis on the objective features of the traumatic event or the child's subjective perceptions and appraisals of threat and personal impact. Pynoos and Eth (1985) previously suggested returning to Freud's (1926) mature model of traumatic helplessness where he envisioned an intimate linkage between objective features and subjective experience. Freud defined a traumatic situation as one where "external and internal, real and instinctual dangers *converge*" [emphasis added]. However, the appraisal of external danger, the appraisal and tolerance of internal dangers, expectations of outside intervention, and self-efficacy—and the degree to which these are influenced by reliance on parents, adult caretakers, siblings, and peers—all vary with the maturation of the child.

Typology of Trauma in Children

The range of traumatic exposures reported in the literature on PTSD in children and adolescents falls into four major categories, which are presented in Table 4–1.

Over the past several years, the study of PTSD has begun to be embedded within refined typologies of childhood traumatic experiences; these are supplanting earlier conceptual frameworks that typically referred to acute, cumulative, strain, or chronic traumatic circumstances (Terr 1991). Researchers are beginning to consider the interaction of traumatic exposure to single or recurring extrafamilial violence within an environment of chronic danger, the impact of acute or repeated intrafamilial traumatic experiences within the context of a more general pathogenic family environment, and the potential interaction over time of these extra- and intrafamilial traumatic experiences and their associated ecologies (Bell and Jenkins 1991; Cicchetti 1989; Garbarino et al. 1991; Richters and Martinez 1993).

In addition, traumatic exposures have been more clearly conceptualized as involving specific sequences of traumatic experiences. There

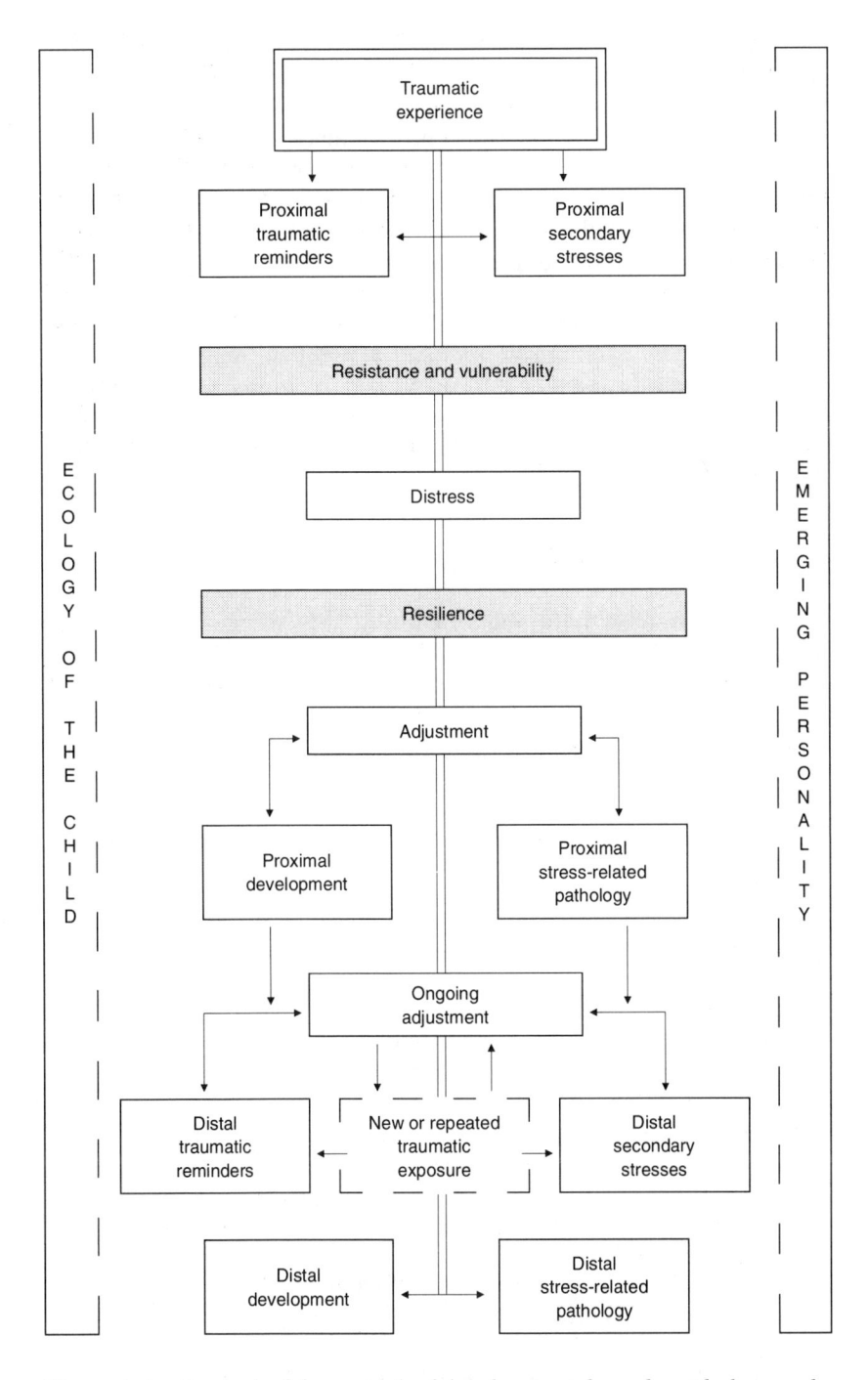

Figure 4–1. Conceptual framework of developmental psychopathology and posttraumatic stress disorder in children and adolescents.

may be a characteristic sequence associated with a type of traumatic situation, for example, under conditions of violent political persecution (Keilson 1992) or major disaster (Sugar 1988). On the other hand, in circumstances of family or community violence, children may experience a highly variable series of exposures occurring at different developmental stages. Young children exposed to life-threatening illness and life-endangering medical procedures represent a special category in which traumatic exposures require parental consent (Stuber et al. 1991).

The typology of trauma should also include characterization of the developmental cycle of the family, which includes the current developmental phase of each family member as well as the developmental phase of the family as a whole (Brown 1980). A familial trauma and loss time line (including parental history of trauma and loss) recognizes that traumata may occur at varying or multiple points in development, both of the child and the family.

Objective Features of Childhood Trauma

Paralleling progress in the study of adult PTSD, more refined descriptions of the nature and degree of children's exposure are being developed. The result has been a more precise identification of the specific features of traumatic experiences associated with risk for PTSD and other reactions. For example, studies of disasters and transportation

Table 4–1. Typology of reported traumatic exposures in children and adolescents

- **Small and large-scale natural and technological disasters** (earthquake, flood, fire, tornado, hurricane, lightning-strike, cyclone, nuclear reactor accident)
- **Accidents**
  Transportation calamities (train, airplane, ship, automobile)
  Severe accidental injury (burns, hit-and-run accidents, accidental shooting)
- **Intra- and extrafamilial violence**
  Kidnapping and hostage situations
  Community violence (gang violence, sniper attacks)
  Political, racial, or religious-related violence (terrorism, war, atrocities, torture)
  Massive catastrophic trauma (concentration camp)
  Witnessing rape, murder, interspousal violence and suicidal behavior
  Sexual molestation, incest, exploitation, physical abuse
- **Life-threatening illnesses and life-endangering medical procedures**

accidents indicated that such factors as exposure to direct life-threat and injury to self, witnessing of mutilating injury or grotesque death (especially to family members or friends), and hearing unanswered screams for help and cries of distress are strongly associated with the onset and persistence of PTSD in children and adolescents (Pynoos et al., in press; Yule and Williams 1990).

The literature related to violence has identified additional objective risk factors, which include proximity to violent threat, the unexpectedness and duration of the experience(s), the extent of violent force and the use of a weapon or injurious object, the number and nature of threats during an episode, the witnessing of atrocities, the relationship to the assailant and other victims, the use of physical coercion, the violation of the physical integrity of the child, and the degree of brutality and malevolence. The posttrauma viewing of graphic details, such as photographs of atrocities or the mutilated corpse of a family member or friend, may constitute an important secondary source of risk (Nader and Pynoos, in press).

One reason for the discrepancies in prior reports of rates of PTSD in children following disasters, war, and victimization has been the use of general categories of traumatic events rather than refined qualitative and quantitative exposure measures to define subject populations (Yule and Williams 1990). This inadequacy confounded the literature after World War II, when there was a common failure to differentiate among the broad range of wartime experiences. For example, being under general threat during an air raid (Burt 1943) is quite different from being strafed by an airplane (Mercier 1943) or witnessing atrocities and being subjected to daily life-threat in a concentration camp (Kuch and Cox 1992). Children or adolescents exposed to specific risk factors such as those noted above in major disasters or catastrophic political violence have been found to exhibit uniformly high rates of chronic PTSD (Kinzie et al. 1986; Nader et al. 1990; Pynoos et al., in press; Yule and Williams 1990). In reviewing similar issues in the study of incest, sexual molestation, and sexual exploitation, Hartman and Burgess (1989) emphasized the need for consistent definitions and refinement of measurements of the degree of force, violence, aggression, and sexual activity in assessing the association of sexual abuse with traumatic reactions in children.

Differential Risk of Exposure in Children and Adolescents

Age, sex, and family and community environments contribute to a child's risk of exposure to various types of traumatic stress. As children get older, school and neighborhood environment increasingly become risk factors, along with behavior and activities independent of family and school. Personality may contribute to the risk of exposure, for example, by children placing themselves in situations in which there is an added risk of violence or injury. In adolescence, peer group affiliation may increase the risk of violent and accidental life-threat, injury, and death. Adolescents are also more likely to be involved in combat and disaster rescue work.

Family factors associated with increased risk of intrafamilial violent experiences for children include parental psychopathology, lack of supervision, marital discord, maladaptive assortative mating, recent unemployment, and alcohol or other substance abuse by adult caretakers (Daly and Wilson 1981). Children are at special risk of witnessing violence to a family member, for example, rape, murder, suicide behavior, and interspousal violence or abuse of a sibling (Black and Kaplan 1988; Pynoos and Eth 1985; Pynoos and Nader 1988; Rosenberg 1987). Changing family patterns also influence the rate of intrafamilial sexual abuse, such as the increased risk of sexual molestation by stepfathers (Russell 1986).

Sociopolitical conditions generate differential risks, such as military conscription, terrorism, war, atrocities against civilians, racial or religious-directed violence, and political oppression and torture. Increased access to firearms, as is occurring in the United States, is associated with children increasingly being victims, witnesses, and perpetrators of violent acts or accidental shootings involving guns (Cotton 1992). Socioeconomic factors such as housing conditions, school building standards, advanced warning and evacuation plans, and disaster relief capabilities affect the nature and frequency of traumatic exposures in natural or technological disasters. Whereas the morbidity and mortality rates of disasters is decreasing in the more industrialized countries, similar natural disasters in developing countries often result in widespread death, injury, and destruction, with large numbers of affected child survivors (Pynoos et al., in press).

Complexity of Traumatic Experience(s) in Children and Adolescents

Empirical studies of acutely traumatized school-age children and adolescents have increased clinical awareness of the complexity of their traumatic experiences. There are intense moment-to-moment perceptual, kinesthetic, and somatic experiences accompanied by appraisals of external and internal threats. These may include misperceptions and primary appraisals that either minimize or exaggerate the extent of threat or harm. Internally, the child may be challenged by the intensity and duration of the physiological arousal, affective responses, and psychodynamic threats. During the traumatic experience, the child makes continuous efforts to address the situation in behavior, thought, and fantasy and to manage physiological and emotional reactions.

In the appraisal of external threat, infants and young toddlers rely on social referencing to attachment figures to respond to situations of uncertainty regarding safety and risk (Klinnert et al. 1983) and initiate motor and mental efforts aimed at searching for the protective figure (Krystal 1991). Preschool children begin to rely on natural clues that elicit fearful responses and to seek the company of attachment figures to diminish fearful apprehensions (Bowlby 1979a). With maturity, school-age children rely less on cues from their caretakers and more fully understand situations of potential threat; they envision increasing self-efficacy in the face of danger and experience a sense of ineffectualness or responsibility when that fails. Adolescents rely on their own appraisals of threat and motivation, more fully envision the threatened harm and its later consequences, and struggle with decisions about whether to intervene actively.

The human infant, helpless to take any direct action in the face of external danger, is equipped with alarm reactions to elicit parental response and protection (Krystal 1991). In preschool children, disruption of the expectation of a protective shield, coercive violation of physical integrity and psychological autonomy, and betrayal of basic affiliative assumptions are associated with intense fear, rage, or shame and agitated motor behavior or extreme passivity. Emerging catastrophic emotions "presage catastrophe" and enable the child to act more self-protectively to threats of invasion and injury to the body; failure to prevent harm is accompanied by terror (Rangell 1991). The school-age child may experience an abrupt dissolution of expectations about a socially modulated world that elicits frightening, even murderous, impulses. The more mature sense of surrender to a moment of unavoidable danger may evoke narcissistic rage in an adolescent (Krystal 1991; van der Kolk 1985).

As the traumatic event proceeds, simultaneous or sequential responses to the experience change the vantage point of concern or attention in the child. Young children may have their attention drawn away from (or suppress fear for) their own safety when there is imminent danger (or actual injury) to a parent, sibling, or friend and experience unalleviated empathic distress (Hoffman 1979). Alternatively, when there is immediate threat or injury to a child, the child may experience a moment of unconcern, even estrangement from other family members who may also be under threat. When injury to self or other occurs, children may become suddenly preoccupied with concerns about the severity of injury, rescue, and repair. In violent circumstances, children may also feel compelled to inhibit wishes to intervene or to suppress retaliatory impulses out of fear of provoking counterretaliatory behavior.

At the moment when a child's physical integrity or autonomy begins to be compromised, the child's attention may be directed away from the monitoring of an assailant or imagining outside intervention and more toward fears of internal psychological and physical harm. As this transition occurs, the child may try to use self-protective mechanisms to meet the internal threats. These may include "dissociative responses" that allow the child to feel a physical distancing from what is happening, to feel it is not happening to him or her, to control autonomic arousal and anxiety, to protect certain ego functions, and to decrease any sense of active participation (Rose 1991). During an incestuous violation, an attempt to ward off any sense of active participation may require disclaiming internal affiliative needs and desires (Bernstein 1990). In contrast, invoking these affiliative emotions during a sexual molestation or hostage taking may mitigate against the child's awareness of the physical menace, psychological abasement, and the accompanying distress.

In addition to its progression, a traumatic experience is often multilayered. For example, worry about the safety of a family member or friend, whether in the next room or at a different location, may be an additional source of extreme stress. The danger may also remind the child of a previous situation, renewing old fears and anxieties that influence the immediate appraisal of threat and exacerbate physiological and psychological responses. Witnessing the death of an attachment figure or peer evokes concurrent acute reactions to the loss, even while the life-threat to the child continues.

Secondary Stresses and Adversities

Traumatic events are commonly associated with secondary stresses and adversities, which may vary considerably with both the type of trauma and environmental responsiveness to the child. They constitute additional sources of distress and increase the risk of initial comorbidity of posttraumatic stress reactions with other adverse reactions. They complicate efforts at adjustment and may interfere with normal opportunities for developmental maturation or initiate maladaptive coping responses that, over time, may be associated with chronic non-PTSD psychopathology. They may substantially interfere with the availability or effectiveness of support to the child from parents, family, school, and community.

These adversities fall into four different, interrelated categories: social structure and values, community and school organization, family function, and individual challenges to the child. Social structure and societal values govern the recognition of the needs of traumatized children and the allocation of resources. They help determine the extent of adversities associated with war, disasters, and interpersonal violence. Social institutions contribute to characteristics of the recovery environment, including the adjudication of blame and provision of restitution, and the type of resources for rehabilitation and child welfare services.

Community disruption resulting from war and large-scale disasters may be associated with deprivation, malnutrition, organic illness, family disruption, dislocation, emigration, and resettlement. Community disorganization and involuntary unemployment after the Mount Saint Helens volcanic eruption in the state of Washington in May 1980 was associated with increases in intrafamilial violence, adult substance abuse, and juvenile delinquency (Adams and Adams 1984). The loss of schooling or the lack of recovery of a school community, including ongoing distress in school personnel, is a significant source of secondary adversity for children (Nader and Pynoos 1993; Yule 1991).

A direct impact on family functioning may include parental loss and subsequent impaired caretaking or separation of children from family members. Lack of parental responsiveness and impairment in role function may be secondary to parental trauma or grief-related preoccupations, exacerbation of preexisting psychopathology, or the demands of secondary adversities. Disharmonious offers and need of support due to differences in exposure among family members often occur (Pynoos 1992a).

Situations of chronic extra- and intrafamilial violence can erode the sense of safety, security, and affiliative commitments on which family life is predicated. In chronically violent environments, child-rearing practices may become more authoritarian and restrictive, thus altering parent-child interactions, decreasing opportunities for play, disturbing family communication (Jensen et al. 1991), and restructuring extended family relationships. Such environments may compromise the parental roles of disciplinarian, affection giver, and role model, which may influence long-term moral development in children (Garbarino et al. 1991; Hoffman 1979). Parental depression and demoralization has been found to be a strong predictor of increased distress among children exposed to military actions (Punamaki 1987).

Children may face a series of individual stressful challenges. They must respond to altered role performance in family or school due to their trauma-related symptoms, disruption of peer relationships, and the need to make new friends due to loss of residence or relocation. The aftermath of violent trauma may include the stress of disclosure, forensic examination, participation in criminal proceedings, engagement with social agencies with possible temporary placement, foster care or removal of a parent from the home, custody hearings, stigmatization, and the need to learn new social skills to respond to social questioning, including by peers. Physical injury to the child may require ongoing medical procedures, rehabilitation, adjustment to disability or handicap, and reintegration among one's peer group.

Traumatic Reminders

Traumatic reminders are ubiquitous in the aftermath of trauma. They represent trauma-specific references to external and internal threats and reactions of the child. Along with secondary stresses, traumatic reminders serve as an important additional source of ongoing distress. Responsivity to them contributes to the periodic or phasic nature of renewed traumatic anxiety or avoidant behavior. The unexpected nature of the reminders may reevoke a sense of unpreparedness and lack of control. Because of the complexity of a traumatic experience and its occurrence in a natural setting, there may be a large number of cues whose previous more neutral or even positive associations are now superseded by associations with the traumatic experience(s).

There is a continuum of frequency of exposure to traumatic reminders that ranges from relatively infrequent to daily—for example, around the anniversary of a specific trauma, once every 6 months when it thunders and rains heavily, or every night going to bed in the room where a brother discovered the body of his sibling after a suicide. Even fictional portrayals in fairy tales, in novels, or on television may further challenge the child. In cases of intrafamilial violence, especially where there are unresolved issues of accountability in conjunction with conspiracies of silence, an abusing parent, for example, may continue to serve as a traumatic reminder of previous sexual abuse, even if that abuse has been discontinued. After physical injury, a scar or handicap may act as a daily reminder of how it was incurred, threatening to bring back remembrance of the circumstances and associated distress.

Clinical descriptive accounts suggest a typology of reminders that refer to the circumstances; precipitating conditions; characteristics of an assailant; signs of danger; endangering objects; associated affective exchanges; indicators of distress; unwanted results and signs of injury or death; parent or teacher reactions during or at reunion; and internal reactions, including kinesthetic, sensory, and bodily sensations, a sense of helplessness or fear, ineffectualness, or feelings of aloneness, shame, guilt, anger, and sadness. It is often overlooked that a child may be challenged by two or more sets of reminders, to both current and past experiences (Pynoos et al. 1991).

RESISTANCE AND VULNERABILITY TO THE TRAUMATIC EXPERIENCE(S)

Resistance and vulnerability refer to factors that mediate the impact of traumatic stress and affect the type and severity of acute posttraumatic distress. Such factors include current developmental competencies and challenges, temperament, self-esteem and locus of control, history of previous trauma, prior psychopathology, and the child's ability to make cognitive discriminations and to tolerate the internal changes and reactivity to reminders. The strength and importance of affiliative attachments constitutes one critical vulnerability factor for experiencing distress (Lazarus and Folkman 1984). Because of the nature and intensity of children's affiliative needs and desires, they are particularly vulnerable to posttraumatic distress from witnessing threat or harm to a parent or family member, or being victim to a violent betrayal of affiliative assumptions. Adolescents who were worried about a younger sibling have reported greater postdisaster distress and more somatic complaints than their peers (Dohrenwend et al. 1981). Separating children from their parents during rescue efforts or postdisaster cleanup can measurably increase their postdisaster morbidity (Friedman and Linn 1957; McFarlane et al. 1987).

A crucial mediator of a child's distress associated with catastrophic threat is the response during the event(s) of the parent or adult caretaker (Bat-Zion and Levy-Shiff, in press). During air raids or evacuation for impending disaster, children reported more anxiety if their parents or adult caretakers overreacted, appeared unable to respond competently, or appeared in conflict with each other over the appropriate response (Handford et al. 1986). When adult caretakers remained calm and appeared in control, children's anxiety during and after the event was reduced. When adult caretakers underreact or minimize an imminent danger that results in injury or death, children may exhibit increased anxiety and distrust (Nader and Pynoos 1993).

Vulnerability is also mediated and affected by preexisting personality, temperament, or psychopathology. Shy or anxious children may be inclined to display more social reticence or to overgeneralize trauma-related fears; depressed children may suffer undue guilt and, therefore, a more severe than expected posttraumatic stress reaction; and impulsive children may increase their problematic behaviors.

Factors contributing to resistance may not necessarily be positive mental health attributes; similarly, factors contributing to vulnerability may not be negative ones. Lack of empathy in a conduct-disturbed child may lead to less overt acute distress. Conversely, intelligence and empathy can increase distress when, for example, such a child more fully recognizes the behavior of a hostage taker as erratic and disturbed. Studies have begun to examine the contribution of children's subjective perception of threat to findings of intraexposure group differences in severity of posttrauma distress (Schwarz and Kowalski 1991; Yule et al. 1992). Guilt over acts of omission or commission perceived to have endangered others has been found to be associated with increased severity and persistence of posttraumatic stress reactions (Pynoos et al. 1987, in press; Yule and Williams 1990). Familiarity with deceased victims is also associated with grief reactions that can exacerbate PTSD reactions (Nader et al. 1990).

DISTRESS

Distress is the term used to encompass the biological, psychological, and behavioral manifestations of posttraumatic stress reactions. Comprehensive assessment procedures include self-report instruments that can provide a continuous scaling of severity and frequency of symptoms, special in-depth interview formats to explore the subjective experience of the child, structured clinical interviews that can reliably establish the presence of a disorder, and multiassessment methods, including instruments designed to obtain information from parents, teachers, and significant others (Earls et al. 1988; McNally 1991; Pynoos and Eth 1986; Pynoos et al. 1987; Saigh 1989; Yule and Williams 1990).

There is compelling evidence to suggest that, by school age, children can provide adequate self-reports of their posttraumatic distress, including the full range of posttraumatic stress symptoms. The assessment of the preschool child remains somewhat more problematic for a number of reasons related to development; however, methods to increase validity and reliability in this age range are beginning to receive more systematic consideration (Marans et al. 1991; Nader et al. 1991).

Measuring the dose of exposure to catastrophic violence at an elementary school, Pynoos et al. (1987) found a correlation between degree of exposure to the violence and severity of posttraumatic stress reaction; a symptom profile among the most severely distressed children that is similar to that for adults; and a pattern of symptom accrual, suggesting that specific symptoms are accumulated as exposure and severity of reaction increase. Mild reactions were associated with general apprehension and anxiety; moderate reactions included more intrusive phenomena and a wish to avoid feelings; and severe reactions included the full range of posttraumatic stress symptoms. In the most severe reactions, estrangement and interference with learning became more prominent. There seems to be a pattern of symptom improvement over the first year, with the rate of recovery primarily dependent on the severity of posttraumatic stress reactions reported at the end of the first month (Nader et al. 1990). Interactive processes may underlie the findings of concordant PTSD reactions among family members where parents and children have been directly exposed.

Reexperiencing phenomena are as central to the disorder in children as they are in adults, as exemplified by the strong association found among exposure, intrusive images, and severity of PTSD reaction (Pynoos et al. 1987, in press; Stuber et al. 1991). These phenomena serve as markers of moments of traumatic helplessness and as indicators of ongoing mental preoccupations. The nature and content of these phenomena are, in part, related to the maturity of both iconic memory (integration of isolated pictures into a single percept) and echoic memory (the brief sensory story), as components of autobiographical episodic memory. Typically, the younger the child, the more the recollection is confined to a single image, sound, or smell, usually representing the action most associated by the child with immediate threat or injury. In adolescence, the occurrence of full flashback phenomena has been reported (Yule and Williams 1990).

Children's portrayal of traumatic images and themes in drawing and play underscores their important role as developmental intermediates between symbolic play and the mental image (Winnicott 1971) and between the realms of external and internal reality (Nader and Pynoos 1991). Evolution in the traumatic dream content from specific trauma-related elements to more general threat to self or family may reflect the developmental reliance on the safety and security of a protective shield. Dreams of their own death may represent not only a sense of life-threat but a perceived absence, failure, or inadequacy of this shield.

Reenactment behavior manifested by specific behavioral responses to subsequent situations or cues that are associated with trauma-related actions, taken or imagined, may represent a developmental tendency toward "action memories" (Terr 1988). Reenactments represent both an "anticipatory bias" in response to perceived threat and unconscious efforts to offset in action the original moments of traumatic helplessness. Older children and adolescents may actively seek out opportunities to engage in reenactments ranging from thrill seeking and controlled risk-taking behavior to more aggressively dangerous or violent actions.

Avoidance and psychological numbing indicate that a child continues to restrict behavior or regulate emotions in a effort to control the recurrent impressions and negative affect. Avoidance and emotional constriction are difficult to measure in children. However, children do report becoming avoidant of specific thoughts, locations, concrete items, themes in their play, and human characteristics and behaviors that remind them of the traumatic incident. Children may exhibit a reduced interest in usual activities, including pleasurable ones, not only in response to a depressed mood, but in an effort to avoid further trauma by reducing involvement with the external world. Children may tend to experience a sense of estrangement, feeling that others, including parents, cannot fully understand or even recognize what they went through. Emotional constriction may be evidenced by children indicating they do not want to know how they are feeling, or by the lack of relevant emotion in their recounting.

Memory disturbances may reflect specific modifications that occur during recall as well as perceptual, encoding, or storage errors (Bjork and Richardson-Klavehn 1989). Developmental maturation governs the capacity to integrate information from different sensory modalities, to synthesize various moments of an episode, to form recall strategies, or for recall to rely less on contextual cues. Developmental vulnerabilities may underlie disunion or repression of traumatic moments due to intolerance of the distress associated with the biological tendency toward stimulus completion. Distortions, omissions, reframing of aspects of the experience, and spatial or temporal misrepresentations of threat may reflect early efforts to minimize the objective threat and to regulate emotional distress during recall (Pynoos and Nader 1989). Reconstruction of the experience when attention had been inwardly directed is especially problematic: there are fewer recorded external memory markers, less well-defined memory registration of internal states, and interference with recall due to shame or guilt.

Children appear to show the same pattern of tonic and phasic physiological reactivity observed in adults. After a disaster or violent occurrence, many children may exhibit a transient increase in anxiety at bedtime or difficulty going to sleep; highly exposed children may exhibit a more serious sleep disturbance associated with changes in sleep architecture and the occurrence of parasomnia symptoms (Ornitz and Pynoos 1989). In the morning, they may report feeling unrested. Symptoms may persist for weeks, months, even years. They may be intermittent and associated with recent traumatic reminders or sounds at night, leading to increased awakenings due to fear-enhanced arousal. Children may become afraid of sleep because of the autonomic reactivity associated with stage four awakenings. A chronic sleep disturbance should not be overlooked as a contributing etiology to problems with daytime concentration and learning.

As has also been noted in adult disaster victims (Weisaeth 1989), exaggerated startle reactions may be a good indicator of overall severity of response in children exposed to major disasters or catastrophic violence (Pynoos et al., in press; Yule and Williams 1990). Persistent hypervigilance and exaggerated startle may alter a child's usual behavior by leading to constant efforts to ensure personal security or the safety of others. These recurrent "bouts of fear" may seriously affect a child's emerging self-concept. In addition, temporary or chronic difficulty in modulating aggression can make children more irritable and easy to anger. This may result in reduced tolerance of the normal behaviors and slights of peers and family members, followed by unusual acts of aggression or social withdrawal (Pynoos et al. 1991).

Despite their absence from DSM-III-R (American Psychiatric Association 1987) criteria, acquisition of incident-specific new fears commonly occurs in children. Children may become afraid of specific elements that remind them of the trauma or may exhibit more generalized fears at moments of feeling vulnerable (e.g., when alone in the bathroom or when going to bed). Several investigators have found sex differences in the reporting of fears and fear-related anxiety, with increased rates among girls, perhaps due to differences in perception of personal vulnerability and self-efficacy or cultural discouragement of male expression of fears (Green et al. 1991; Lonigan et al. 1991; Pynoos and Nader 1988; Pynoos et al., in press). In a comprehensive study of English students involved in a ferry disaster, Yule et al. (1990) found that, opposed to an increase in generalized fearfulness among survivors compared with control subjects, the survivors developed new fears specifically linked to trauma-related cues. Two explanations for trauma-related fear acquisition in children have been proposed: a generalization gradient consistent with classical conditioning theory (Dollinger et al. 1984) and an interaction between perceived efficacy and anticipated consequences (Saigh 1985).

Disparities in reports of a child's distress by the child, parent, and teacher have been repeatedly found (Nader and Pynoos 1992; Yule and Williams 1990). Children report more subjective symptoms, such as intrusiveness and emotional avoidance, whereas parents typically report changes in their children's aggressive, fearful, or regressive behaviors. Parents notice traumatic play when it is dramatic, disturbing, or dangerous. The least visible symptoms to parents are the self-imposed restrictions on emotional range and daily activities. Parents often interpret children's avoidance of any mention of the trauma as successfully putting it behind them.

Associated features of posttraumatic stress reactions include guilt, grief, worry about a significant other, and reactivation of symptoms associated with a previous life experience (Pynoos and Nader 1993). These reactions are not necessarily found to be related to degree of exposure, although they may increase the severity of posttraumatic stress reactions and contribute to other comorbid conditions. Recent findings regarding the complex nature of childhood bereavement are providing new perspectives on the complicated interplay of grief and posttraumatic stress reactions (Pynoos 1992a).

COMPLEX OF PROXIMAL STRESS-RELATED PATHOLOGY

The posttrauma psychopathology of children and adolescents has been reported to include PTSD, phobic and overanxious disorders, trauma-related disorders of attachment and conduct, new-onset attention-deficit disorder, depression, substance abuse, dissociative disorder, sleep disorder, and somatization disorder. ICD-10 (World Health Organization 1990) includes an attachment disorder secondary to intrafamilial abuse and violence. Current diagnostic research focuses on the possibly spurious comorbidity resulting from overlap between criteria sets and the potential confounding of other diagnoses by PTSD symptoms.

In one study of catastrophic community violence, the most frequent diagnoses correlated with degree of exposure were, in order of decreasing frequency, PTSD, depression, attention deficit, and phobic disorder (Pynoos and Nader 1992). Depression was also found to be correlated with the frequency and intensity of grief reactions. Overanxious behavior and separation anxiety were found to be associated with other factors, including worry about a significant other and past history or threats to important attachments (e.g., parental illness, separation, divorce, loss). Persistent worry about a significant other may lead to morbid fears of catastrophe befalling family members, nightly checking on the safety of a family member, continued apprehension about a sibling or parent being out of sight, and a child's emotional detachment and impairment of daily functioning (Pynoos et al. 1991).

Perry (in press) proposed that the onset of secondary disorders to PTSD may be linked to specific familial predispositions, accounting for some of the variability in the onset or exacerbation of psychiatric disorders. The rate of comorbidity may represent an interplay between specific trauma-related reactions and those associated with the accumulation of secondary adversities (Rutter and Quinton 1984). Traumatic events can also exacerbate preexisting conduct or learning disorders, which in turn can hamper the ability of the child to process traumatic experiences. Such reciprocal exacerbation may be especially characteristic of substance-abusing adolescents, who may come to rely on drugs as a maladaptive coping strategy. The rate of adolescent substance abuse after trauma has been found to be culturally influenced (Kinzie et al. 1986).

POTENTIAL EFFECTS OF TRAUMATIC STRESS ON PROXIMAL DEVELOPMENT

The assessment of posttraumatic distress in children and adolescents should include consideration of proximal developmental tasks, including the ontogenesis of developmental competencies (Cicchetti 1989), interpersonal and intrafamilial developmental transitions (Rutter 1988), and biological plasticity and consolidation (Ornitz 1991). Recently acquired developmental achievements may be particularly vulnerable to disruption (Rutter 1988). The continuous establishment of a sense of safety and security throughout childhood provides a foundation for developmental maturation and achievement of age-appropriate competencies (Sandler 1987).

Reexperiencing phenomena affect the processing of real-world information by skewing selective attention either toward or away from concrete and symbolic reminders. This process has strong developmental determinants. Preschool children may experience cognitive confusions that interfere with the achievement of narrative coherence and exhibit a general decrease in verbalization or more precocious use of trauma-related expressions. School-age children may engage in trauma-related "detective" work, exhibit selective inhibition of thought and nonreflexive daydreaming, or make repeated use of traumatic details and meanings that compromise their expanded use of metaphor. Adolescents may search for or shun motivational explanations and may be challenged in the acquisition of abstract concepts where these concepts subsume more trauma-specific reminders. Further, an impairment in attention or learning may have quite different proximal impact for a child who is just learning to read than for a high school student whose sudden scholastic decline affects application to college. The marginal student may be at greatest academic risk (Yule 1991). School decline and failure may lead to a significant loss of self-esteem and increased risk of secondary psychiatric morbidity (Saigh and Mrouegh 1991).

The generation of intense negative emotions challenges the maturing mechanisms of emotional regulation (Parens 1991). Fear of affective intensity may interfere with the preschool task of increasing differentiation of affective states, with the capacity for school-age children to elaborate on their affective expression, and with the effort of adolescents to achieve a more sophisticated understanding of the origin and consequences of negative emotions. Somatic complaints and wariness of even intense pleasurable responses may result from similarities to the traumatic state of arousal. Self-attributions of shame, ineffectualness, or blame can *initiate* negative self-images that immediately challenge adaptive functioning. The generation of these intense, self-conscious emotions (Lewis 1991) may lead to significant alterations in the privatization of internal life, empathy, tendencies toward reparative behavior, and prosocial actions.

Autonomous striving may be subverted by trauma-related avoidant behavior that adversely restricts exploration and normal pleasurable activities; it may also be accelerated by trauma-generated adventuresome pursuits that may be beyond the child's developmental capabilities. Early assault on the physical integrity of a young child or intentional psychological harm may interfere with establishing a sense of physical and psychological autonomy, and thereby a recognition of similar boundaries with others, including peers.

A child's interpretation (or those proffered by others) of his or her own behavior during and after a traumatic experience may transform perceptions of self-efficacy. These perceptions include a sense of physical prowess or weakness, of passivity or activity, of cowardice or courage and heroism, and of self-enhancement or diminishment. These appraisals may be linked to changes in self-confidence, self-esteem, and pride that mediate the acquisition or consolidation of new competencies in the immediate posttrauma period (Emde 1991).

Specific traumatic features may correspond to phase-specific psychodynamic psychosexual and narcissistic concerns (Eth and Pynoos 1985; Pynoos and Nader 1993), sometimes "actualizing" prior fantasy elements. Acute separation of young children from parents during a disaster may lead to exceptionally intense posttrauma preoccupation with fears of abandonment or desertion that may forestall attempts at individuation. A 5-year-old boy witnessing the use of a dildo during a mother's rape may subsequently be preoccupied with accentuated fears of dismemberment. A preadolescent boy's experience of lying helpless on the floor during a violent rampage in a fast-food restaurant, where women were mutilated and killed, may generate unremitting conflicts over masculine and feminine self-attributions.

Unaddressed revenge and counterretaliatory fantasies may challenge the child's maturing capacity for restraint of aggression and appropriate assertiveness. Witnessing or being victim to adult violence compromises the school-age child's reliance on adult augmentation of emerging impulse control. The immediate social consequences of a dysregulation of aggression differ with age. By adolescence, the combination of vengeful fantasy, narcissistic rage, and a sense of invulnerability, and the accessibility of weapons, provides the precursors to injurious or fatal violence.

The proximal impact on moral development, especially if there is nonadjudication of a violent crime or war-related atrocity, can be profound. In the preschool child, catastrophic violence represents an instantiation of the concept of "bad" that is far beyond its use in the child's daily life. Consequently, there may be interference with the emergence of moral concepts, resulting in behavior that is overly regulated by considerations of good or bad or, alternatively, manifestly amoral. Nonadjudication of a parent's murder may undermine a school-age child's evolving reliance on rules to govern behavior. The early adolescent may experience an intense exaggeration of moral confusion (Stilwell et al. 1991), and the late adolescent and young adult may incorporate themes of the threat of violence and revenge into a political ideology (Pynoos 1992b).

Trauma disturbs the emerging awareness of historical continuity of the self. In preschool children, traumatic experiences embedded in "action memories" may result in their inaccessibility to the emerging verbal self (Stern 1985; Terr 1988; Wilson and Malatesta 1989). Trauma-generated negative emotions may disturb the "affective core of the self," which contributes to one's sense of continuity across developmental progression (Emde 1991). A trauma-induced sense of discontinuity can have a disrupting influence on the adolescent task of integrating past, present, and future expectations into a lasting sense of identity. Changes in future orientation, if they represent a discontinuity in expectation and forecast, may adversely affect the adolescent's emerging ambition, initiative, and assertiveness (Krystal 1991) and may alter current behavior by limiting the range of constructive plans for the future (Bowlby 1979a).

Changes in the representation of self and other can effect critical transitions in child-parent relationships, upsetting the developmental balance between independent and dependent behavior. Evolving forms of attachment serve the biological function of protecting children from danger while they develop skills to protect themselves (Cicchetti et al. 1990). The introduction of fear into a primary relationship has been found central to the development in infants and toddlers of disorganized and disoriented attachment relations (Cicchetti 1989). The mutual sense of a disrupted protective shield may alter a young child's reliance on parental efficacy and assurances of safety or security, and parental confidence in their own ability to protect their child. Posttraumatic stress–related estrangement may deter a mid-adolescent from seeking the counsel of parents at a critical juncture of decision making or risk taking. In late adolescence, there may be a rapid thrust toward self-sufficiency or, out of concern for other family members' safety and security, postponement of plans to leave home.

Critical transitions in establishing peer relationships may be affected. Withdrawal, emotional constriction, and disrupted impulse control may interfere with the preschool tasks of cooperation, sharing, and discovery of the self in relationship to other children. Traumatic play may limit the flexibility of play for other developmental purposes and distort age-specific forms of play (e.g., preschool coordinated fantasy play). The school-age child may suffer an acute disturbance in relatedness to a best friend, may experience a sense of isolation from peers, or may be ostracized as "different" because of posttraumatic behavior or physical injury. Reenactment behavior, especially inappropriate sexual or aggressive behavior, may acutely disrupt normative patterns of peer relationships and result in being labeled as "deviant." The adolescent may experience abrupt shifts in interpersonal attachments or heightened attachment in already existing relationships, increased identification with a peer group as a protective shield, or extreme isolation or ostracism, and a tendency toward aberrant rather than mainstream relationships.

There are different effects of traumatic stress during development periods characterized by relative neurophysiological plasticity or consolidation. The startle reaction provides a good example of potential neurophysiological vulnerability. It involves a well-elucidated neuroanatomical and biochemical pathway with known developmental maturation. Ornitz and Pynoos (1989) provided preliminary evidence that consolidation of the inhibitory control of the startle reflex may be interfered with by traumatic exposure, leading to a "neurophysiological regression" to an earlier pattern of startle modulation. The central nucleus of the amygdala regulates fear-enhanced startle (Ornitz 1991) and, perhaps, the reactivity to novel stimuli of inhibited children (Kagan 1991). The loss of inhibitory control over the startle reflex may interfere with the acquisition of a number of latency skills, for example, increased control over activity level, and capacity for reflection, academic learning, and focused attention.

RESILIENCE AND ADJUSTMENT

Resilience and adjustment refer to the child's early and ongoing processes to effectively tolerate, manage, or alleviate the psychological, physiological, behavioral, and social consequences of traumatic experience(s) without major deviation in developmental course, and with the achievement of adequate understanding of the experience and subsequent reactions. The child may require different means of coping and support to adjust to trauma-specific features of the experience(s), subsequent distress, contextual or affective reminders, proximal developmental disturbances, secondary stresses, and renewed responses to past experiences.

The cumulative goal of cognitive reprocessing is an enhanced, age-appropriate understanding of the circumstances and meaning of the traumatic experience(s). Reconciling primary and secondary appraisals (Lazarus and Folkman 1984) may require increasing a child's appreciation of the extent of threat or modifying the child's overestimation. It includes efforts to formulate constructive prevention and intervention strategies in relation both to what has occurred and to future situations. Emotional reprocessing represents an effort to understand the origins, legitimacy, and content of negative emotional reactions generated by the experience to increase tolerance, to diminish self-punitive attributions, and to maintain or repair the subjective sense of relatedness.

Parental responsiveness to the child in assisting cognitive and emotional reappraisals may facilitate adjustment in providing a co-construction of the contextual situation and meaning, as well as an empathic legitimization of the child's emotional experience. Parents, however, may be reluctant to participate with the child because they may feel too challenged by the traumatic material and by certain revelations that raise issues of accountability or call for interventions they are not prepared to undertake. Discrepancies in degree of exposure and occurrences of intrusive recollections among family members may lead parents or siblings to expose children secondarily to additional traumatic details and reminders.

Children may be under pressure from adult caretakers to disregard their own registration and attribution of meaning to a traumatic experience, through misleading explanations, prohibition, threats, or a covert conspiracy of silence. These tend to curtail efforts at adjustment, leading to impaired cognitive and emotional processing and failure to address issues of accountability (Bowlby 1979b; Kestenberg 1972).

A key indicator of how children are addressing trauma-specific features is the content and evolution of intervention fantasies. Pynoos and Nader (1989) observed that these are highly specific to the child's appraisals and wished-for actions and are commonly incorporated into the memory representation of the experience(s). These fantasies represent complex mental efforts influenced by age, gender, and life experience and demonstrate a developmental hierarchy in children's efforts to address the external and internal dangers (Pynoos and Nader 1993). Types of intervention fantasies include efforts to alter the precipitating events, to interrupt the traumatic action, to reverse the lethal or injurious consequences, to gain safe retaliation, and to prevent future trauma and loss. The organization of episodic memory as well as the intervention fantasies and psychodynamic attributions may differ as children focus on different moments of the experience.

Psychodynamic considerations are particularly germane in understanding the progressive developmental modifications of intervention fantasies as children attempt both to maintain a reality-based veridical memory representation, as well as to modify that representation to be more internally tolerable (Pruett 1984). Unchanging intervention fantasies or role identification may lead to an inflexible, intrapsychic maladjustment that underlies processes that have been variably referred to as "repetition compulsion," "fixation to the trauma," or "identification with the aggressor." This may result in a behavioral disposition that may become manifest in particular circumstances that serve as contextual or emotional reminders.

Among the most difficult issues are those of accountability and the associated psychodynamic meaning and affects. These issues vary depending on whether there is a perceived human agency, and if so whether it is inside or outside the family or group affiliation. Intrafamilial accountability causes profound disturbances in the family matrix by creating intense conflicts of loyalty, different attributions of blame by family members, severe challenges to basic affiliative assumptions, and difficulties in resolving feelings of shame and guilt, as well as rage, hatred, and revenge. An extrafamilial agency can provoke extreme, conscious fantasies of retaliation and counterretaliation that can be terrifying and, at the same time, deeply challenging to the child's emerging sense of moral and social conscience. Family, group, or society may attempt to mobilize these intense retaliatory wishes into group hatreds, persecution, and armed violence. The child can be assisted to understand better the origin of these revenge fantasies in his or her experience of initial helplessness and the after-the-fact wish to be rid of the threat. Responsiveness of the judicial system can help the child by shifting the burden to society for resolving issues of accountability and punishment.

Unrealistic expectations about recovery on the part of the child, and his or her family, friends, and teachers, may exacerbate the child's distress, generate additional negative self-images, and prevent help-seeking behaviors (Silver and Wortman 1980). Successful efforts at adjustment to traumatic distress increase the child's understanding that these reactions are expectable, enhance the child's tolerance of them, and, over time, decrease their frequency and intensity. Recognition of reactivation of prior distress can prevent misinterpretations of these responses as "overreactions," temperamental traits, or moments of parental failure.

Fear of recurrence is a common reaction across varying exposure levels. Addressing myths, rumors, and misconceptions can assist the child in diminishing anxieties that interfere with daily functioning. Proactive interventions on the part of adult caretakers may be essential to restoring a sense of safety and security. A lack of responsiveness on the part of a parent, family, school, or community to real dangers of recurrence may not only exacerbate the child's distress but also initiate primitive modes of accommodation to anticipatory fears.

Many PTSD symptoms reflect a subjective experience that requires a well-maintained interrelatedness with parent, sibling, or teacher for these reactions to be empathically understood or communicated at moments of renewed distress. A child may need overt permission, encouragement, and assistance in describing specific intrusive symptoms, avoidant wishes based on fear, or arousal disturbances. Shared affective exchanges with a child, often requiring parental courage, are necessary to assist in increasing tolerance for negative emotions associated with the experience. Being able to listen to a child's subjective experience and distress can generate a sense of authentic mutuality (Stern 1985) that bridges a private feeling of estrangement.

Proper understanding of the basis of arousal symptoms in disrupted neurophysiological function and reactivity to reminders will prevent inappropriate expectations about the course of their recovery. Appropriate strategies include assisting a child in contextual discriminations to reduce the frequency of phasic reactivity, providing timely support to reduce its intensity and duration, and tolerating time-limited occurrences of unusual or regressive behaviors.

Children often experience traumatic reminders without any adequate assistance from others, increasing their sense of isolation, lack of protection and intervention, and inability to tolerate and understand their own reactions. Attention to actual or anticipated reminders can enable adult caretakers to provide enhanced behavioral and emotional support. The child can be assisted to increase support seeking, understanding of the traumatic reference, emotional tolerance, and cognitive discrimination (Pynoos and Nader 1993). Similar considerations apply in diminishing both the acquisition and intensity of new fears.

A proactive stance is essential to prevent or minimize secondary stresses and to enhance specific individual and family means of coping. The impact of secondary stresses on children is often mediated by parental mood, behavior, and responsiveness. Relief of parental distress or intervention for stress-related psychopathology can make a significant contribution to strengthening the recovery environment. Promoting reunion with at least one parent, sibling, or relative after catastrophic family losses can improve outcome and help preserve or restore a sense of historical continuity (Danielli 1985; Kinzie et al. 1986).

Schools can also assist in this effort. Restoration of the school milieu may be critical to academic and behavioral adjustment among students after major disasters or catastrophic community violence. Temporary modification of classroom activities and requirements may help restore or maintain an individual child's self-esteem during a period of recovery (Nader and Pynoos 1993; Yule 1991). Attention to the posttraumatic stress origins of acute changes in school and peer behavior can prevent misattributions of such behavior to other "deviant" etiologies.

The same factors found to mediate resilience and adjustment to childhood stress in general are applicable to trauma-related secondary stresses. These include a positive relationship with a competent adult, skill at learning and problem solving, engaging personality, competence and perceived efficacy by self or society, high IQ score, positive school experience, mastery motivation, and previous successful experiences (Masten et al. 1990).

In violent environments, each exposure may cause immediate traumatic reactions from which there is only incomplete recovery, thus increasing the risk of significant deviation in developmental trajectory. In an environment of ever-present threats of coercive violation of physical integrity and autonomy, coping mechanisms leading to primitive monitoring strategies, such as autohypnotic vigilance, serve as a means of gaining some sense of anticipatory control (Shengold 1989; Terr 1991). When these circumstances are seen as uncontrollable, primitive mechanisms of emotional regulation and avoidance may also be utilized (Band and Weiss 1988). Many of these mechanisms, including those subsumed under the terms *dissociation* and *repression*, are complex mental operations, directed not only at diminishing immediate or delayed distress, but also at related issues of accountability or perceived involvement (Pynoos and Nader 1993; Shengold 1989). These mechanisms may then be incorporated into prominent intervention fantasies, not only in fear of repetition but also in apprehension over fears of escalation in threats or violence.

EFFECTS ON EMERGING PERSONALITY AND DISTAL DEVELOPMENT

Traumatic exposures in childhood occur during critical periods of personality formation when there are ongoing revisions of the inner model of the world, self, and other. This working model includes expectations about others and one's own behavior and forecasts about the future. There may be a developmental tendency for veridical and nonveridical representations of traumatic exposures to initiate the formation of coexisting, frequently incompatible working models (Bowlby 1979a). These internal models, once organized, tend to operate outside of conscious awareness and to resist dramatic change (Cicchetti et al. 1990). They may result in isolated areas of decision making or behavior that are inconsistent with other personality attributes or may lead to global patterns of incongruent interpersonal behavior.

Traumatic stress interacts with the emerging personality in several areas: 1) achievement of psychological and physiological maturation; 2) hierarchical integration of competencies; 3) intrapsychic structure of internal and external dangers, inner representation of self and other, and mechanisms of cognitive and emotional regulation; 4) schematization of security, safety, risk, injury, loss, protection, and intervention; 5) behavioral attributes of fear, courage, and fearlessness; and 6) evolving intervention fantasies and their relationship to internal scripts, constructive actions, and creativity.

What appears to be a discontinuity after experiencing trauma may in fact reflect an exaggeration of preexisting temperament or personality attributes. On the other hand, the emerging personality of a child may be particularly susceptible to traumatic influences, resulting in marked deviations in character and life attitude. One central personality axis affected by traumatic exposure is that of fear, courage, and fearlessness (Rachman 1980), with reported oscillations toward each of the extremes (Gislason and Call 1982). Successful adjustment restores a normative level of fear and promotes the capacity for courage in the face of ongoing subjective apprehension, conflicts over traumatic helplessness, and discomforting affects (Rachman 1980).

Changes in the form and content of intervention fantasies over time reflect increasing maturity, additional outside information, and future life experiences. They may incorporate new reappraisals as well as revised intrapsychic conflicts and narcissistic accommodations. The evolving intervention fantasies, with embedded traumatic elements, can be instrumental in the construction of specific internal scripts that guide expectations and goals as well as real interpersonal interactions (Emde 1991). They may direct a child's attention toward future constructive actions, both short- and long-term, and may serve as an ongoing source of creativity in career or artistic pursuits. On the other hand, unaddressed or maladaptive revenge fantasies may contribute to a chronic pattern of dangerous reenactment behaviors. Compensatory fantasies of omnipotence and underestimation of the degree of threat may interfere with the development of appropriate self-protective capabilities and caution. Mental modification in the form of spatial misrepresentation of threat may, if incorporated into an evolving mental schema, increase the risk of further victimization. Lack of adequate schematization of protective intervention may compromise self-preservative and self-caring functions in children (Hartman and Burgess 1989) and interfere with adult protective behavior (Wyatt et al. 1992). The impact on later parental competencies is an important area for future investigation (Solkoff 1992).

Acutely traumatized children demonstrate a flexibility in identificatory roles, varying even within a single interview session, in their identification with assailant, victim, or rescuer. Over time, there may be a rigidity and prominence of one such role that becomes dominant in the emerging personality. Williams (1987) described one set of children who became totally involved with aggressive revenge fantasies and another set that turned the aggression inward. Character traits and career interests may also reflect a lifelong preoccupation with rescue or reparative roles or motivation for altruistic behavior. There may also be a chronic struggle against identification with a parent or sibling who died under traumatic circumstances (Furman 1974). Negative self-attributions that arise out of the original experience(s) may, if uncorrected, also become embedded in character; adult studies suggest that these negative self-images are vulnerable to reactivation after future traumatic exposure (see Foa and Riggs, Chapter 6).

Childhood masturbation fantasies may incorporate traumatic themes that, by adulthood, may become, as Stoller (1989) noted, repetitive, compulsive, and aesthetic elements of erotic life. He also suggested that consensual forms of sadomasochistic behavior in adults may derive from schematization of danger, risk, mystery, secrecy, and negotiated consent relating to early childhood experiences with life-threatening medical illness, painful medical procedures, and required trust in parental oversight and medical restraint.

A developmental psychopathology model of PTSD underscores the complex impact on developmental progression and personality of serial or sequential traumatization. There are long-range influences on psychosexual and narcissistic maturation, with the risk of prolonged psychosexual disturbances, narcissistic deficits, and impaired development of conscience. In situations of child abuse, additional exposures to spousal abuse and parental suicidal and homicidal behavior (at different points in the child's life) help shape the form and content of these disturbances. The nature and circumstances of physical or sexual abuse or witnessing of violence necessarily change over time, as both the child and the circumstances develop. A parent's expressed reason or threat, the child's attribution of meaning, and the content of retaliatory rage, protection, and escape fantasies may vary with developmental maturation. Mones (1991) provided vivid descriptions of the extreme of this evolution, culminating in conscious and detailed parricidal plans carried out by a late adolescent after failed attempts to evoke familial, school, and societal intervention.

Trauma-induced developmental changes in the reactivity of central catecholamine systems may produce a biological analogue of altered expectations by governing the attention of the central nervous system toward specific traumatic-related information, including reminders, and away from other "less pressing" information that requires less immediate action. These changes may initiate "anticipatory bias" in the perception of environmental information, including context errors, a "state of preparedness" for extremely negative emotions, and "anxiety of premonitions," which involve expectations of potentially dangerous future events (Kagan 1991). Trauma-induced release of stress hormones in early childhood is likely to influence the selection and formation of neuronal networks that extend throughout the school-age years and into adolescence (Chugani et al. 1987).

In situations where there is chronic environmental threat, arousal disturbances may be interpreted by the child and family as situationally appropriate monitoring, confrontational, or avoidant responses. The impact on personality and development may not be apparent until long after the perceived threat is over. This is what makes the assessment of children in war zones so problematic, where self-perception as a good soldier or resistance fighter may maintain a child's self-esteem (Baker 1990). Children and adolescents may, in the future, seek out situations where heightened arousal and accompanying intervention fantasies will feel ego-syntonic.

The influence of distal traumatic reminders may depend on the extent to which they are embedded in the circumstances of future everyday life. The more they involve intricacies of interpersonal interactions, bodily sensations, and internal affective states, the more likely their occurrence, and the more difficult they are to identify as sources of renewed hypervigilance or other arousal behavior, anxiety, or avoidance. Disturbances or distortion in a sense of historical continuity and conscious veridical representation increase the difficulty of making this association. The inability to identify the historical referent to a response to a distal traumatic reminder may lead to increased negative self-attributions for current actions that further compromise self-esteem and self-concept. The influence of traumatic reminders may become apparent only in quite specific, future challenging adult situations, and the troubling aspects of the exposure are variable over time.

Distal secondary stresses may be a continuation of stresses that occurred in the immediate aftermath of the trauma, or they may arise out of new developmental challenges or life circumstances. There may be need for future medical treatment related to injuries received during the event or accommodations to disabilities or handicaps deriving from it. There may be involvement in later criminal or civil proceedings or efforts at societal restitution. Further, there may be renewed apprehension or concerns about release of an assailant from prison, future encounters with an abusive adult caretaker or sibling, or contact of an abusive parent or relative with children of the next generation. Additionally, there may be the need to acquire social skills to explain trauma-related behavior to intimate persons in one's later life, including spouse, children, selected colleagues, and friends. Such revelations may then induce secondary changes in the development cycle of the family of origin, nuclear family, or interpersonal relations. Self-revelation, disclosure, and social communication mediate the long-term repercussions of childhood trauma, including psychosomatic symptoms. Conversely, ongoing inhibition of disclosure may operate as a distal secondary stress that may adversely affect physical and psychological well-being (Pennebaker and Susman 1988).

COMPLEX OF DISTAL POSTTRAUMATIC STRESS–RELATED PATHOLOGY

Distal posttraumatic stress–related pathologies include chronic PTSD, comorbid mental and physical conditions, developmental and personality disturbances, and age-appropriate indications of dissatisfaction and lack of well-being. In addition to the central role of traumatic insults at different developmental phases, pathology also derives from the interaction with other pathogenic environmental factors, the ongoing influences of secondary stresses and traumatic reminders, and the damaging consequences of the use of maladaptive coping mechanisms. The proposed DESNOS (disorder of extreme stress not otherwise specified) classification (see Davidson, Chapter 1) may best be understood from a developmental standpoint as involving an interdigitating or layering of many of the above factors. Self-injurious behavior in adults presents an example in which childhood trauma, neglect, and deprivation each contribute to the factorial analysis of risk (van der Kolk et al. 1991). A history of multiple victimization in childhood serves as one of several complex antecedents to borderline personality disorder (Herman et al. 1989).

A study of adolescents with multiple personality disorder found that, in treatment, improved integrated ego functions lead to increased reporting of posttraumatic stress reactions to specific past traumatic experiences (Dell and Eisenhower 1990). This study also reported that core "personalities" originated during preschool years. The central types included fearful, protective-intervening, and avenging or aggressive selves, each of which was associated with specific traumatic episodes. A developmental psychopathology model would suggest investigating to what degree these "selves" reflect a rigidification and persistence of age-related intervention fantasies and solitary and coordinated role play.

There have not as yet been prospective long-term follow-up studies of PTSD in children and adolescents using appropriate multimethod assessments. Adult clinical research suggests that after 3–6 months there may be relative stability of untreated PTSD symptoms (see Foa and Riggs, Chapter 6). Short-term posttrauma studies in children have so far supported the persistence of untreated posttraumatic stress symptoms in those who experienced several initial reactions (Dyregrov and Raundalen 1992; Nader et al. 1990; Yule 1991). A longitudinal controlled comparison study of adolescent Cambodian refugees, now young adults, revealed that although chronic PTSD remained related to the initial traumatic exposures, current depression was most strongly associated with current secondary stresses (Sack et al. 1991). One study of adolescents in residential treatment showed the advantage of rigorous adherence to DSM-III-R criteria to discern the frequency of chronic PTSD among other comorbid conditions, including mood and disruptive behavioral disorders. Rediagnosis permitted more accurate identification of the role of current traumatic reminders in precipitating otherwise unexplained aggressive and avoidant behaviors (Doyle and Baver 1989).

Elements of childhood traumatic experiences may contribute to presentation of selective symptoms in adolescence and adulthood. Symptoms of self-mutilation and suicidal behaviors in adolescents and young adults may include trauma-related behavioral reenactments and accompanying intervention fantasies. Cooper (1986) suggested that an unusual, isolated adult symptom may be etiologically related to a specific childhood traumatic experience. Stoller (1989) commented that the more fixed and compulsive a perverse adult behavior, the more likely it is to find traumatic exposures and family forces that participated in its origin and maintenance.

Among a group of children in a residential treatment setting, Perry (in press) reported chronic alterations in neurochemical regulation and physiological function. These included tachycardia, alterations in α_2 platelet receptors, and marked reduction of symptoms in response to clonidine, an α_2-adrenergic blocker. He hypothesized that prolonged "alarm reactions" in childhood may induce chronic abnormal patterns of catecholamine activity altering brain stem functioning, including cardiovascular dysregulation, affective lability, increased anxiety, increased startle response, sleep abnormalities, and "sensitization" to future stressful events. A future avenue for investigation concerns the contribution of these chronic biological changes to adult personality, psychopathology, and deleterious effects on physical health. In addition, physical health problems may be due to chronic maladjustment, such as substance abuse.

CONCLUSION

A developmental psychopathology framework can provide a more comprehensive approach to the scientific investigation of child and adolescent trauma and its consequences. There should be attention to the complexity of traumatic experiences and the interactions of traumatic reminders, secondary stresses, posttraumatic distress, development and its effects on emerging personality, and psychopathology. Having established more reliable and valid measurements of PTSD in children and adolescents, there is now the opportunity for use of more expanded research designs and statistical methods, including developmental epidemiology and path analysis, and multidisciplinary approaches to address salient questions of resilience, adaptation, and psychopathology.

The conceptual schema presented in this chapter has a number of implications for developing and evaluating preventive and therapeutic interventions. This model suggests the interaction over time of many critical factors that play a role in the progression from traumatic exposure(s) to subsequent psychopathology. Each of these factors can be seen as a potential focus for prevention and treatment. It also suggests the importance of early intervention to promote developmental progression; the further along the pathway the child continues, the more likely that multifaceted treatment approaches will be needed.

The assistance and support provided to children in their adjustment efforts by parents, family members, school, community, and society help reshape trauma-induced disturbances in internal representations of self, other, and the world. As Solnit (1989) argued, if these efforts are positive and successful, they may promote long-term growth; preserve a sense of personal coherence, competence, and integrity; and provide the child with the courage and personal resources to undertake subsequent reprocessing that may occur with maturation and to address future adversities.

REFERENCES

Adams PR, Adams GR: Mount St. Helens' ashfall: evidence for a disaster stress reaction. Am Psychol 39:252–260, 1984

American Psychiatric Association: Diagnostic and Statistical Manual of Mental Disorders, 3rd Edition, Revised. Washington, DC, American Psychiatric Association, 1987

Baker AM: The psychological impact of the intifada on Palestinian children in the occupied West Bank and Gaza: an exploratory study. Am J Orthopsychiatry 60:496–505, 1990

Band EB, Weiss JR: How to feel better when it feels bad: children's perspectives on coping with everyday stress. Developmental Psychology 24:247–253, 1988

Bat-Zion N, Levy-Shiff R: Children in war: stress and coping reactions under the threat of the scud missile attacks and the effect of proximity, in Effects of War and Violence in Children. Edited by Lewis L, Fox N. Hillsdale, NJ, Lawrence Erlbaum (in press)

Bell CC, Jenkins EJ: Traumatic stress and children. J Health Care Poor Underserved 2(1):175–186, 1991

Bernstein AE: The impact of incest trauma on ego development, in Adult Analysis and Childhood Sexual Abuse. Edited by Levine HB. Hillsdale, NJ, Analytic Press, 1990, pp 65–91

Bjork RA, Richardson-Klavehn A: On the puzzling relationship between environmental context and human memory, in Current Issues in Cognitive Processes: The Tulane Flowertree Symposium on Cognition. Hillsdale, NJ, Lawrence Erlbaum, 1989, pp 313–344

Black D, Kaplan T: Father kills mother: issues and problems encountered by a child psychiatric team. Br J Psychiatry 153:624–630, 1988

Bowlby J: The Making and Breaking of Affectional Bonds. London, Tavistock, 1979a

Bowlby J: On knowing what you aren't supposed to know and feeling what you are not supposed to feel. Can J Psychiatry 24:403–408, l979b

Brown SL: Developmental cycle of family: clinical implications. Psychiatr Clin North Am 3:369–381, 1980

Burt C: War neuroses in British children. Nervous Child 2:324–337, 1943

Chugani H, Phelps ME, Mazziotta JC: Positron emission tomography study of human brain functional development. Ann Neurol 22:487–497, 1987

Cicchetti D: How research on child maltreatment has informed the study of child development: perspectives from developmental psychopathology, in Child Maltreatment: Theory and Research on the Causes and Consequences of Child Abuse and Neglect. Edited by Cicchetti D, Carlson V. New York, Cambridge University Press, 1989, pp 377–431

Cicchetti D, Cummings M, Greenberg M, et al: An organizational perspective on attachment beyond infancy: implications for theory, measurement and research, in Attachment During the Preschool Years: Theory, Research and Intervention. Edited by Greenberg M, Cicchetti D, Cummings M. Chicago, IL, University of Chicago Press, 1990, pp 3–49

Cooper AM: Toward a limited definition of psychic trauma in the reconstruction of trauma: its significance, in Clinical Work, Workshop Series of the American Psychoanalytic Association Monograph 2. Edited by Rothstein A. New York, International Universities Press, 1986, pp 41–56

Cotton P: Gun-associated violence increasingly viewed as public health challenge. JAMA 267:1171–1174, 1992

Daly M, Wilson J: Child maltreatment from a sociobiological perspective. New Dir Child Dev 11:93–112, 1981

Danielli Y: Treatment and prevention of long-term effects of intergenerational transmission of victimization: a lesson from the Holocaust survivors and their children, in Trauma and Its Wake. Edited by Figley C. New York, Brunner/Mazel, 1985, pp 295–313

Dell P, Eisenhower JW: Adolescent multiple personality disorder: a preliminary study of eleven cases. J Am Acad Child Adolesc Psychiatry 29:359–366, 1990

Dohrenwend BP, Dohrenwend BS, Warheit GJ, et al: Stress in the community: a report to the president's commission on the accident at Three Mile Island. Ann N Y Acad Sci 365:159–174, 1981

Dollinger SJ, O'Donnell JP, Staley AA: Lightning-strike disaster: effects on children's fears and worries. J Consult Clin Psychol 52:1028–1038, 1984

Doyle JS, Baver SK: Posttraumatic stress disorder in children: its identification and treatment in a residential setting for emotionally disturbed youth. Journal of Traumatic Stress 2:275–288, 1989

Dyregrov A, Raundalen M: The impact of the Gulf War on the children of Iraq. Paper presented at the International Society for Traumatic Stress Studies World Conference "Trauma and Tragedy." Amsterdam, The Netherlands, June 1992

Earls F, Smith E, Reich W, et al: Investigating psychopathological consequences of a disaster in children: a pilot study incorporating a structured diagnostic interview. J Am Acad Child Adolesc Psychiatry 27:90–95, 1988

Emde RN: Positive emotions for psychoanalytic theory: surprises from infancy research and new directions. J Am Psychoanal Assoc 39:5–44, 1991

Eth S, Pynoos RS: Developmental perspective on psychic trauma in childhood, in Trauma and Its Wake, Vol 1. Edited by Figley C. New York, Brunner/Mazel, 1985, pp 36–52

Freud S: Inhibitions, symptoms and anxiety (1926), in The Standard Edition of the Complete Psychological Works of Sigmund Freud, Vol 20. Translated and edited by Strachey J. London, Hogarth Press, 1959, pp 87–156

Friedman P, Linn I: Some psychiatric notes on the Andrea Doria disaster. Am J Psychiatry 114:426–432, 1957

Furman E: A Child's Parent Dies: Studies in Childhood Bereavement. New Haven, CT, Yale University Press, 1974

Garbarino J, Kostelny K, Dubrow N: What children can tell us about living in danger. Am Psychol 46:376–383, 1991

Gislason IL, Call J: Dog bite in infancy: trauma and personality development. Journal of the American Academy of Child Psychiatry 22:203–207, 1982

Green BL, Korol M, Grace MC, et al: Children and disaster: age, gender, and parental effects on PTSD symptoms. J Am Acad Child Adolesc Psychiatry 30:945–951, 1991

Handford HA, Mayes SD, Mattison RE, et al: Child and parent reaction to the Three Mile Island nuclear accident. Journal of the American Academy of Child Psychiatry 25:346–356, 1986

Hartman CR, Burgess AW: Sexual abuse of children: causes and consequences, in Child Maltreatment: Theory and Research on the Causes and Consequences of Child Abuse and Neglect. Edited by Cicchetti D, Carlson V. New York, Cambridge University Press, 1989, pp 95–128

Herman JL, Perry JC, van der Kolk BA: Childhood trauma in borderline personality disorder. Am J Psychiatry 146:490–495, 1989

Hoffman ML: Development of moral thought, feeling, and behavior. Am Psychol 34:959–966, 1979

Jensen PS, Richters J, Ussery T, et al: Child psychopathology and environmental influences: discrete life events versus ongoing adversity. J Am Acad Child Adolesc Psychiatry 30:303–309, 1991

Kagan J: A conceptual analysis of the affects. J Am Psychoanal Assoc 39:109–130, 1991

Keilson H: Sequential Traumatization in Children (1979), English Edition. Translated by Bearne Y, Coleman H, Winter D. Jerusalem, Israel, Magnes Press, 1992

Kestenberg JS: How children remember and parents forget. International Journal of Psychoanalytic Psychotherapy 1:103–123, 1972

Kinzie D, Sack W, Angell R, et al: The psychiatric effects of massive trauma on Cambodian children, I: the children. Journal of the American Academy of Child Psychiatry 25:370–376, 1986

Klinnert MD, Campos J, Source JF, et al: Social referencing, in The Emotions in Early Development. Edited by Plutchik P, Kellerman H. New York, Academic Press, 1983, pp 123–134

Krystal H: Integration and self-healing in post-traumatic states: a ten-year retrospective. American Imago 48:93–117, 1991

Kuch K, Cox BJ: Symptoms of PTSD in 124 survivors of the Holocaust. Am J Psychiatry 149:337–340, 1992

Lazarus RS, Folkman S: Stress, Appraisal and Coping. New York, Springer, 1984

Lewis M: Self-conscious emotions and the development of self. J Am Psychoanal Assoc 39:45–73, 1991

Lonigan CJ, Shannon MP, Finch AJ, et al: Children's reactions to a natural disaster: symptom severity and degree of exposure. Advances in Behavior Research and Therapy 13:133–154, 1991

Marans S, Mayes L, Cicchetti D, et al: The child-psychoanalytic play interview: a technique for studying thematic content. J Am Psychoanal Assoc 39:1015–1036, 1991

Masten AS, Best KM, Garmezy N: Resilience and development: contributions from the study of children who overcome adversity. Development and Psychopathology 2:425–444, 1990

McFarlane AC, Policansky SK, Irwin C: A longitudinal study of the psychological morbidity in children due to natural disaster. Psychol Med 17:727–738, 1987

McNally RJ: Assessment of posttraumatic stress disorder in children. Psychological Assessment 3:001–007, 1991

Mercier MH: Children in an occupied land: the suffering of French children. Nervous Child 2:308–312, 1943

Mones P: When a Child Kills: Abused Children Who Kill Their Parents. New York, Simon & Schuster, 1991

Nader K, Pynoos RS: Drawing and play in the diagnosis and assessment of childhood post-traumatic stress syndromes, in Play, Diagnosis and Assessment. Edited by Schaefer C, Gitlan K, Sandgrun A. New York, Wiley, 1991, pp 375–389

Nader K, Pynoos RS: Parental report of children's responses to life threat. Paper presented at the American Psychiatric Association annual meeting, Washington, DC, May 1992

Nader K, Pynoos R: School disaster: planning and initial interventions. Journal of Social Behavior and Personality (suppl, Handbook of Post-Disaster Interventions) 8:1–22, 1993

Nader K, Pynoos RS: The children of Kuwait following the Gulf crisis, in Effects of War and Violence in Children. Edited by Lewis L, Fox N. Hillsdale, NJ, Laurence Erlbaum (in press)

Nader K, Pynoos RS, Fairbanks L, et al: Children's PTSD reactions one year after a sniper attack at their school. Am J Psychiatry 147:1526–1530, 1990

Nader K, Stuber M, Pynoos R: Posttraumatic stress reactions in preschool children with catastrophic illness: assessment needs. Comprehensive Mental Health Care 1:223–239, 1991

Ornitz EM: Developmental aspects of neurophysiology, in Child and Adolescent Psychiatry: A Comprehensive Textbook. Edited by Lewis M. Baltimore, MD, Williams & Wilkins, 1991, pp 38–51

Ornitz EM, Pynoos RS: Startle modulation in children with post-traumatic stress disorder. Am J Psychiatry 147:866–870, 1989

Parens H: A view of the development of hostility in early life. J Am Psychoanal Assoc 39:75–108, 1991

Pennebaker JW, Susman JR: Disclosure of traumas and psychosomatic processes. Soc Sci Med 26:327–332, 1988

Perry BD: Neurobiological sequelae of childhood trauma: posttraumatic stress disorders in children, in Catecholamine Function in Posttraumatic Stress Disorder: Emerging Concepts. Edited by Murberg M. Washington, DC, American Psychiatric Press (in press)

Pruett K: A chronology of defensive adaptations to severe psychological trauma. Psychoanal Study Child 39:591–612, 1984

Punamaki RL: Psychological stress response of Palestinian mothers and their children in conditions of military occupation and political violence. The Quarterly Newsletter of the Laboratory of Comparative Human Cognition 9:76–79, 1987

Pynoos RS: Grief and trauma in children and adolescents. Bereavement Care 11:2–10, 1992a

Pynoos RS: Violence, personality and politics, in The Mosaic of Contemporary Psychiatry in Perspective. Edited by Kales A, Pierce CM, Greenblatt M. New York, Springer-Verlag, 1992b, pp 53–65

Pynoos RS, Eth S: Children traumatized by witnessing acts of personal violence: homicide, rape and suicide behavior, in Post-Traumatic Stress Disorder in Children. Edited by Eth S, Pynoos RS. Washington, DC, American Psychiatric Press, 1985, pp 17–43

Pynoos R, Eth S: Witness to violence: the child interview. Journal of the American Academy of Child Psychiatry 25:306–319, 1986

Pynoos RS, Nader K: Children who witness the sexual assaults of their mothers. J Am Acad Child Adolesc Psychiatry 27:567–572, 1988

Pynoos RS, Nader K: Children's memory and proximity to violence. J Am Acad Child Adolesc Psychiatry 28:236–241, 1989

Pynoos RS, Nader K: Children exposed to catastrophic school violence. Paper presented at the American Psychiatric Association annual meeting, Washington, DC, May 1992

Pynoos RS, Nader K: Issues in the treatment of post-traumatic stress in children and adolescents, in The International Handbook of Traumatic Stress Syndromes. Edited by Wilson JP, Raphael B. New York, Plenum, 1993, pp 535–549

Pynoos RS, Frederick C, Nader K, et al: Life threat and posttraumatic stress in school age children. Arch Gen Psychiatry 44:1057–1063, 1987

Pynoos RS, Nader K, March J: Childhood post-traumatic stress disorder, in The Textbook of Child and Adolescent Psychiatry. Edited by Wiener J. Washington, DC, American Psychiatric Press, 1991, pp 955–984

Pynoos RS, Goenjian A, Karakashian M, et al: Posttraumatic stress reactions in children after the 1988 Armenian earthquake. Br J Psychiatry (in press)

Rachman S: Emotional processing. Behav Res Ther 18:51–60, 1980

Rangell L: Castration. J Am Psychoanal Assoc 39:3–23, 1991

Richters J, Martinez P: NIMH Community Violence Project, I: children as victims of and witnesses to violence. Psychiatry 56:7–21, 1993

Rose DS: A model for psychodynamic psychotherapy with the rape victim. Psychotherapy 28:85–95, 1991

Rosenberg MS: New directions for research on the psychological maltreatment of children. Am Psychol 42:166–171, 1987

Russell D: The Secret Trauma. New York, Basic Books, 1986

Rutter M: Epidemiological approaches to developmental psychopathology. Arch Gen Psychiatry 45:486–495, 1988

Rutter M, Quinton D: Parental psychiatric disorder: effects on children. Psychol Med 14:853–880, 1984

Sack WH, Clarke G, Goff B, et al: Three forms of stress in Cambodian adolescent refugees. Paper presented at the 25th annual Association for Advancement of Behavior Therapy Annual Convention, New York, November 1991

Saigh PA: Adolescent anxiety following varying degrees of war exposure. Journal of Clinical Child Psychology 14:311–314, 1985

Saigh PA: The validity of the DSM-III posttraumatic stress disorder classification as applied to children. J Abnorm Psychol 98:189–192, 1989

Saigh PA, Mrouegh A: Academic variations among traumatized Lebanese adolescents. Paper presented at the 25th annual Association for Advancement of Behavior Therapy Annual Convention, New York, November 1991

Sandler J: The background of safety, in From Safety to Superego: Selected Papers of Joseph Sandler. Edited by Sandler J. New York, Guilford, 1987, pp 1–8

Schwarz ED, Kowalski JM: Malignant memories: PTSD in children and adults after a school shooting. J Am Acad Child Adolesc Psychiatry 30:936–944, 1991

Shengold L: Autohypnosis and soul murder: hypnotic evasion, autohypnotic vigilance and hypnotic facilitation, in The Psychoanalytic Core. Edited by Blum HP, Weinshel EN, Rodman FR. Madison, CT, International Universities Press, 1989, pp 187–206

Silver RL, Wortman CB: Coping with undesirable life events, in Human Helplessness: Theory and Applications. Edited by Garber J, Seligman MEP. New York, Academic Press, 1980, pp 279–340

Solkoff N: Children of survivors of the Nazi Holocaust: a critical review of the literature. Am J Orthopsychiatry 62:342–358, 1992

Solnit A: Memory as preparation, in Dimensions of Psychoanalysis. Edited by Sandler J. Madison, CT, International Universities Press, 1989, pp 193–217

Steinberg AM, Ritzmann RF: A living systems approach to understanding the concept of stress. Behav Sci 35:138–146, 1990

Stern D: The Interpersonal World of the Infant. New York, Basic Books, 1985

Stilwell BM, Galvin M, Kopta SM: Conceptualization of conscience in normal children and adolescents, ages 5–17. J Am Acad Child Adolesc Psychiatry 30:16–21, 1991

Stoller R: Consensual sadomasochistic perversions, in The Psychoanalytic Core. Edited by Blum HP, Weinshel EN, Rodman FR. Madison, CT, International Universities Press, 1989, pp 265–282

Stuber ML, Nader K, Yasuda P, et al: Stress responses after pediatric bone marrow transplantation: preliminary results of a prospective longitudinal study. J Am Acad Child Adolesc Psychiatry 30:952–957, 1991

Sugar M: Children and the multiple trauma in a disaster, in The Child in His Family: Perilous Development: Child Raising and Identity Formation Under Stress. Edited by Anthony Et, Chilano C. New York, Wiley, 1988, pp 429–442

Terr L: What happens to early memories of trauma? a study of twenty children under age five at the time of documented traumatic events. J Am Acad Child Adolesc Psychiatry 27:96–104, 1988

Terr L: Childhood traumas: an outline and overview. Am J Psychiatry 148:10–20, 1991

van der Kolk BA: Adolescent vulnerability to post-traumatic stress. Psychiatry 48:365–370, 1985

van der Kolk BA, Perry JC, Herman JL: Childhood origins of self-destructive behavior. Am J Psychiatry 148:1665–1671, 1991

Weisaeth L: The stressors and the post-traumatic stress syndrome after an industrial disaster. Acta Psychiatr Scand Suppl 355:25–37, 1989

Williams W: Reconstruction of an early seduction and its after effects. J Am Psychoanal Assoc 35:145–163, 1987

Wilson A, Malatesta C: Affect and the compulsion to repeat: Freud's repetition compulsion revisited. Psychoanalytic Contemporary Thought 12:265–312, 1989

Winnicott DW: Therapeutic Consultations in Child Psychiatry. New York, Basic Books, 1971

World Health Organization, Division of Mental Health: ICD-10 Chapter V: Mental and Behavioral Disorders. Geneva, DCR World Health Organization, Division of Mental Health, 1990, p 22

Wyatt GE, Guthrie D, Notgrass CM: The differential effects of women's child sexual abuse and subsequent sexual assault. J Consult Clin Psychol 60:167–173, 1992

Yule W: Resilience and vulnerability in child survivors of disasters, in Vulnerability and Resilience in Human Development. Edited by Tizare B, Varma V. London, Jessie Kingsley, 1991, pp 182–197

Yule W, Williams RM: Post-traumatic stress reactions in children. Journal of Traumatic Stress 3:279–295, 1990

Yule W, Udwin O, Murdoch K: The "Jupiter" sinking: effects on children's fears, depression and anxiety. J Child Psychol Psychiatry 31:1051–1061, 1990

Yule W, Bolton D, Udwin O: Objective and subjective predictors of PTSD in adolescence. Presentation at the World Conference of the International Society for Traumatic Stress Studies, Amsterdam, The Netherlands, June 1992

Chapter 5

An Integrated Approach for Treating Posttraumatic Stress

Charles R. Marmar, M.D.,
David Foy, Ph.D.,
Bruce Kagan, M.D., Ph.D., and
Robert S. Pynoos, M.D., M.P.H.

The past decade has seen advances in the understanding of the psychodynamic, cognitive-behavior, and neurobiological factors contributing to the development of posttraumatic stress disorder (PTSD), as well as newly emergent models for the treatment of this prevalent condition. Although further preclinical and clinical research is required, and few controlled treatment trials have been reported (Solomon et al. 1992), the findings to date support an interactive model in which traumatic stress exposure, against a background of psychological and biological vulnerability, combines to influence the severity and course of PTSD. Further, the rationale for integrated treatment is supported not only by clinical observations of recovering trauma victims, but more broadly in the field of anxiety disorders. As noted by Fishman (1992), there is increasing evidence that pharmacotherapy of anxiety disorders results in changes in cognitive and behavioral processes and that effective psychotherapy and cognitive-behavior therapy are associated with changes in neurotransmitter systems. In the following review, we address advances in the psychological and biological models of traumatic stress response, treatment approaches derived from these theoretical perspectives, and the integration of approaches from these perspectives keyed to distinct forms of traumatic stress response varying in severity, chronicity, and comorbidity.

FACTORS INFLUENCING THE RESPONSE TO TRAUMA

The course of response following traumatic stress exposure is affected by multiple factors. Four broad factors with relevance to diverse treatments are discussed below: the circumstances of the trauma, reactivation of latent trauma from earlier developmental periods, the phase of development at which trauma occurs, and the social context during and after the trauma.

Circumstances of the Trauma

The psychological sequelae following traumatic life events are in part determined by the circumstantial factors of the trauma. In combat trauma, repeated endangerment to the self, witnessing the death and dismemberment of buddies, witnessing or participating in atrocities, and physical injury with permanent disability increase the risk for more chronic and severe traumatic stress reactions (Kulka et al. 1990). For rape trauma victims, use of physical force, display of a weapon, and injury to the victim are associated with increased risk of PTSD (Bownes et al. 1991). For battered women, the risk for PTSD has also been shown to be associated with the characteristics of the battery experience (Kemp et al. 1991). Not only are different levels of exposure within a similar traumatic event associated with different outcomes, but different classes of traumatic events are associated with different psychological sequelae. For example, rape trauma victims suffer more acute guilt, shame, and suicidal ideation when compared with individuals experiencing civilian accidents or industrial disasters (Dahl 1989).

Traumatic grief responses are complicated when there have been mutilative injuries to the deceased that have been witnessed by the survivor and when there are frequent, protracted court proceedings that lead to compulsive inquiry with frustrated efforts to provide a frame of meaning for a tragic death (Pynoos, in press). These preoccupations with the circumstances of the death reinforce the occurrence of painful unbidden visual imagery and the preoccupation with the brutality and the meaninglessness of the death and interfere with the survivor's capacity to modulate the loss by reminiscing about positive memories of the deceased.

The course of traumatic stress response may be further complicated by a domino-like progression of secondary adversities that frequently follow violent experience. For example, rape, assault, and accident victims may require repeated hospitalization and reconstructive surgery and may suffer variable lengths of disability. The repeated medical procedures may be traumatic in and of themselves. They may serve as inevitable reminders of the original trauma and, in combination with scarring or other physical stigmata, constitute unavoidable reminders of the trauma (Pynoos, in press). Financial compensation for the trauma in the form of disability payments are frequently a mixed blessing, providing needed financial help during a transition back to health but risking the development of chronic dependency and ultimately a profound self-concept disturbance in a reorganized identity as a victim. Once established, such identity shifts constitute powerful resistances to recovery.

Reactivation of Latent Trauma

Trauma in adulthood can transiently, and in some cases permanently, alter the gains made in building a healthy self-concept over the course of development. For those adult victims of trauma without a history of prior traumatization, the trauma in adulthood frequently recruits two classes of problematic self-concepts. Consciously felt and expressed concerns relate to problematic weak and defective feelings about the self, including fear, helplessness, vulnerability to repetition of the trauma, grief over losses, and shameful feelings about being unable to control one's emotional reactions or fate. There is a second set of a problematic self-concepts, which are usually warded off and operating outside of the person's conscious awareness, in which the self is viewed as dangerously powerful and responsible for victimizing the self or others during the trauma (Marmar 1991). The latter problematic powerful self-concepts are associated with exaggerated feelings of personal responsibility, intense survivor guilt, and self-defeating behaviors linked to the magical belief of personal responsibility for the trauma.

The picture is further complicated when feelings of helplessness and victimization at the time of adult trauma reinvoke memories of childhood experiences of victimization. Similarly, views of the self as dangerously powerful and responsible for inflicting harm during the adult trauma may recruit real or fantasized views of the self as having victimized others during childhood or adolescence. These changes recapitulate cognitive, affective, and physiological reactions that were experienced at the time of the original trauma. As a result, the trauma victim is flooded with intrusive memories of the current adult trauma, as well as thoughts, images, memories, and dreams of trauma that occurred years or decades earlier, and with compounded levels of hyperarousal.

Impact of Developmental Phase on Traumatic Stress Response

Pynoos (in press) summarized the high risks of childhood physical and sexual abuse and exposure to family violence. The representational world of the normal developing child is in flux, with constant revisions of inner models of the self, others, and the world. Compared with adults, identity is more fluid, with positive and negative representations of the self and others less well integrated. The child is dependent on the social, emotional, and physical environment of the family, which may itself be the source of the abuse or may become severely strained in an effort to cope with the consequences of trauma affecting the family unit.

Abuse of infants and toddlers may have far-reaching influence on attachment behavior. Preschool children are limited in the capacity to represent trauma verbally, and even with increasing maturity these early experiences are not readily assimilated into verbal representation. For these reasons, the trauma may be represented for the very young child primarily at the level of nonverbal communication, bodily representation, and play with compulsive behavioral reenactments. Chronic or repetitive trauma in childhood is associated with profound restrictions in emotional responsiveness, social isolation and detachment, difficulties with impulse control, self-injurious behaviors, traumatic reenactments, and increased frequency of dissociative responses (Pynoos and Nader 1993; Terr 1991). In extreme cases, fragmentations of self-representation occurs with long-lasting or permanent dissociation of part self-concepts expressed later in development as multiple personality (Putnam 1985; Spiegel and Cardena 1991) or as borderline personality (Herman et al. 1989).

Trauma exposure during early adolescence interferes with stage-appropriate tasks of integration of past, present, and future orientations; separation from parents; moral development; and the development of symbolic thinking (Pynoos and Nader 1993). Repetitive severe traumatization during later adolescence, as seen in young combat veterans, can result in severe personality disorders. These effects are not limited to troubled adolescents who are subsequently traumatized, but may occur in late adolescent military personnel whose prior academic, social, and moral development was in the normal range (Horowitz et al. 1987; Marmar 1991).

Models of traumatization have not always adequately addressed the impact of adult developmental phases on trauma response. The traumatic event may impact at varying time periods with respect to the adult's achievement of interpersonal and occupational goals and health status (Pynoos and Nader 1993). As an example, the young adult who is sexually assaulted by a stranger at the time of forming an important love relationship may suffer consequences not limited to the nightmares, flashbacks, and arousal reactions of PTSD. The current love relationship is at risk of disruption; subsequent love relationships may be delayed; and marital and family goals may be derailed. Avoidance of intimacy, including sexuality, may lead with time to impaired social skills.

For traumatized adults, the profound experience of helplessness associated with the traumatic event is at variance with adult self-conceptualizations as competent, in control, and invulnerable, leading to subsequent changes in ambition, assertiveness, and initiative. Representations of the world as a violent, unpredictable, and uncontrollable place are not readily assimilated into existing schemas, requiring modified views of the self and others that take account of the reality of trauma without swamping trusting, safer, and more predictable views of relationships and life experience. These strains, particularly in vulnerable individuals, can intensify borderline (Marmar and Horowitz 1986), narcissistic (Marmar and Freeman 1988), and other severe personality disturbances (Horowitz et al. 1984).

Inadequate attention has been given to the nuances of traumatic stress response in older adults. Physical, material, medical, and emotional abuse of elders has been identified (Finklehor and Hotaling 1984). When natural and human-caused disasters strike older adults, they occur at a sensitive developmental period in which the individual is attempting to come to terms with declining social status, loss of relatives and friends, diminishing income, and increasing dependency on others (Pynoos, in press). The older adult's perception of self-efficacy in addressing and coping with traumatic events may be low. A large percentage of older adults are widows living alone, without spousal, financial, and social support.

Older adults physically traumatized from assaults or natural disasters may experience relatively greater physical injury and slower recovery. Trauma may necessitate changes in living situations and social routines that are more difficult for older adults. The combination of physical vulnerability, difficulty adjusting to change, and limited financial resources increases the risk of depression secondary to traumatization in the elderly (Maida et al. 1989).

Mediating Role of the Interpersonal Environment

Victims of natural and human-caused disasters have a heightened need for reliance on appropriate social support, within the context of the immediate family, the community, and the more narrow group of those sharing a common traumatic event. The availability of social support from family, friends, and community may be compromised when those called on for support have had their own lives adversely changed by the traumatic event, a phenomena referred to as indirect victimization. Family members and friends of trauma survivors may directly witness the traumatic event or receive graphic information about the circumstances of the trauma, resulting in both intrusive and avoidant reactions in members of the support system. The support system may be greatly strained, for example, when waiting to hear the outcome of hostage or kidnapping events, rescue and recovery operations, or posttrauma emergency care. Family and friends may be further depleted when called on to assume supportive roles for a longer period of time.

Even when supports are available, the trauma victim may decline help, in part because of the invitation for disclosure of disturbing memories and in part because of realistic or exaggerated worries about burdening others with emotional reactions to the trauma. The trauma victim may erect a "trauma membrane," allowing intimacy and disclosure only with those who have shared the immediate trauma or those who have survived a similar past trauma (Lindy 1985). The barrier of the trauma membrane is erected to prevent access to the trauma victim by any individual who is not conferred the status of a safe and protective figure by virtue of having shared a similar life experience. The assumption is that a similar life experience will automatically confer empathy. In erecting such a barrier, trauma victims may deprive themselves of much needed help.

Further adding to the traumatized individual's ambivalent approach toward support is a conflict between the need to address increased dependency following victimization and a heightened need for autonomy. Well-meaning family and friends may offer help that undermines rather than builds the traumatized individual's need to reassert autonomy, mastery being more difficult in those with a history of difficult childhood and adolescent attachment, separation, and autonomy experiences.

The family environment provides a fundamental context for reconferring a sense of safety and security following trauma. A well-functioning family serves as a natural buffer, helping a traumatized member to legitimize and validate the traumatic experience, express painful reactions, clarify issues of realistic responsibility, and encourage return to full functioning in work and love relations (McCubbin and McCubbin 1989). These normal self-maintaining functions of the intact family may be compromised when all family members are exposed to a common traumatic event or when dysfunctional patterns of the family unit preexist the traumatic event. In the former case, family members may be at different phases of traumatic stress response. One member may experience a compulsive need to discuss the trauma, whereas another rigidly wishes to deny the event and avoid reminders, creating strains in the support system. In the latter case, dysfunctional patterns increase the risk of regression in family functioning following family trauma, with greater divisiveness, blaming, unrealistic expectations for rapid recovery, distorted communication patterns, isolation, and risk of rupture of an already fragile family cohesion with greater rigidity or chaos in family functioning.

Group support structures such as mutual help groups, community support groups, and formal group therapy may play a decisive role for the victim of trauma. A well-functioning support group will provide practical support for the individual temporarily overwhelmed by trauma, reinforce the normative nature of stress reactions and recovery patterns, share mutual concerns, address common fears and traumatic memories, increase the capacity to tolerate disturbing emotions, and share strategies for coping (Marmar et al. 1988).

DYNAMIC PSYCHOTHERAPY OF PTSD

Psychodynamic Models of Traumatic Stress Response

Psychodynamic approaches to the understanding of traumatic stress emphasize the impact of a traumatic event on the person's self-concepts and view of others, affects resulting when conscious and unconscious representations of the self and others triggered by the trauma are discrepant with usual views, and defenses mobilized to cope with the discrepant meanings and painful emotions. Psychodynamic approaches emphasize meaningful conscious and unconscious associations linked to each moment within the traumatic event and its aftermath. These associations or themes may recruit earlier conflicts from preexisting developmental periods. Traumatic events activate earlier mental schemas concerning danger, injury, and protection, activating concerns from childhood and adolescence regarding safety, trust, risk, injury, loss, parental protection, dependency, and autonomy. Adult trauma may activate specific preoedipal or oedipal constellations, particularly those concerning maternal protection and nurturance, control of emotions and bodily functions, and conflicts about potency, rivalry, and fears of retaliation. The trauma-activated themes are seen as bridges from current concerns to self-representations, representations of others, affect states, and defenses arising during early developmental periods.

When these posttraumatic shifts in self-concept are unaddressed over time, a deterioration in character functioning may result. Shifting views of the self as victim or as victimizer interfere with mastery of the trauma. The adult who is functioning reasonably well before the trauma occurred may develop posttraumatic narcissistic or borderline personality features with fracturing of a coherent positive sense of self; traumatic disillusionment in self, others, and institutions; use of more primitive defenses, including splitting (Marmar and Horowitz 1986) and dissociation (Spiegel and Cardena 1991); poorly controlled affect states; heightened impulsivity; and increased vulnerability to future narcissistic injuries (Fox 1974; Horowitz and Zilberg 1983; Marmar and Freeman 1988). As part of this regression in psychological functioning, victims of trauma have a tendency to repeat situationally inappropriate, immature, or conflicted relationship patterns that have been internalized during formative relationships. These relationship patterns prominently feature shifting views of the self and others as victims, victimizers, and rescuers (Pynoos and Nader 1993; van der Kolk 1992). The result is more turbulent current interpersonal relationships and intensified transference reactions during treatment, which can threaten the patient's capacity and willingness to engage in the therapeutic process (Horowitz 1986; Marmar 1991; Marmar and Horowitz 1986).

Dynamic Approaches for Treating Posttraumatic Stress

Normal stress response. The majority of adults who are relatively well functioning prior to traumatic life events who have adequate social supports, who do not have a history of childhood or adolescent trauma or psychiatric illness, and who experience a single discrete traumatic event in adulthood will have a normal stress response. The reaction usually lasts from several weeks to months and leads to full recovery. As described by Horowitz (1986), the typical phases are as follows: 1) an immediate painful registration and outpouring of terror, grief, rage, and other emotions, lasting minutes to hours; 2) several weeks of denial, numbing, and unreality, which yield to reexperiencing the trauma in the form of nightmares and daytime unbidden thoughts and images; and 3) working through with recovery by 3–5 months.

Interventions that have been demonstrated to facilitate normal recovery from traumatic stressors and reduce the occurrence of PTSD and other posttraumatic psychological problems include education and support; avoidance of maladaptive coping through isolation, alcohol and drugs, or compulsive work; and individual or group debriefing. Armstrong et al. (1991) described a dynamically informed multiple stressor debriefing model aimed at reducing complications following traumatic stress exposure. The model derived in part from earlier work by Mitchell (1983) and Raphael (1986), modified for use in debriefing emergency services personnel following multiple repeated stress events in the aftermath of the 1989 Loma Prieta earthquake in California and the 1991 Oakland Hills fire storm in California. The multiple stressor debriefing model provides a single 2-hour debriefing session in four stages: 1) disclosure of events; 2) exploration of troubling reactions; 3) identification of practical coping strategies; and 4) exploration of feelings about leaving the disaster, plan of action regarding transition, and requests for referrals.

Acute catastrophic stress reactions. Acute catastrophic stress reactions occur within hours or a few days following traumatic stress exposure and are characterized by panic reactions, cognitive disorganization, disorientation, dissociation, severe insomnia, tics and other movement disorders, paranoid reactions, and incapacity to manage even basic self-care, work, and interpersonal functions (Marmar 1991; Rahe 1988).

Treatment strategies for acute catastrophic stress reactions include immediate support, removal from the scene of the trauma, time-limited use of antianxiety medications for daytime anxiety and insomnia, brief supportive-expressive dynamic psychotherapy aimed at abreaction and integration of the trauma, and careful follow-up (Forster and Marmar 1991). Brief supportive-expressive dynamic psychotherapy is conducted within a crisis intervention framework, emphasizing anxiety reduction; shoring up of defenses; restabilization of the feelings of safety, predictability, and coherence of self that have been fragmented by catastrophic stress exposure; and provision of caring and empathic support in the framework of a holding environment aimed at countering posttraumatic narcissistic regression (Marmar and Freeman 1988). Therapists offer assistance in processing the event, modulating overwhelming affect, and making decisions, as well as provide other related supportive functions that allow the acute catastrophic stress victim to identify with the therapist's calm step-by-step problem-solving approach.

Uncomplicated PTSD. PTSD, in a pure form uncomplicated by comorbid conditions and extensive secondary adversities, is most frequently seen 6–18 months following exposure to catastrophic events. The individual's mental state is dominated by reexperiencing, avoidant, and arousal symptoms that persist, do not remit with the passage of time and support of family and friends, and interfere with work and interpersonal functioning. For individuals whose PTSD problems persist beyond 3–5 months following the trauma, treatment is strongly indicated. Left untreated, the majority of this group will not remit with further passage of time and are at risk for depression, alcohol and substance abuse, panic disorder and multiple phobic avoidances, marital and family disturbances, and work impairment (Windholz et al. 1985).

Brief dynamic psychotherapy (Horowitz 1986; Marmar 1991; Weiss and Marmar, in press) is effective for uncomplicated PTSD (Brom et al. 1989) and for pathological grief reactions (Marmar et al. 1988). At the beginning of treatment, the patient is encouraged to retell the story of the traumatic event. The opportunity to retell the event in the presence of an expert healer who remains calm, empathic, compassionate, and nonjudgmental begins to depressurize the trauma response for the patient and facilitate a working collaboration with the therapist.

The rapid establishment of a therapeutic alliance, central to brief therapy approaches, may take on special nuances with recently traumatized individuals. The threat that emotions may escalate to unmanageable proportions, leaving the patient disorganized and overwhelmed, or that the therapist may not tolerate the expression of rage, sorrow, panic, and other intense emotions, may inhibit self-disclosure. A further threat to the therapeutic alliance derives from the tendency of the trauma victim to repeat situationally inappropriate, immature, or conflicted relationship models that have been internalized during sensitive developmental periods and heightened following traumatic stress exposure. Common transferential views of the therapist include victim, victimizer, and rescuer representations (Lindy 1986; Rose 1991; van der Kolk 1992).

For individuals with PTSD, the impact of a traumatic event on self-concept serves as an organizer for the unfolding treatment process. The initial focus of treatment centers on the therapist's empathic response to the patient's feelings of helplessness, shame, and vulnerability. Later, when the patient reexperiences a greater sense of self-cohesion, utilizes better functioning defense and coping strategies, and more successfully modulates the powerful affects related to uncovering of the trauma, the therapist addresses the warded-off conflict-laden meanings of the traumatic event. The latter include angry reactions and feelings of exaggerated responsibility (Marmar and Freeman 1988). The pace and depth of the uncovering processes are also adjusted to take account of the patient's level of functioning prior to the trauma (Horowitz et al. 1984).

For the trauma victim who has experienced a failure of control resulting in intrusive breakthrough of imagery and undermodulated feeling states, the therapeutic effort is directed at resurrecting adaptive defenses. Interventions include provision of support, asking questions or repeating comments, helping the patient to compartmentalize elements of the trauma experience to examine them in tolerable doses, and helping to organize information by reconstructing sequences. Further support is provided by recommending reduced interpersonal and work demands as well as removal of environmental cues that trigger memories of the trauma, and by encouraging the adaptive use of suppression and avoidance techniques so the person can function while struggling to master the trauma.

For an individual who presents with overcontrol, avoidant coping, and emotional numbing, the therapist's efforts are directed at creating a safe environment for the exploration of warded-off images and feelings related to the traumatic event. The therapist directs the patient's attention to characteristic avoidant coping strategies, including use of alcohol and drugs, workaholism, compulsive spending, compulsive eating or sexual behavior, thrill-seeking behavior, and avoidance of events associated with the trauma. Transference-based fantasies of injuring the therapist or self if feelings emerge in the treatment are addressed. The therapist encourages the patient to use imagery rather than words in reconstructing the trauma, to associate to the images, to express the feelings experienced at the time of the trauma, and to elaborate conflicted meanings.

Patients with PTSD most commonly present with rigid overcontrolled states alternating with poorly controlled undermodulated states. The result is an approach-avoidance struggle, with difficulty staying with feelings without taking defensive flight or being overwhelmed. The working-through process is marked by the patient's increasing capacity to review memories of the trauma, express feelings, revive distorted meanings, and plan for the future in a way that takes account of the consequences of the trauma. The capacity to dose the intensity and duration of work on the trauma depends heavily on the therapist's intervention early in treatment. Readiness for termination is signaled when the patient can talk about the trauma without being overwhelmed and can also put the trauma out of mind to cope with interpersonal and work responsibilities.

Just as weak and strong problematic self-concepts characterize trauma responses in patients, parallel weak and strong views of the self can occur as countertransference reactions. As trauma victims relate the details of their experiences, therapists frequently experience helplessness, fear, disgust, and grief. In a process of secondary traumatization, therapists may experience intrusive images and dreams in response to material disclosed by patients. Traumatized patients may, for conscious or unconscious reasons, attempt to shock their therapist with recapitulation of the trauma, in part to test the safety of the relationship and in part to evacuate painful memories of the trauma.

Therapists struggling with trauma victims may also experience feelings of anger, exaggerated responsibility, and identification with the aggressor. As an example, therapists working with rape trauma victims may experience ego-alien aggressive and sexual impulses toward patients (Rose 1991). Transference reactions can be managed by supervision and provision of peer support groups, approaches particularly important for clinicians whose work is specialized in addressing traumatic stress disorders.

For all patients in time-limited psychotherapy, but especially for recent trauma victims, termination represents the loss of a recently acquired meaningful relationship. During the termination phase, there is often a reactivation of feelings of helplessness and loss that may have been experienced at the time of the trauma. Negative transferences, which have been successfully managed during the initial alliance-building and later working-through phases, may greatly intensify during termination. Reactivation of memories of childhood and adolescent losses may further complicate the termination response. The patient may develop a transference-based belief that the treatment is ending because the patient is undeserving of further help or because the therapist cannot tolerate further exploration of the trauma. Patients struggling with survivor guilt may feel they have gotten more than their just share of help. For patients who were functioning well prior to the trauma transference interpretations, linking here-and-now responses to the therapist with the trauma and earlier formative relationships leads to manageable expression of anger and sadness and more complete mourning of loss. The patient is encouraged to view the period after termination as an opportunity for further working through in the privacy of personal reflection, with the support of family and friends, and in the formation of new relationships.

Pynoos and Nader (1993) described modifications of brief dynamic psychotherapy for acutely traumatized children and adolescents. Debriefing, designated psychological "first aid," is adjusted for the developmental level of the child. Attention is given to both proximal and distal impact on developmental stages. For example, a sexually abused 3-year-old who responds to treatment at age 4 is at risk for reactivation of PTSD during early adolescence. For this reason, a postintervention model is recommended, with reassessment and booster treatments as necessary to prevent derailment at later developmental crossroads.

PTSD comorbid with other disorders. Individuals with PTSD are at risk for developing secondary affective, alcohol and substance abuse, and panic and phobic disorders. The occurrence of these secondary conditions is greater in those with pretraumatic histories of these conditions. Treatment of the comorbid conditions is essential to the management of PTSD. Alcohol and substance abuse treatment generally precedes psychotherapy for PTSD. Relapse prevention for alcohol and substance abuse is provided concurrent with PTSD treatment. Use of tricyclic antidepressants or serotonin reuptake inhibitors, for treatment of major depression or panic disorder that develops in the course of PTSD, has the advantage of reducing reexperiencing and arousal symptoms in addition to targeted depressive and panic disorders.

Posttraumatic personality disorder. A variant of PTSD is seen many years or decades after unresolved trauma in adults who present for treatment with histories of childhood sexual or physical abuse, in Holocaust survivors, and in combat veterans. These individuals may show all the prototypical features of PTSD, multiple secondary adversities with poor physical health, unstable work identities, and turbulent interpersonal relations, resulting over time in a clinical picture complicated by avoidant, narcissistic, or borderline personality disturbances. The invasion of the sphere of personality functioning by the long-term maladaptive consequences of chronic PTSD produces a condition designated as posttraumatic personality disorder (Horowitz et al. 1987). Although genetic and early developmental factors contribute, the development of personality disorders in these cases is greatly influenced by the impact of decades of unresolved PTSD and associated cumulative secondary adversities on character functioning. High rates of comorbidity with alcohol and substance abuse, depression, and psychosomatic disorders are seen in individuals with posttraumatic personality disorder.

Treatment is long term and multimodal for this difficult population. Long-term group therapy (Koller et al. 1992) plus pharmacotherapy with antidepressant medication provides a cost-effective treatment approach. Treatment must be tailored to the needs of the individual, with consideration given to long-term supportive-expressive individual psychotherapy, family therapy, and mood-stabilizing agents. Inpatient treatment may be required during periods of regression to permit a safe uncovering of traumatic memories. As the individual with severe posttraumatic personality disorder recovers, vocational rehabilitation, social skills training, and alcohol and drug abuse relapse prevention improve functioning and stabilize gains.

Group treatment provides an opportunity to reconstruct and master trauma and addresses multiple secondary adversities. These approaches have formed the cornerstone for treatment of chronic PTSD in war veterans (Egendorf 1975; Lifton 1973; Rozynko and Dondershine 1991; Scurfield et al. 1984). Koller et al. (1992) developed a model of treating posttraumatic personality disorder in combat veterans in group therapy incorporating psychodynamic principles. In each group, 8–12 combat veterans with PTSD are accepted, with the goal of retaining 6–10 working members. The group is conducted on a weekly basis for 1.5-hour sessions. A 1-year total period of treatment allows adequate time to address trauma in the war zone and pre- and postmilitary service problems affecting the course of response. A 1-year period has further advantage of recapitulating the typical veteran's tour of duty, heightening anniversary reactions and enriching the symbolic meaning of the group experience as an effort to master the war zone experience. Over the course of treatment, the first 6-month block is directed primarily at processing traumatic experiences related to military service. The second 6-month block focuses on developmental issues that preceded combat and postmilitary experiences, including maladaptive coping strategies and secondary adversities arising out of failed efforts to deal with combat trauma and influencing the development of posttraumatic personality disorder.

COGNITIVE-BEHAVIOR TREATMENT OF PTSD

Theoretical Models

Several cognitive-behavior models have been advanced to account for the development and maintenance of PTSD symptoms, and these have influenced the evolution of methods for both assessment and treatment of PTSD. In one of the earliest formulations, Kilpatrick et al. (1979) used Mowrer's (1956) two-factor learning theory to conceptualize reactions in adult rape victims. Keane et al. (1989) later extended the application of two-factor theory to explain the development of combat-related PTSD.

In the two-factor theory, principles of both classical and operant conditioning are posited to be critical in development and persistence of fear to cues associated with the original trauma. From the perspective of classical conditioning, the traumatic event acts as an aversive unconditioned stimulus, which evokes the original unconditioned response to extreme fear. Cues, both external and internal, that are present in the traumatic experience become conditioned stimuli through their pairing with the overwhelming emotional and physical reaction to the trauma. Subsequent exposure to these cues then elicits a painful conditioned fear reaction. Through principles of instrumental conditioning, the individual learns to escape or avoid contact with these threatening cues. This avoidant response pattern is negatively reinforced by relief from the conditioned fear response. In this way, the conditioned fear response is protected from natural extinction, which would occur if the conditioned stimuli were repeatedly encountered without reinforcement of the conditioned fear response.

Two-factor theory prediction is consistent with the findings of many studies showing strong linkage between severity of trauma exposure and increased risk for PTSD in both combat and rape survivors. It is also helpful in explaining the persistence of hyperarousal and avoidance symptoms in cases of chronic PTSD. However, the theory cannot adequately account for the lack of development of acute PTSD in cases of extreme trauma exposure. Similarly, the theory cannot be used to explain why some cases of acute PTSD resolve, whereas other cases with equal trauma exposure evolve into chronic PTSD.

Other models have been formulated that rely on information processing and cognitive variables such as perceived threat, predictability, and controllability to predict development and maintenance of PTSD (Foa et al. 1989; Jones and Barlow 1990). In addition to stressing the importance of cognitive perception, these models place emphasis on response elements that become cues in the trauma memory network that elicit reexperiencing symptoms of repetitive thoughts, dreams, and alarm reactions. Other cognitive models stress the importance of victims' attributions about causality and appraisal of meaning in relation to the traumatic experience(s) (Janoff-Bulman 1985; Veronen and Kilpatrick 1983).

Finally, Jones and Barlow (1990) and Foy et al. (1992) proposed comprehensive mediational models that posit interactions between individual and stressor characteristics in development and maintenance of PTSD. Both of these models suggest that variables such as social support, coping, family history, and past history of psychopathology may serve as either predisposing or protective factors in determining outcome following exposure to a potentially traumatic stressor. The models differ, however, in the stage at which these variables are hypothesized as operating. Jones and Barlow (1990) posited that these mediational variables may actually determine initial reactions to trauma; Foy et al. (1992) proposed that stressor characteristics are necessary and sufficient for producing an acute reaction, whereas mediational variables play a greater role in determining whether symptoms resolve or become chronic. In their PTSD etiological hypothesis, trauma-exposed individuals become "at risk" for disorder when the overwhelming stressor occurs, and the immediate emotional reaction is hypothesized as a critical link in the causal chain mechanism producing acute distress (Foy 1992).

In recent studies of PTSD etiology, disorder rates in exposed individuals have been found to vary directly as a function of the degree of exposure. Studies of clinical samples comparing PTSD rates in "high versus low" exposed subjects consistently show that high exposure is associated with more than twice the risk found for low exposure in combat veterans (e.g., Foy et al. 1987), in adult (Rowan et al. 1990) and child sexual assault survivors (Koverola et al. 1990), and in battered women (Houskamp and Foy 1991). In these studies, high exposure has been defined as personal involvement including both physical injury and perceived life-threat. Frequent cases of multiple trauma exposure have also been found. For example, many battered women also reported childhood physical and sexual abuse and marital rape, in addition to battering by their current intimate partner. Similarly, delinquent youths currently involved in perpetrating violence through gang-related activities show high rates of prior physical abuse, traumatic deaths in their immediate family, and personal victimization by having been beaten, shot, or stabbed.

Symptom patterns in PTSD include physiological, cognitive, and behavioral manifestations. Autonomic arousal on presentation of trauma-related cues is consistently found among combat veterans for approximately two-thirds of PTSD-positive cases. Although other trauma populations have not yet been assessed for physiological reactivity in laboratory-analogue situations, hypervigilance, exaggerated startle responses, and panic symptoms are frequently reported by these survivors. Thus, it seems reasonable to expect that physiological arousal to traumatic cues is an important feature in these cases as well.

Cognitive distortions as an indication of "shattered" life assumptions are also frequently observed (Janoff-Bulman 1985). Critical assumptions about personal invulnerability, equitability and fairness of life, and personal self-worth may shift radically after traumatic victimization. Extreme self-blame, inability to trust others, and constant fear for personal safety may develop to the extent that survivors are rarely free of the need to monitor their interpersonal and physical environments constantly for signs of danger.

Avoidance of trauma-related cues may come to characterize the lifestyles of survivors who are unable to overcome their immediate trauma crisis reactions successfully. Feared stimuli eliciting escape or avoidance responses may not be limited to the physical environment. Strong negative emotions such as rage, grief, and intense anxiety or panic may elicit patterns of responding very similar to the individual's original trauma reactions (reenactment), thereby establishing escape or avoidant behaviors in a much wider range of situations.

Implications for Treatment

Behavioral models of PTSD development provide direct implications for current assessment and treatment strategies. For assessing trauma victims, it is important to gather systematic information about: 1) exposure characteristics of the trauma; 2) initial behavioral, emotional, cognitive, and psychophysiological reactions during and immediately following the traumatic experience; 3) stimulus and response components that have become part of a fear memory or signal for danger; 4) previous exposure to other trauma(s); and 5) other biological, psychophysiological, or psychosocial characteristics that may interact to influence likelihood of PTSD development and maintenance.

In terms of treatment, cognitive-behavior formulations underscore the importance of direct therapeutic exposure to elements of the stimulus-response complex to reduce trauma-related fear and to desensitize trauma-related cues. In addition, cognitive restructuring to facilitate accurate and adaptive interpretations of trauma is indicated. Information-processing models also suggest that direct therapeutic exposure is needed to modify faulty perceptions of danger or other maladaptive, generalized interpretations associated with stimulus and response elements of the traumatic memory (Foa and Kozak 1986; Foa et al. 1989; Jones and Barlow 1990).

Cognitive-Behavior Treatment Methods

In previous work describing behavior treatment methods for PTSD, distinctions have been made between types according to the primary goal of intervention (Foy et al. 1990). Accordingly, exposure strategies are employed in the reduction of intrusive memories, flashbacks, and nightmares related to the original traumatic experience(s) and current related symptoms of hyperarousal. Cognitive restructuring strategies are designed to deal with problems of meaning attributed to traumatic experiences or related associations and assumptions that are maladaptive. Finally, skills training strategies are oriented toward teaching coping skills that either reduce personal distress or provide additional means of meeting interpersonal demands.

Exposure strategies include systematic desensitization, flooding, and implosive therapy. These techniques are used to treat the positive symptoms of PTSD, which are characterized by their intrusive and recurrent presence. Flashbacks, nightmares, and exaggerated startle responses are common examples. An imaginal modality for presentation of feared stimuli is used primarily in the treatment of combat veterans, although actual combat sights and sounds are often used in systematic pretreatment assessment procedures. In most reports, 10–15 exposure trials are used to reduce conditioned emotional arousal to traumatic cues. Treatment sessions typically last 60–120 minutes and are held once or twice weekly.

A commonsense rationale is given to patients about the use of exposure therapy. They are told that painful experiences must be dealt with psychologically in order for healing to occur. These memories that have not been worked through are connected to many reminders of the experience. When these reminders occur, painful memories of the original experience are activated. The patient has learned to stop the pain by escaping or avoiding these reminders but now lives in fear of both the painful memories and the reminders. Exposure therapy is described as a way to reexperience the painful memories in a safe place where it is permissible for the feared emotional reactions to occur. The potential benefit is that it may be possible to reduce the reactivity to the painful memories so that the patient is less fearful of them. In this way, the individual may regain control, rather than continuing to be controlled by PTSD symptoms.

Cognitive restructuring methods are used to deal with specific issues related to patients' appraisals of their traumatic experiences and related changes in their worldviews. Key cognitive elements include issues of foreseeability, controllability, and culpability. Foreseeability refers to whether the occurrence of a catastrophic outcome could have been anticipated in advance. Controllability involves assessment of the extent to which a traumatic outcome could have been modified through human actions. Similarly, culpability refers to the extent to which the actions or inactions of particular persons are directly implicated in the outcome.

Basic life assumptions that may be altered by traumatic victimization include self-invulnerability, life meaningfulness and equitability, and positive self-esteem in life experiences (Janoff-Bulman 1985). These implicit assumptions or cognitive schemas serve the individual by allowing "automatic" psychological functioning in which these needs are assumed to be met without requiring evaluation of each environment and situation. However, these key assumptions may be polarized by the experience of traumatic victimization so that extreme fearfulness, mistrust, and self-blame become prominent. By explicit review of the patient's life assumptions both before and after the traumatic experiences, the patient acknowledges these fundamental assumptions and gains the choice of moderating extreme reactions in favor of a more balanced perspective. The role of the therapist is to facilitate the patient's discovery of these implicit assumptions, thereby making them explicit and modifiable.

Cognitive restructuring is used to "correct" misattributions of predictability, causality, and responsibility associated with remembered traumatic experiences. This can be done in conjunction with exposure therapy immediately following exposure trials over the traumatic scene, or it can be done independently in individual therapy sessions devoted primarily to that task. In actual practice, a combination of the two strategies is often used so that restructuring of a specific trauma is done in conjunction with flooding, while addressing the "victim" worldview is accomplished in sessions devoted to that task.

Skills training approaches represent a third type of behavioral strategy for treating PTSD and related interpersonal difficulties. These techniques include relaxation training, anger management, problem-solving skills, assertion training, and family or dyadic communication skills training. Currently, they are most often used in combination with other methods.

One area in which PTSD studies have identified a particular need for a skills training approach is that of marital and family discord often found in conjunction with chronic PTSD (Carroll et al. 1991). Communication skills training can be used to promote the initially painful but necessary self-disclosure of the traumatic experience by survivors to their partners. Correspondingly, the spouse's or partner's active listening skills can also be targeted so that the survivor's avoidance of topics, activities, and emotions associated with the trauma is not inadvertently reinforced.

Clinical decisions about the use of cognitive-behavior treatment methods are influenced by the length of time that has elapsed since the traumatic experience(s). During the aftermath of the trauma, social skills training methods may be used to help recent survivors establish and maintain interpersonal boundaries to prevent unintended retraumatization. For example, a survivor may need to practice assertion skills in telling family members, friends, and co-workers when their trauma-related questions are unhelpful reminders. In the first 6 months following the trauma, stress inoculation and cognitive restructuring methods may be indicated when the survivor is struggling to reestablish psychological equilibrium by reducing intrusive thoughts, obtaining relief from painful arousal, and finding meaning in the experience. Reexposure techniques may be indicated for those survivors who, after a longer period of time, show a preponderance of avoidance behaviors.

Exposure Therapy Research Summary

Three controlled studies featuring randomized assignment to experimental treatment to evaluate the use of direct exposure therapy in treating combat-related PTSD were recently reported (Boudewyns and Hyer 1990; Cooper and Clum 1990; Keane et al. 1989). Psychiatric inpatients served as subjects, and each of these studies evaluated flooding in the context of a hospital milieu containing multiple therapeutic modalities. Uncontrolled pharmacologic treatments were also included in the treatment regimen in two of the studies. However, in each of the studies, there was some evidence of incremental benefit beyond treatment outcome obtained by hospital milieu treatment alone.

Results of these controlled trials generally support the use of exposure therapy in cases of chronic combat-related PTSD, when used in combination with other more traditional psychiatric treatment. However, the findings of Boudewyns and Hyer (1990) suggested that individuals diagnosed as PTSD positive who did not show physiological reactivity to traumatic cues ("nonresponders") were less likely to benefit from direct therapeutic exposure. This finding was also reported in a study using single case design to evaluate effects of exposure therapy for combat-related PTSD (Mueser et al. 1991). Thus, the relationship between PTSD treatment outcome and pretreatment physiological reactivity bears further controlled investigation.

PSYCHOPHARMACOLOGIC TREATMENT OF PTSD

Neurobiology of PTSD

Perhaps the most consistent research finding in PTSD has been that of physiological arousal. Patients may exhibit baseline increases in heart rate, blood pressure, or other measures or may show enhanced reactivity to traumatic stimuli (Friedman 1991). These physiological responses track activation of the sympathetic nervous system as part of a larger stress response of the organism. This response includes behavioral, neural, endocrine, and metabolic adaptations that help the organism cope with a dangerous situation. Major centers in the brain coordinating the stress response include corticotropin-releasing hormone neurons in the paraventricular nucleus of the hypothalamus, norepinephrine neurons of the locus coeruleus, opioid neurons of the arcuate nucleus of the hypothalamus, mesocortical and mesolimbic dopamine neurons, and the amygdala and hippocampal complex (Chrousos 1992). Although a review of the generalized stress response is beyond the scope of this chapter, several animal models of stress shed some light on possible pharmacologic treatments for PTSD.

Fear-enhanced startle. PTSD patients frequently exhibit an increased startle response. A similar response in animals has been shown to be mediated by a relatively small number of brain stem pathways involving the thalamus and amygdala (Krystal et al. 1989). Fear enhancement appears to be an associative learning process that may be blocked by a variety of agents, including clonidine, benzodiazepines, alcohol, opiates, and neuroleptics. Treatment with antidepressants (tricyclics and monoamine oxidase inhibitors) does not block fear-enhanced startle (Krystal et al. 1989). These results may underlie the clinical reports suggesting a role for clonidine in the treatment of PTSD.

Inescapable shock. Exposing animals to inescapable shock produces a syndrome of "learned helplessness," characterized by behavioral depression, impaired learning, decreased appetite, decreased reproductive behavior, decreased immunity, and increased ulcer formation (Krystal et al. 1989). This pattern, reminiscent of changes seen in major depression, has also been likened to PTSD (van der Kolk 1987). Clonidine, benzodiazepines, tricyclics, and monoamine oxidase inhibitors all prevent the development of learned helplessness (Krystal et al. 1989). These agents also can reduce the intensity of deficits induced by learned helplessness once established. These results are consistent with a role for noradrenergic systems in learned helplessness and might account for the reported usefulness of these agents in PTSD and depression.

Kindling. Kindling has been proposed as a mechanism for the generation of seizures, affective disorders, and PTSD (Friedman 1991). Repeated traumatization through actual events or reexperiencing phenomena may be the kindling stimulus in PTSD. Carbamazepine, a drug that prevents kindling in animals, has also been reported to have efficacy in PTSD in an open trial (Lipper et al. 1986). If this mechanism has relevance, early and chronic pharmacologic intervention may be important in preventing long-term complications of acute PTSD.

Basic Principles of Pharmacotherapy

Pharmacotherapy is usually an adjunctive treatment. Although it is technically difficult to prove the efficacy of psychotherapeutic interventions, a broad base of clinical evidence has accumulated to show that psychotherapeutic techniques are often effective in treating PTSD. This is especially true for acute uncomplicated forms of PTSD. Both psychodynamic and cognitive-behavior therapies have been shown to be beneficial in the treatment of acute PTSD. Both schools of therapy aim to help the victim reintegrate the traumatic experience into the self and worldview in a more fruitful manner. Both techniques are also likely to accomplish a good deal of desensitization to the traumatic stimuli by reexposing the victim to the stimuli in a safe and controlled environment.

Pharmacotherapy can assist in the victim's ability to participate in psychotherapy. Panic attacks, fear, hallucinations, insomnia, and other disturbing symptoms can interfere with the patient's ability to participate meaningfully in the intellectual and emotional tasks of psychotherapy. By reducing the intensity of these debilitating symptoms, medications can actually facilitate the psychotherapeutic process, permitting symptom reduction to be achieved.

In PTSD complicated by comorbidity, medications can alleviate conditions such as mania or severe depression, which make psychotherapy impossible. Although the efficacy of psychotherapy is less certain in the more severe and chronic forms of PTSD, it is still regarded as the core treatment for most patients, along with group and family interventions.

In the most severe and psychotherapy-refractory patients, medications may be the only viable alternative. Patients with disabling flashbacks, nightmares, startle, panic, and other debilitating symptoms may find relief only in psychotropic medication. Although we have several animal models that reflect aspects of PTSD, there is no one model that clearly parallels all the symptoms of PTSD. Thus, pharmacologic agents that block symptoms in animal models appear to have only limited symptomatic utility in humans. Further model development and research is needed to find psychopharmacologic agents that can directly target the core biological dysfunctions in PTSD.

Pharmacotherapy should to be tailored to the stage of illness. As detailed above, a spectrum of disorders can be observed following trauma. The utility of pharmacotherapy will vary according to the stage and severity of the PTSD. Many uncomplicated acute cases will not require medication or even psychotherapy. Other cases may require only brief time-limited symptom-related courses of medication. Sometimes a few days of medication may suffice to give the patient rest, support, and the ability to begin the psychotherapeutic trauma processing. In complicated PTSD, medications may be needed for longer periods of time to treat the illness completely. For example, in PTSD with accompanying major depression, antidepressant medication might be continued for 6–12 months to prevent depressive relapse even if psychotherapy had successfully treated the PTSD. In the most severe, chronic forms of PTSD, chronic administration of medications may be required to suppress dysfunctional symptoms. In some patients, polypharmacy may be required to optimize treatment response.

Pharmacotherapy should address symptoms that interfere with psychotherapy or cause significant dysfunction. Since the time course of action of psychopharmacologic agents is generally faster than psychotherapy, medications can be used to bring about rapid symptomatic relief to patients in acute distress. Pharmacologic goals should first target symptoms that prevent psychotherapy from taking place, since this will allow the definitive treatment to proceed. Second, symptoms that cause undue hardship, emotional, financial, or otherwise, should be remedied as soon as practical for humanitarian reasons. For example, intrusive thoughts and irritability that impair work function may be ameliorated by adrenergic blockers such as clonidine or propranolol. Severe insomnia can be treated rapidly with benzodiazepines or trazodone. These symptomatic interventions may help prevent secondary adversities that can lead to demoralization.

Some moderate anxiety may be necessary for successful psychotherapy and should not be medicated. In the acute phases of PTSD, patients must be helped to regulate their fear and anxiety levels so that they are not overwhelmed by fear and phobias but are not robbed of their adaptive fear mechanisms. The interaction of medications and psychotherapy in the treatment of PTSD is at least as controversial as it is in other psychiatric disorders. Since many clinicians and theoreticians believe that patients must relive the traumatic experience in order to recover, medications have the potential for interfering with this process by reducing anxiety, by intensifying denial and numbing, and by creating a medicated brain state in which psychotherapeutic learning may not be effective in other nonmedicated brain states. Furthermore, many clinicians believe that an optimal level of working anxiety is a necessary motivator for doing the painful, difficult work of trauma processing. In addition, anxiety is an important marker of the uncovering of significant trauma. Although more careful research is needed to examine these possibilities, evidence from other psychiatric disorders suggests that medications and other therapies can work together quite well and that the combination can be more effective than either modality used alone.

Comorbidity conditions can and should be treated in the standard manner. Numerous other psychiatric conditions can become comorbid with PTSD. Common ones include depression, panic disorder, alcohol and substance abuse, simple phobias, generalized anxiety disorder, and bipolar disorder. In general, the psychopharmacologic approach to these conditions should follow the usual standards of practice. There is evidence from controlled studies of chronic PTSD that tricyclic antidepressants and monoamine oxidase inhibitors can be useful in treating major depression associated with PTSD. Clinical evidence suggests that the PTSD of patients with comorbid conditions is much more difficult to treat. Depression, bipolar affective disorder, generalized anxiety disorder, and substance abuse can all interfere with the patient's ability to participate in specific PTSD treatment and with the ability to process information necessary to successful treatment.

Adequate duration of treatment is essential. Antidepressants, for example, should be continued for at least 6–12 months after recovery to prevent early relapse. Maintenance of therapeutic levels of mood stabilizers such as lithium or carbamazepine is also critical, especially if the patient is undergoing psychotherapeutic interventions. There is evidence to suggest that patients undergoing successful psychotherapy may have transient increases in depressive and anxiety symptoms. Full-blown mood episodes can be triggered by therapy, and the alert clinician must be on the lookout for this to avoid complications in patients prone to depression and other DSM-III-R (American Psychiatric Association 1987) Axis I disorders. Although there is no hard evidence as yet to suggest that antidepressants or mood stabilizers can actually prevent relapses during PTSD psychotherapy, the strong evidence that these agents can prevent relapses for related disorders suggests that maintenance therapy makes good clinical sense.

Psychoses must be carefully assessed to ensure the appropriate therapy. Flashbacks, which are the hallmark of PTSD, can often contain vivid sensory phenomena such as visual, auditory, olfactory, or tactile hallucinations. If the phenomena are exclusively trauma related, they may not require neuroleptic treatment, and standard psychotherapeutic procedures can be used. Bizarre or trauma-incongruent hallucinations should be treated with standard neuroleptic therapy. Paranoia is a common symptom in PTSD, and clinical judgment should be exercised as to the utility of neuroleptics. Our experience has suggested that low-dose neuroleptic therapy (e.g., haloperidol 2 mg/day) can be quite effective in some PTSD patients in reducing paranoia or severe flashback phenomena. Some chronic and treatment-refractory patients may require long-term maintenance for adequate symptom control. Because of the frequent misuse of neuroleptics in the 1970s, partially due to the misdiagnosis of PTSD patients as schizophrenic, the rationale for neuroleptic treatment must be carefully explained to the patient along with the risks and benefits of treatment. Pharmacotherapy for PTSD, alone and in association with comorbidity, is summarized in Table 5–1.

Positive symptoms are generally more responsive to pharmacotherapy than negative symptoms. Reexperiencing and arousal (insomnia, increased startle, hypervigilance) symptoms are commonly referred to as positive symptoms, and avoidance (emotional numbing, isolation) symptoms are referred to as negative symptoms. Most clinical studies have found that positive symptoms are far more responsive to medications than negative symptoms. The reason for this difference is unclear, but the resistance of negative symptoms to pharmacotherapy serves to underline the importance of psychotherapy for the total treatment process.

The meaning of medication should be explored. As with any illness, patients should be educated about the disorder and its treatment. The utility of medication should be explained along with the role of medication in the larger treatment program. Side effects and risks of medication should also be explored so that patients are not taken by surprise if adverse reactions should emerge. We found a medication "group" useful for this educational purpose. The meaning of medication for the individual patient should also be explored. Patients may feel that accepting medication is a sign of failure or a sign of lack of interest in the causes of their distress. More paranoid patients may believe that

Table 5–1. Pharmacotherapy of posttraumatic stress disorder (PTSD)

Category	First choice	Second choice	Others
Normal stress response	None		
Acute catastrophic stress reaction	Adrenergic blockers	BZDs for anxiety/insomnia	Neuroleptics for hallucinations
PTSD without comorbidity	Adrenergic blockers	TCAs or BZDs	MAOIs
PTSD and depression	TCAs or MAOIs	Serotonin reuptake inhibitors	Lithium/carbamazepine
PTSD and panic	TCAs or MAOIs	BZDs	Serotonin reuptake inhibitors, adrenergic blockers
PTSD and bipolar disorder	Lithium or carbamazepine	Valproate	Neuroleptics
PTSD and alcohol abuse	Disulfiram		
PTSD and cocaine abuse	Desmethylimipramine		
PTSD and opiate withdrawal	Clonidine		
Chronic PTSD comorbid with secondary Axis II disorders	TCAs or MAOIs	Adrenergic blockers, serotonin reuptake inhibitors	BZDs, lithium, carbamazepine, neuroleptics

Note. BZDs = benzodiazepines. TCAs = tricyclic antidepressants. MAOIs = monoamine oxidase inhibitors.

the therapist is trying to control them or muzzle their behavior with medications. The history of injudicious use of neuroleptics for PTSD patients at many facilities has also contributed to negative attitudes toward medications on the part of many patients. Severely depressed patients may refuse medications for the same reasons other depressed patients do (e.g., "I don't deserve to get better"; "There's no help for me"; "I can't tolerate the side effects"). These misconceptions must be aggressively explored and corrected to engage the patient's full cooperation in the treatment program.

Noncompliance is common and must be vigorously monitored. Many people believe they ought to be able to cope with PTSD symptoms through sheer force of will. Failure to do so is seen as a moral or character weakness. Other victims may feel self-blame and guilt. When medication is indicated, the clinician must ensure compliance through active monitoring, including obtaining serum levels when appropriate.

The potential risks of medications, including side effects, dependence, and suicide, must be weighed against therapeutic potential of the agents. Many centers prescribe benzodiazepines quite commonly for PTSD symptoms. Others discourage the use of benzodiazepines largely because of the potential for dependence and abuse. Although this potential must be carefully evaluated, some patients may have symptoms that respond only to benzodiazepines. Others may require high-dose benzodiazepines or long-term treatment. These patients must be evaluated on a case-by-case basis. Blanket rules for an agent or class of medications do not make sense given the current state of knowledge.

Suicide potential should be evaluated in PTSD patients, especially those suffering from depression or substance abuse. Victims who are older, male, or medically ill or have access to firearms are likely at higher risk of suicide. If necessary, medications should be limited to small amounts, to limit the danger of overdose.

Nonpharmacologic methods of symptom control should not be neglected. Aside from individual, family, and group psychotherapy, there are several simple techniques that may help reduce PTSD symptom intensity. Paying attention to sleep hygiene (e.g., having a regular bedtime, sleeping only in the bed, having a quiet bedroom) may help improve disturbed sleep. Regular exercise may also help relieve depressive and anxiety symptoms if the patient has no major contraindications to exercise. Relaxation techniques, including meditation or yoga, may help decrease PTSD symptoms and allow increased tolerance of anxiety.

Early intervention may help reduce chronicity. There is some evidence that early psychotherapeutic interventions, including debriefing, may help prevent PTSD from becoming chronic and severe. Biological evidence suggests that chronic symptomatology and release of stress hormones, including cortisol, may produce chronic symptoms through kindling or neurotoxicity. Certainly the secondary adversities associated with unrelieved symptoms (e.g., job loss, incarceration, fatigue, poor relationships) can be devastating and create psychopathology of their own. Not all models suggest that early use of medications may block the production of some PTSD symptomatology. Still, there is little hard clinical evidence to go on in this area, so clinical judgment must guide any decision to use medication for prophylactic purposes.

Patients may be resistant to standard doses of medication. PTSD clinical lore is full of tales of patients who showed little or no response to massive doses of potent medications such as neuroleptics, benzodiazepines, or barbiturates. This may reflect the vital survival nature of the stress response system, or it may simply be an expression of the most severe cases. Clinicians should be alert for medication resistance and must always evaluate possible causes of resistance such as noncompliance, medical illness, or incorrect diagnosis. Still, some patients may respond only at very high doses of standard medications, and these should be cautiously considered if the patient is tolerating medication well. There is virtually no information about the utility of polypharmacy in PTSD patients, although many clinicians clearly use combinations of psychotropic agents in refractory cases.

Pharmacotherapy of Specific Forms of Traumatic Stress Response

Normal stress response. In general, no medications are indicated for treating a normal stress response. Symptoms are usually time limited and without risk of complications or progressing to chronicity. Possible exceptions to the rule might include patients with severe medical illness (e.g., cardiovascular disease) or severe psychiatric disability (e.g., bipolar disorder) who might require medication to prevent exacerbation of their preexisting disorder by a normal stress response.

Acute catastrophic stress reactions. Adrenergic blockers (e.g., the beta-blocker propranolol or the α_2 presynaptic agonist clonidine) can dampen the peripheral sympathetic stress response or the central locus coeruleus stress response, respectively. These agents have long records of clinical safety and efficacy in cardiac illness and have been used more recently to suppress the arousal and reexperiencing symptoms of stress reactions (Kinzie and Leung 1989; Kolb et al. 1984). Advantages include a relative lack of side effects, especially sedation and memory loss, which can be damaging to function at work, at school, or in social relationships. In addition, since these medications are not routinely known as psychotropic agents, their use carries less stigma in the general population. Furthermore, they lack dependence potential and are of no street value as recreational drugs. Although controlled studies of their use are lacking, since Kolb et al.'s (1984) pioneering report there is a growing body of clinical experience with these agents supporting efficacy. From a biological point of view, these agents are the most rational to use since they were effective in blocking the effects of fear-enhanced startle and other animal models for PTSD.

Benzodiazepines are also a good choice for brief time-limited treatment of acute catastrophic stress reactions. These agents are also effective in animal models of PTSD and can provide reduction of re-experiencing and arousal symptoms. Furthermore, benzodiazepines have direct effects on sleep and anxiety that can be quite helpful for patients with severe problems in these areas. Treatment is usually aimed at the restoration of vital functions such as sleep and enhancing the patient's ability to cope with work and interpersonal demands and to participate in the psychotherapeutic process. Because of the potential for dependence (Forster and Marmar 1991; Friedman 1988), use of these agents should be carefully time limited. Neuroleptics can be useful for patients with severe hallucinatory phenomena, paranoia, or agitation and anxiety. Because of past misuses of neuroleptics, their use has declined dramatically, but they still may have important utility in reactions with frank psychotic features. Clinicians should remember that the sedative effects of neuroleptics are rapid (hours to days), whereas the antipsychotic effects are slower (about 10–14 days).

Pure uncomplicated PTSD. Multiple psychopharmacologic agents have been advocated for PTSD, with few controlled trials reported as of this writing (Davidson 1992; Friedman 1988, 1991). As discussed above, the adrenergic blockers and benzodiazepines have theoretical and clinical bases justifying their use for PTSD. Antidepressants (tricyclics and monoamine oxidase inhibitors) may also have a role to play in victims whose symptoms persistent beyond a few weeks. The slower-acting agents have been reported to be effective in suppressing positive symptoms of PTSD. However, only three placebo-controlled trials have been reported as of this writing, all employing chronic combat-related PTSD patients: Shestatsky et al. (1988) found no difference between phenelzine and placebo; Frank et al. (1988) showed a slight edge for phenelzine and imipramine over placebo; and Davidson et al. (1990) reported some advantages for amitriptyline over placebo after 8 weeks. Thus, although numerous anecdotal and clinical reports suggest a useful role for antidepressants, the evidence from controlled studies is limited, even in the comorbid depressed group, and lacking in the pure PTSD group.

Promising uncontrolled reports have described the use of fluoxetine in PTSD, but these must await confirmation in controlled trials. Our own open trial of fluoxetine in chronic combat-related PTSD veterans showed a beneficial effect of drug treatment only on depressive and anxiety symptoms.

PTSD and comorbidity. The majority of clinical psychopharmacologic trials have reported results on veterans with chronic combat-related PTSD with comorbidity. As discussed above, there is controlled evidence suggesting antidepressants can be effective for PTSD patients with comorbid depression. Tricyclic antidepressants, monoamine oxidase inhibitors, and serotonin reuptake inhibitors have all had positive reports in their favor (Davidson 1992; Friedman 1991). Although hard evidence is lacking, anecdotal reports suggest that comorbid panic disorder, generalized anxiety disorder, and bipolar disorder are also responsive to standard pharmacologic treatments. Other psychoses such as schizophrenia should also be treated with standard therapy. The relationship between PTSD and these other disorders remains unclear.

Posttraumatic personality disorder. This category encompasses chronic PTSD that has become hardened into traits of lasting stability. Effectiveness of any treatment in this population has yet to be proven. Still, there is a growing literature on pharmacologic therapies for chronic PTSD. Although tricyclic antidepressants and monoamine oxidase inhibitors have a demonstrated benefit, this is largely limited to depressive and anxiety symptoms and not specific for PTSD-related symptoms. Adrenergic blockers have been less well studied, but logically should have beneficial effect. Benzodiazepines should be used with caution because of the potential for abuse and tolerance. Mood stabilizers have shown great promise in open trials, but await verification in controlled studies (Fesler 1991; Kitchner and Greenstein 1985). Neuroleptics may have a very important role to play in the treatment of patients with chronic psychotic features such as hallucinations. We have seen dramatic effects of these agents in selected patients at low neuroleptic doses. This is consistent with neurobiological evidence implicating mesocortical dopamine pathways in animal models of PTSD.

COMMON GOALS AND CHANGE MECHANISMS

Common Treatment Goals

Dynamic, cognitive-behavior, and psychopharmacologic treatment of PTSD share in common a number of fundamental aims:

- To increase the capacity to respond to threat with realistic appraisal rather than exaggerated or minimized responses
- To maintain normal levels of arousal rather than hypervigilance or psychic numbing
- To facilitate return to normal development, adaptive coping, and improved functioning in work and interpersonal relations
- To restore personal integrity and normalize traumatic stress response, in part by validating the universality of stress symptomatology and by establishing a frame of meaning
- To conduct treatment in an atmosphere of safety and security to ensure that the threat of retraumatization is modulated
- To regulate level of intensity of traumatic aspects to facilitate cognitive reappraisal
- To increase capacity to differentiate remembering from reliving of the trauma, for both external reminders and internal cues
- Neither to eradicate the memories of the trauma nor to avoid and overreact rigidly to reminders, but rather to place trauma in perspective and regain control over life experiences
- To attend to early risk factors that shape trauma response
- To intervene actively to address secondary adversities and prevent future complications, including the risk for spreading comorbidities
- To regard self-concept as impacted by changes in dynamic, cognitive, behavioral, and neurobiological systems
- To facilitate a transformation from a victim identity to a sense of constructive engagement in daily life and future goals
- To enhance a sense of personal courage in approaching the memories and reminders of the trauma

Contrasting Treatment Goals

Psychodynamic approaches stress associative meanings for the trauma registered from a wider network, including unconscious as well as conscious representations, unconsciously motivated defenses against remembering, the contribution of early psychological development to trauma-based self- and other representations, and the management of transference, countertransference, and resistances in the treatment setting.

Behavior treatments focus in-depth on overt behavioral avoidance and reenactment, stimulus and response components that have become part of the fear memory or signal for danger, and a detailed understanding of biological and psychological conditioning occurring during trauma exposure. Cognitive-behavior treatments emphasize revision of pathogenic beliefs in the course of direct therapeutic exposure. Pharmacotherapy targets underline psychobiological mechanisms regarding chronic hyperarousal, cue-specific hyperreactivity, insomnia, and comorbid anxiety and depressive disorders. Table 5–2 summarizes comparative features of dynamic, cognitive-behavior, and pharmacologic approaches, anchored to specific forms of traumatic stress response.

Combined Treatment Approaches

Integrated approaches to treating PTSD take account of the forms of traumatic stress response and interactions of dynamic, cognitive-behavior, and pharmacotherapeutic approaches. The management of normal stress response includes psychoeducation, support, caution against maladaptive coping, debriefing, and support groups. The management of acute catastrophic stress reactions emphasizes brief supportive-expressive dynamic psychotherapy conducted within a crisis intervention framework, time-limited cognitive-behavior techniques aimed at anxiety reduction, and short-term pharmacotherapy with adrenergic blockers or benzodiazepines for overwhelming daytime anxiety. Insomnia in acute catastrophic stress reactions can be safely managed with sedative antidepressants, including low-dose trazodone or short-term use of benzodiazepines for those without a history of alcohol or sedative dependency.

For uncomplicated PTSD, brief dynamic psychotherapy or time-limited cognitive-behavior treatments emphasizing exposure strategies and cognitive restructuring are effective treatments. Both the dynamic and the cognitive-behavior methods emphasize revision of pathogenic beliefs and dosing of exposure to traumatic images and affects. When PTSD is comorbid with panic disorder, partial agoraphobia, major depressive episode, and related disorders, the addition of specific psychotherapeutic and pharmacotherapeutic treatments for these conditions is indicated.

Long-term multimodal integrated treatment offers the greatest hope for the treatment of posttraumatic personality disorder in trauma victims with decades of unresolved traumatic stress symptomatology, extensive secondary adversities, and complex comorbidities. Long-term psychodynamic group therapy, in combination with long-term pharmacotherapy emphasizing tricyclic antidepressants, serotonin reuptake inhibitors, adrenergic blockers, and mood-stabilizing agents in an individualized approach, provides a cost-effective treatment. The initial phase of treatment is directed at exploration of the trauma and modulation of intrusive, avoidant, and arousal symptoms. Inpatient treatment may be required in severe cases to permit a safe uncovering of traumatic memories. As the individual with severe posttraumatic personality disorder is able to tolerate reconstruction of the trauma and reduce conditioned emotional arousal to traumatic cues, long-term recovery depends on the integration of pharmacotherapy to reduce

Table 5–2. Comparative treatment approaches for posttraumatic stress disorder (PTSD)

Traumatic stress category	Dynamic	Cognitive-behavior	Pharmacologic
Normal stress response	Debriefing	Debriefing	None
Acute catastrophic stress reaction	Debriefing, abreaction, support, self-cohesion, adjunctive pharmacotherapy	Debriefing, restructuring of erroneous ideas, prevention of avoidant behavior	BZDs for sleep and anxiety, adrenergic blockers for intrusion and arousal
PTSD without comorbidity	Time-limited dynamic psychotherapy, establish therapeutic alliance, focus on self-concepts, working through conflicts, linkage to prior trauma, attention to transference and countertransference	Desensitization to trauma, restructuring of erroneous beliefs, gradual activation of avoidant behaviors	None or BZDs, adrenergic blockers for intrusion/arousal, TCAs/MAOIs for intrusion/arousal, serotonin reuptake inhibitors
PTSD with Axis I comorbidity	Time-limited dynamic therapy, treat alcohol and substance abuse first, treat other comorbidities concurrently	Treat comorbidity first, then cognitive-behavior treatments	Treat comorbidity as usual, then medication for PTSD if needed
Chronic PTSD with secondary Axis II comorbidity	Multimodal; long-term dynamic group and pharmacologic; inpatient at times for uncovering or crises; individual, marital, and family treatment; vocational rehabilitation and social skills training	Cognitive-behavior treatments, chronic intermittent skills training, relapse prevention	TCAs/MAOIs, serotonin reuptake inhibitors, BZDs with caution, neuroleptics for hallucinations, lithium/carbamazepine for irritability/aggressivity

Note. BZDs = benzodiazepines. TCAs = tricyclic antidepressants. MAOIs = monoamine oxidase inhibitors.

irritability, arousal, and insomnia; communication and social skills training; vocational rehabilitation; and alcohol and drug abuse relapse prevention.

REFERENCES

American Psychiatric Association: Diagnostic and Statistical Manual of Mental Disorders, 3rd Edition, Revised. Washington, DC, American Psychiatric Association, 1987

Armstrong K, O'Callahan W, Marmar CR: Debriefing Red Cross disaster personnel: the multiple stressor debriefing model. Journal of Traumatic Stress 4:481–491, 1991

Boudewyns PA, Hyer L: Physiologic response to combat memories and preliminary treatment outcome in Vietnam veteran PTSD patients treated with direct therapeutic exposure. Behavior Therapy 21:63–87, 1990

Bownes IT, O'Gorman EC, Sayers A: Assault characteristics in post-traumatic stress disorder in rape victims. Acta Psychiatr Scand 83:27–30, 1991

Brom D, Kleber RJ, Defares PB: Brief psychotherapy for posttraumatic stress disorders. J Consult Clin Psychol 57:607–612, 1989

Carroll EM, Foy DW, Cannon BJ, et al: Assessment issues involving the families of trauma victims. Journal of Traumatic Stress 4:25–40, 1991

Chrousos GP: Concepts of stress and stress system disorders. JAMA 267:1244–1252, 1992

Cooper NA, Clum GA: Imaginal flooding as a supplementary treatment for PTSD in combat veterans: a controlled study. Behavior Therapy 20:381–391, 1990

Dahl S: Acute responses to rape: a PTSD variant. Acta Psychiatr Scand 80 (suppl 355):56–62, 1989

Davidson J: Post-traumatic stress disorder. Br J Psychiatry 160:309–314, 1992

Davidson J, Kudler H, Smith R, et al: Treatment of posttraumatic stress disorder with amitriptyline and placebo. Arch Gen Psychiatry 47:259–266, 1990

Egendorf A: Vietnam veterans rap groups and themes of postwar life. Journal of Social Issues 4:111–124, 1975

Fesler FA: Valproate in combat-related posttraumatic stress disorder. J Clin Psychiatry 52:361–364, 1991

Finklehor D, Hotaling GT: Sexual abuse in the National Incidence Study of Child Abuse and Neglect: an appraisal. Child Abuse Negl 8:23–32, 1984

Fishman H: Integrated treatment of panic disorder and social phobia (introduction). Bull Menninger Clin 56:1–2, 1992

Foa EB, Kozak MS: Emotional processing of fear: exposure to corrective information. Psychol Bull 99:20–35, 1986

Foa EB, Steketee G, Rothbaum BO: Behavioral/cognitive conceptualizations of post-traumatic stress disorder. Behavior Therapy 20:155–176, 1989

Forster P, Marmar CR: Benzodiazepines in acute stress reactions: benefits, risks, and controversies, in Benzodiazepines in Clinical Practice: Risks and Benefits. Edited by Roy-Byrne PP, Cowley DS. Washington, DC, American Psychiatric Press, 1991, pp 73–89

Fox PP: Narcissistic rage and the problem of combat aggression. Arch Gen Psychiatry 31:807–811, 1974

Foy DW (ed): Treating Post-Traumatic Stress Disorder: Cognitive Behavioral Strategies. New York, Guilford, 1992

Foy DW, Resnick HS, Sipprelle RC, et al: Premilitary, military and postmilitary factors in the development of combat-related post-traumatic stress disorder. Behavior Therapy 10:3–9, 1987

Foy DW, Resnick HS, Carroll EM, et al: Behavior therapy in post-traumatic stress disorder, in Handbook of Comparative Treatments for Adult Disorders. Edited by Bellack AS, Hersen M. New York, Wiley, 1990

Foy DW, Osato SS, Houskamp BM, et al: Etiological factors, in Post-Traumatic Stress Disorder: A Behavioral Approach to Assessment and Treatment. Edited by Saigh PA. New York, Allyn & Bacon, 1992

PTSD

treatment:
- stress inoculation
- cognitive restructuring

Address
- intrusion
- avoidance
- arousal

Possible perceptions of client
- world is indiscriminating, dangerous
- self is an inadequate coper

Coping Strategies
- relaxation techniques
- deep breathing
- tapes
- positive self talk

Frank JB, Giller EL, Kosten TR, et al: A randomized clinical trial of phenelzine and imipramine for post traumatic stress disorder. Am J Psychiatry 145:1289–1291, 1988

Friedman MJ: Toward rational pharmacotherapy for posttraumatic stress disorder. Am J Psychiatry 145:281–285, 1988

Friedman MJ: Biological approaches to the diagnosis and treatment of post-traumatic stress disorder. Journal of Traumatic Stress 4:67–92, 1991

Herman JL, Perry JC, van der Kolk BA: Childhood trauma in borderline personality disorder. Am J Psychiatry 146:490–495, 1989

Horowitz MJ: Stress-Response Syndromes, 2nd Edition. Northvale, NJ, Jason Aronson, 1986

Horowitz M, Zilberg N: Regressive alterations in the self-concept. Am J Psychiatry 140:284–289, 1983

Horowitz MJ, Marmar CR, Krupinick J, et al: Brief Psychotherapy and Personality Styles. New York, Basic Books, 1984

Horowitz MJ, Weiss DS, Marmar CR: Diagnosis of post-traumatic stress disorder. J Nerv Ment Dis 175:267–268, 1987

Houskamp BM, Foy DW: The assessment of posttraumatic stress disorder in battered women. Journal of Interpersonal Violence 6:368–376, 1991

Janoff-Bulman R: The aftermath of victimization: rebuilding shattered assumptions, in Trauma and Its Wake. Edited by Figley CR. New York, Brunner/Mazel, 1985

Jones JC, Barlow DH: The etiology of posttraumatic stress disorder. Clinical Psychology Review 10:299–328, 1990

Keane TM, Fairbank JA, Caddell JM, et al: Implosive (flooding) therapy reduces symptoms of PTSD in Vietnam combat veterans. Behavior Therapy 20:245–260, 1989

Kemp A, Rawlings EI, Green BL: Post-traumatic stress disorder (PTSD) in battered women: a shelter sample. Journal of Traumatic Stress 4:137–148, 1991

Kilpatrick DG, Veronen LJ, Resick PA: Assessment of the aftermath of rape: changing patterns of fear. Journal of Behavioral Assessment 1:133–148, 1979

Kinzie JD, Leung P: Clonidine in Cambodian patients with post traumatic stress disorder. J Nerv Ment Dis 177:546–550, 1989

Kitchner I, Greenstein R: Low dose lithium carbonate in the treatment of post traumatic stress disorder: brief communication. Mil Med 150:378–381, 1985

Kolb LC, Burris BC, Griffiths S: Propranolol and clonidine in the treatment of posttraumatic stress disorders of war, in Post-Traumatic Stress Disorder, Psychological and Biological Sequelae. Edited by van der Kolk BA. Washington, DC, American Psychiatric Press, 1984, pp 97–107

Koller P, Marmar CR, Kanas N: Psychodynamic group treatment of post-traumatic stress disorder in Vietnam veterans. Int J Group Psychother 42:225–246, 1992

Koverola C, Foy DW, Heger A, et al: Relationship of PTSD to sexual abuse trauma assessed by medical findings and child disclosure. Paper presented at Society for Traumatic Stress Studies Annual Meeting, New Orleans, October 1990

Krystal JH, Kosten TR, Southwick S, et al: Neurobiological aspects of PTSD: review of clinical and preclinical studies. Behavior Therapy 20:177–198, 1989

Kulka RA, Schlenger WE, Fairbank JA, et al: Trauma and the Vietnam War Generation. New York, Brunner/Mazel, 1990

Lifton R: Home From the War. New York, Simon & Schuster, 1973

Lindy JD: The trauma membrane and other clinical concepts derived from psychotherapy work with survivors of natural disasters. Psychiatric Annals 15:153–160, 1985

Lindy JD: An outline for the psychoanalytic psychotherapy of post-traumatic stress disorder, in Trauma and Its Wake, Vol 2. Edited by Figley CR. New York, Brunner/Mazel, 1986, pp 195–202

Lipper S, Davidson JRT, Grady TA, et al: Preliminary study of carbamazepine in post-traumatic stress disorder. Psychosomatics 27:849–854, 1986

Maida C, Gordon N, Steinberg A, et al: Psychosocial impact of disasters: victims of the Baldwin Hills fire. Journal of Traumatic Stress 2:37–48, 1989

Marmar CR: Brief dynamic psychotherapy of post-traumatic stress disorder. Psychiatric Annals 21:405–414, 1991

Marmar CR, Freeman M: Brief dynamic psychotherapy of post-traumatic stress disorders: management of narcissistic regression. Journal of Traumatic Stress 1:323–337, 1988

Marmar CR, Horowitz MJ: Phenomenological analysis of splitting. Psychotherapy 23:21–29, 1986

Marmar CR, Horowitz MJ, Weiss D, et al: A controlled trial of brief psychotherapy and mutual help treatment of conjugal bereavement. Am J Psychiatry 145:203–209, 1988

McCubbin MA, McCubbin HI: Theoretical orientations to family stress and coping, in Treating Stress in Families. Edited by Figley CR. New York, Brunner/Mazel, 1989, pp 3–43

Mitchell J: When disaster strikes . . . The critical incident stress debriefing process. Journal of Emergency Medical Services 8:36–39, 1983

Mowrer OH: Two-factor learning theory reconsidered, with special reference to secondary reinforcement and the concept of habit. Psychol Rev 63:114, 1956

Mueser KT, Yarnold PR, Foy DW: Statistical analysis for single case design: evaluating outcome of imaginal exposure treatment of chronic PTSD. Behav Modif 15:134–155, 1991

Putnam FW: Dissociation as a response to extreme trauma, in The Childhood Antecedents of Multiple Personality. Edited by Kluft RP. Washington, DC, American Psychiatric Press, 1985, pp 65–97

Pynoos RS: New perspective on grief and trauma in children and adolescence. Bereavement Care (in press)

Pynoos RS, Nader K: Issues in the treatment of post-traumatic stress in children and adolescents, in The International Handbook of Traumatic Stress Syndromes. Edited by Wilson JP, Raphael B. New York, Plenum, 1993, pp 535–549

Rahe RH: Acute versus chronic psychological reactions to combat. Mil Med 153:365–371, 1988

Raphael B: When Disaster Strikes. New York, Basic Books, 1986

Rose DS: A model for psychodynamic psychotherapy with the rape victim. Psychotherapy 28:85–95, 1991

Rowan AC, Rodriquez N, Gallers J, et al: Sexual abuse exposure factors in the development of PTSD in adult survivors of childhood assault. Paper presented at Society for Traumatic Stress Studies Annual Meeting, New Orleans, October 1990

Rozynko V, Dondershine HE: Trauma focus group therapy for Vietnam veterans with PTSD. Psychotherapy 28:157–161, 1991

Scurfield R, Corker T, Gongla P, et al: Three post-Vietnam "rap/therapy" groups: an analysis. Group 4:3–24, 1984

Shestatsky M, Greenberg D, Lerer B: A controlled trial of phenelzine in post traumatic stress disorder. Psychiatry Res 24:149–155, 1988

Solomon SD, Gerrity ET, Muff AM: Efficacy of treatments for posttraumatic stress disorder. JAMA 268:633–638, 1992

Spiegel D, Cardena E: Disintegrated experience: the dissociative disorders revisited. J Abnorm Psychol 100:366–378, 1991

Terr L: Childhood traumas: an outline and overview. Am J Psychiatry 148:10–20, 1991

van der Kolk B: Drug treatment of post-traumatic stress disorder. J Nerv Ment Dis 13:203–213, 1987

van der Kolk B: Advances in the psychotherapy of post-traumatic stress disorder. Paper presented at the World Conference of the International Society for Traumatic Stress Studies, Amsterdam, The Netherlands, June 1992

Veronen LJ, Kilpatrick DG: Stress management for rape victims, in Stress Reduction and Prevention. Edited by Meichenbaum D, Jaremko ME. New York, Plenum, 1983, pp 341–374

Weiss DS, Marmar CR: Teaching time-limited dynamic psychotherapy for post-traumatic stress disorder and pathological grief. Psychotherapy (in press)

Windholz MJ, Marmar CR, Horowitz MJ: A review of the research on conjugal bereavement: impact on health and efficacy of interventions. Compr Psychiatry 26:433–447, 1985

Chapter 6

Posttraumatic Stress Disorder and Rape

Edna B. Foa, Ph.D., and David S. Riggs, Ph.D.

Epidemiological studies demonstrate that rape has become a monumental problem in our society.[1] Many rapes go unreported to police (Kilpatrick et al. 1988), and the actual incidence is thought to be 3–10 times higher than the number of rapes reported (Law Enforcement Assistance Administration 1975). Results from a national random sample of adult women, reported by the National Victim Center and Crime Victims Research and Treatment Center (1992), indicated that 12.9% of (about 12 million) women had been raped at least once during their lifetime; an estimated 683,000 were raped within the last year. Somewhat higher rates, 15.4%, were found in representative samples of college students (Koss et al. 1987).

The harmful and often debilitating effects of rape have been noted by many authors (e.g., Burgess and Holmstrom 1974; Norris and Feldman-Summers 1981). Early studies focused on specific psychological reactions associated with rape, such as anxiety (Calhoun et al. 1982; Kilpatrick et al. 1982), depression (Atkeson et al. 1982; Frank et al. 1979; Kilpatrick et al. 1979), and sexual dysfunction (Becker et al. 1982). In 1980, posttrauma syndrome was introduced into DSM-III (American Psychiatric Association 1980) as a distinct anxiety disorder called posttraumatic stress disorder (PTSD). Since then, postrape syndrome has been conceptualized as PTSD (Holmes and St. Lawrence 1983; Kilpatrick et al. 1987; Steketee and Foa 1987). In this chapter, we first consider the prevalence and course of PTSD in rape victims. Next, we offer a theoretical model for understanding the development and maintenance of chronic PTSD in trauma victims, and we review studies on

---

[1]Although both males and females are victims of sexual assault, studies of the effects of rape on male victims are extremely scarce. Therefore, in this chapter, we refer exclusively to adult female rape victims.

The theoretical concepts that are advanced in this section have been greatly influenced by numerous discussions between E.B.F. and Drs. John Teasdale, Phillip Bernard, and Marsha Linehan at the Applied Psychology Unit in Cambridge, England, and by conversations with Dr. David Clark that took place both in Oxford, England, and in Philadelphia, Pennsylvania.

Support for the preparation of this chapter was provided in part by NIMH Grant MH42178, awarded to E.B.F.

postrape sequelae, interpreting their results within this theoretical framework. Finally, we summarize studies on treatment outcome for rape-related PTSD and interpret the results in light of the proposed theoretical model.

POSTRAPE PSYCHOPATHOLOGY

Several studies have examined the psychological effects of rape victimization (for reviews, see Burt and Katz 1985; Resick 1990; Steketee and Foa 1987). Intense fear of rape-related situations and pervasive anxiety appear to be the most persistent postrape reactions, observed as long as 16 years after the assault (Calhoun et al. 1982; Kilpatrick et al. 1982). Symptoms of depression are also frequently reported by rape victims; however, they seem to be less persistent than anxiety (Atkeson et al. 1982; Frank and Stewart 1984; Kilpatrick et al. 1979). Rape victims also report intrusive memories, thoughts, and images of the assault, which they attempt to block (Kilpatrick and Veronen 1984; Resick 1987); nightmares and other sleep disturbances (Ellis et al. 1981; Nadelson et al. 1982); and impaired concentration (Nadelson et al. 1982).

Since the conceptualization of postrape syndrome as PTSD, several studies examined the prevalence of this disorder in rape victims. In a representative sample of women in Charleston County in South Carolina, 57% of rape victims met diagnostic criteria for PTSD at some point after the assault; more than 16% of them had PTSD at the time of the assessment, an average of 17 years after the assault (Kilpatrick et al. 1987). Somewhat lower rates were detected in a national sample of women: 31% of rape victims reported having had PTSD at some time subsequent to the rape, and 11% had PTSD at the time of the assessment (National Victim Center and Crime Victims Research and Treatment Center 1992). The disorder appears somewhat more prevalent in victims who reported the rape to police (70%) or to medical professionals (61%) (Bownes et al. 1991; H. Resnick, L. J. Veronen, B. Saunders, D. Kilpatrick, and V. Cornelison: "Follow-Up Study of Rape Victims in a Relationship," unpublished manuscript, 1989).

In a longitudinal study conducted by Foa et al. on 65 rape victims who reported the assault to the police, the prevalence of rape-related PTSD was examined weekly for 3 months after the assault (Rothbaum et al. 1992). Within 2 weeks after the assault, 94% of the victims met DSM-III symptom criteria for PTSD; 65% met criteria after 5 weeks, and 47% 3 months after the assault. Similar rates emerged in our ongoing study using DSM-III-R (American Psychiatric Association 1987) criteria for PTSD. Given the high rate of rape in the United States and the high incidence of PTSD among rape victims, it is likely that rape victims constitute the largest group of people with PTSD in this country.

We have examined the prevalence of specific PTSD symptoms in two samples of rape victims. DSM-III symptoms were assessed in the first sample, and DSM-III-R symptoms were assessed in the second. Three months after the assault, the most prevalent symptom among rape victims with PTSD in the first sample was fear, and the least prevalent was guilt. With the exception of guilt, all symptoms were reported by more than 40% of these victims. Significantly fewer symptoms were reported by non-PTSD victims. Interestingly, many non-PTSD victims reported symptoms of fear, avoidance, and hyperalertness, but few reported reexperiencing and numbing symptoms. A similar, but more distinct, symptom pattern emerged in the second study. Again, many victims who did not meet criteria for PTSD reported fear associated with trauma cues, avoidance, and hypervigilance. What distinguished PTSD from non-PTSD victims was the high prevalence of numbing symptoms reported by the former. These results support Foa et al.'s (1992) suggestion that the tendency to allocate attention to threat information, and at the same time to avoid elaborated processing of such information, characterizes all anxiety disorders, including PTSD. PTSD, however, is distinguished from other anxiety disorders by the presence of numbing symptoms. It appears that two types of psychopathology may occur following a trauma: some victims will meet criteria for PTSD, whereas others will present a symptom pattern similar to that of simple phobia.

ETIOLOGY OF PTSD: AN INFORMATION-PROCESSING PERSPECTIVE

The results described above clearly indicate that not all rape victims incur chronic PTSD. Several researchers have investigated predictors of chronic PTSD following trauma, adopting a model comprising three factors: individual characteristics, trauma characteristics, and characteristics of the recovery environment (e.g., Green et al. 1985; D. S. Riggs, E. B. Foa, B. O. Rothbaum, and T. Murdock: "Post-Traumatic Stress Disorder Following Rape and Non-Sexual Assault: A Predictive Model," unpublished manuscript, June 1992; Wyatt et al. 1990). Research based on these models has advanced knowledge about correlates of PTSD. However, these models have not specified the interrelationship among the three factors, although the presence of such interrelationships has been postulated by several theorists (e.g., Foy et al. 1987; Keane et al. 1985). This interrelationship was described by Horowitz (1986), who noted that "any event is appraised and assimilated in relation to the past history and the cognitive and emotional set of the person who experiences it, and therefore it produces idiosyncratic responses" (p. 17).

Behavior theorists have conceptualized PTSD as a conditioned fear response that over time becomes generalized to many stimuli (e.g., Keane et al. 1985; Kilpatrick et al. 1979). Although this conceptualization can accommodate the phobic avoidance symptoms that are observed in trauma victims, it cannot explain the pervasive anxiety and the alternation between arousal and numbing that characterizes PTSD (Foa et al. 1992; van der Kolk 1987). A more promising approach is presented by information-processing theorists who have proposed that knowledge acquired throughout life is represented in memory in the form of abstract, generic knowledge structures, often referred to as "schemas" (e.g., Bartlett 1932; Mandler and Goodman 1982; Neisser 1976) or "memory networks" (e.g., Anderson and Bower 1973; Bower 1981). Schema theorists agree that an existing schema influences the encoding and interpretation of new information that falls within the domain of that schema (e.g., Alba and Hasher 1983). For example, existing schemas will lead one to interpret a scream in the midst of a lively party as an expression of joy, whereas a scream in the middle of the night, emerging from a forsaken alley, would be taken as a sign of distress or danger. The concept of schema is similar to Epstein's (1980) notion of "theory of reality" and Bowlby's (1969) concept of "world models"; all share the view that knowledge is organized in cognitive structures that influence perception and comprehension of new events.

How can we understand the development of PTSD within an information-processing framework? Adopting this perspective, we propose that chronic PTSD should be conceptualized as the victim's failure to process the trauma successfully. Specifically, we suggest that "individual characteristics" noted by other PTSD researchers can be conceived of as preexisting schematic models, or the "psychological makeup" of the victim prior to the "target" rape. "Trauma characteristics" can be conceptualized as the victim's memory records of the trauma itself (i.e., what the victim recorded "on line" during the rape). This memory depends both on what actually happened during the trauma and on the psychological makeup of the victim. "Characteristics of the recovery environment" can be conceived of as memory records of posttrauma experiences (i.e., what the victim records about her own reactions to the trauma as well as about the reactions of others). The posttrauma records, in turn, are influenced by the pretrauma psychological makeup of the individual as well as by the memory records of the trauma. Like Horowitz (1986), our conceptualization emphasizes the interrelationship between the traumatic event and its cognitive processing by the victim.

Predispositional Factors

Within the framework of information processing we postulate that life events are organized into schemas that influence the processing of a victim's experiences both during and after the rape. Some schemas encompass large bodies of knowledge such that they are called into play in most life experiences. Two such large schemas organize knowledge about "oneself" and about the "world." One important dimension of the world schema is the degree to which the world is perceived as physically and psychologically safe or dangerous. An important dimension of the self-schema is the degree to which a person conceives of himself or herself as competent and self-reliant or incompetent and a "poor coper." Another way to conceive of these dimensions is as the degree to which an individual perceives his or her interaction with the environment as predictable and controllable (Foa et al. 1992). Individuals who perceive the environment as predictable and controllable will develop a self-schema of competence and a schema of the world as safe. On the other hand, the perception of events as unpredictable and uncontrollable will result in a schema of the world as dangerous and oneself as incompetent.

Horowitz (1986) suggested that people have a need to match "new information with inner models based on old information" (p. 92) and that "the revision of both until they agree can be called a completion tendency" (p. 92). It is inconceivable that humans undergo such a matching process for each of the vast number of perceptions that occur in daily life. However, it is likely that significant information, such as possible threats to one's life, does require integration with existing schemas. If such information matches existing schemas, it serves to reinforce them. Conversely, when new information is incongruent or contradictory to information represented in the schemas, two possibilities exist: altering the meaning of the experience so that it fits into existing schemas or altering the schemas to conform with the new information. The former process is known as assimilation and the latter as accommodation (McCann and Pearlman 1990; Piaget 1971).

Research has demonstrated that, in the face of inconsistent information, people are generally resistant to accommodating their schemas (e.g., Fiske and Taylor 1984; Janoff-Bulman 1989; Nisbett and Ross 1980). This conservatism in preserving existing schemas comes from the need for stability and coherence in assigning meaning to daily experiences (e.g., Epstein 1980; Nisbett and Ross 1980). However, despite the resistance to alter schemas, accommodation does ensue under certain circumstances. We propose that two factors will determine when accommodation will occur: the significance of the experience and the extent to which it is incongruent with existing schemas.

Trauma theorists have suggested that the process of accommodating existing safety schemas to incorporate the traumatic event underlies posttrauma psychopathology, including PTSD (e.g., Foa et al. 1989; Horowitz 1986; Janoff-Bulman 1989; Perloff 1983). Horowitz (1986) highlighted this view by stating that "a stressful life event is, by definition, one that is not fully in accord with a person's usual inner working models" (p. 93) and that "after deaths, personal injuries, and other serious life events, the inner model must be revised" (p. 94). A similar view is offered by Janoff-Bulman (1989), who suggested that in the face of a trauma, the preservation of basic assumptions embedded in the "self" and the "world" schemas is threatened. Specifically, she proposed that victimization violates three basic assumptions victims hold about the world and about themselves: the world is benevolent, the world is meaningful, and the "self" is worthy. She further proposed that "the experience of victimization shatters the assumption of invulnerability" (p. 19), replacing it with a new perception of extreme vulnerability. According to this theory, we would expect that "unpredictable" rapes (e.g., those occurring in a safe place, by a friend) would be more likely to lead to chronic PTSD than would rape by a stranger in an unsafe environment.

The mismatch between existing schemas and trauma information is one possible scenario by which a stressful event may lead to PTSD. Foa et al. (1992) noted that such a mismatch was evident in some experimental procedures with animals that produce PTSD-like symptoms. An example of such an experiment is Rescorla's (1971) "superconditioning" procedure in which the pairing of a novel stimulus with an uncontrollable shock resulted in a greater level of behavioral suppression if the novel stimulus was presented together with a stimulus that had undergone prior inhibitory training. In other words, greater fear to an excitatory stimulus was exhibited if the fear conditioning trials occurred in a context that previously signaled safety. Another example of mismatch between safety context and aversive stimuli is Masserman's (1943) procedure in which the animal had formed a strong appetitive association with a stimulus that was later paired with uncontrollable aversive stimuli. It is interesting to note that in Masserman's paradigm, when the expectation for a pleasurable experience was violated, a *single* aversive confrontation produced long-lasting, extreme disturbance.

Models that emphasize the mismatch between trauma information and existing schemas of safety and competence as an important etiological factor of postrape PTSD are quite compelling. However, the underlying assumption of these models, that schemas of a "safe world" and "invulnerable self" are universal, is counterintuitive. Many people are subjected to circumstances that would be expected to foster schemas of the world as dangerous and unpredictable. For these people, a traumatic experience will confirm, rather than shatter, existing schemas. When victimized, then, are these individuals less likely to develop PTSD than the "self-assured," "invulnerable" ones? Although this question has been largely neglected by trauma theorists, McCann and Pearlman (1990) described a rape victim with a negative self-schema who exhibited severe depression and PTSD, apparently because the rape reminded her of having been victimized by an alcoholic father and activated the schema, "I deserve to be punished." This observation implies that the presence of negative self-schemas may exacerbate reactions to trauma and thus appears contradictory to the mismatch hypothesis.

McCann and Pearlman's (1990) observation as well as studies revealing a positive relationship between previous victimization and postrape psychopathology (e.g., Burgess and Holmstrom 1978; Resick 1987) suggest that PTSD is likely to develop when the traumatic event activates already-existing schemas about the world as dangerous and the self as incompetent. To accommodate these findings and the mismatch hypothesis within one conceptual framework, Foa et al. (1992) proposed two scenarios for the development of PTSD. The first entails the violation of preexisting safety schemas; the second scenario occurs when the traumatic event matches existing negative schemas. These schemas may have resided in long-term memory with high activation thresholds and thus may not have resulted in severe psychopathology. The new trauma primes these negative schemas and thereby lowers their activation threshold. Consequently, a whole range of stimuli, even those only remotely similar to the trauma, will activate these schemas and produce PTSD symptoms.

Foa et al. (1992) noted that the second scenario for the development of PTSD parallels the finding that animals who did not have an appetitive association with the uncontrollable, unpredictable aversive stimuli also developed PTSD-like symptoms. In this case, symptoms developed *only after repeated* experience with uncontrollable, unpredictable stress. This repeated experience can be conceived of as forming negative schemas that danger can occur at any time and is inescapable. These findings suggest that, when a trauma does not violate preexisting positive schemas, repeated aversive experiences are necessary for the formation of negative schemas that lead to chronic PTSD.

In summary, we propose that the relationship of PTSD to schemas of safety and competence is curvilinear. Victims with exaggerated notions of a safe world and of invulnerability, as well as victims with exaggerated ideas of danger and personal incompetence, will be especially susceptible to developing PTSD. In contrast, individuals with "flexible" schemas, who perceive the world as sometimes safe and sometimes dangerous and know that their ability to cope may vary from one situation to another, will be most likely to recover following a trauma.

Memory Records of the Rape

The second class of factors that underlies the development of PTSD following a trauma is the victim's memory records of the trauma itself. Foa et al. (1989) proposed that the experience of rape produces an intense, easily activated fear structure. This memory structure includes representations of the rape situation, representations of physiological and overt behavioral responses of the victim, and interpretive information about the meaning of the stimulus and response representations. Further, the authors suggested that the fear structures of persons with PTSD are distinguished from other fear memories in three ways: the fear responses are more intense; the number of representations in the structure is larger; and the threshold for activation is lower. Therefore, the structure is easily primed by a plethora of stimuli.

We propose that in addition to the specific characteristics of the fear structure of rape victims described by Foa et al. (1989), trauma memories are also distinguished from other memories by their disorganized and fragmented nature. Clinical observations of rape victims suggest that their memory of the assault is often fragmented and heavily loaded with representations of intense emotions, incomprehension, confusion, and a sense of dread or "awfulness" (Kilpatrick et al. 1992). The fragmented memory often includes representations of the actions of the perpetrator as well as those of the victim, bodily sensations (e.g., pain, touch, smell), and thoughts that reflect attempts to make sense of the trauma.

The disorganization of the trauma memory record can be explained by the difficulty inherent in processing information under conditions of extreme distress. The effects of anxiety on information processing is particularly relevant to understanding the memory records of rape victims. In summarizing research on the effects of anxiety on information processing, Eysenck and Keane (1990) proposed four ways in which anxiety may affect information processing. First, it increases attention to threat-relevant stimuli and decreases attention to neutral stimuli (e.g., Eysenck et al. 1987; MacLeod et al. 1986), even in the absence of conscious awareness (Mathews and MacLeod 1986). The presence of selective processing in individuals with anxiety disorder was noted by Beck and Emery (1985), who stated that "an anxious person will be hypersensitive to any aspects of a situation that will be potentially harmful but will not respond to its benign or positive aspects" (p. 31).

A second way in which anxiety may affect the processing of information is by elevating distractibility and reducing concentration (for review, see Eysenck 1982). High distractibility and poor concentration are expected to result in disorganized memory records. Third, anxiety (or arousal) narrows the range of stimuli to which one attends. When anxiety is moderate, this process reduces attention to irrelevant cues, thus improving performance. However, it is conceivable that, under extreme anxiety, this narrowing of attention may also degrade the processing of relevant information, resulting in a fragmented, disorganized representation of the traumatic events. A fourth mechanism through which anxiety can interfere with information processing is by limiting attentional capacity in working memory. Eysenck and Keane (1990) suggested that anxiety and self-concern capture much of the available capacity so that less is free for other tasks. In the case of a rape victim, the perception of threat to one's physical and psychological integrity may have appropriated much of the available attentional capacity during the rape, thus interfering with processing the details of the assault.

The four mechanisms described above not only lead to the hypothesis that trauma memories will be fragmented and disorganized but also suggest that the content of these memory records will be highly skewed toward threat representations. We therefore hypothesize that priority will be assigned to remembering actions that are especially related to threat, such as the assailant's use of physical force or the victim's behavior that is perceived as having invited the assault or having failed to terminate it (e.g., being friendly with the assailant, freezing). As with actions, there will be a bias to remember threat-related emotions, such as fear, guilt, and shame. These biased memory records are likely to foster the perception of the world as dangerous and of oneself as incompetent.

When an event produces intense anxiety or dread, an additional mechanism, dissociation, is frequently mobilized. Rape victims often describe dissociative experiences, such as the sensation of watching the rape from outside their bodies. More common are reports of "numbing" experiences during which a victim ceases to feel physical and emotional pain while being brutalized. We suggest that this discrepancy between the representations of actions and the representations of sensations may further contribute to the fragmentation and disorganization of the trauma memory records.

Although all traumatic memories are likely to be somewhat fragmented and disorganized because of the processes discussed above, the degree of disorganization may vary from one victim to another. We propose that the rape victim's preexisting schemas of the world and the self will influence the degree to which her memories will be disorganized and fragmented. We hypothesize that rape victims with either rigid safety schemas or rigid danger schemas will evidence more confused and disorganized memories of the trauma than will rape victims with flexible schemas. Specifically, we predict that victims with distinct safety schemas will have greater difficulty in comprehending the traumatic event, and this difficulty will be expressed through statements such as, "What is he going to do to me?" or "I can't believe this is happening to me." On the other hand, for the "vulnerable" victim, the rape will prime schemas of the world as dangerous, augmenting anxiety during the assault and thereby magnifying the difficulty in processing the trauma information. The "vulnerable" victim will be likely to express thoughts such as, "I won't be able to survive this again" and "This is going to be as terrible as the last time."

Horowitz (1986) suggested that individuals continuously process information to achieve a fit between existing schemas and current reality. We propose that a fragmented and disorganized memory record is more difficult to fit within existing schemas than is an intact memory. This difficulty is caused by the loose relationships among the different memory representations in a fragmented memory. In an organized memory, the priming of a few representations will activate the entire memory structure (Foa and Kozak 1986; Lang 1977). Thus, all the representations within that memory will be processed simultaneously. In contrast, the priming of a few representations in a fragmented memory will not necessarily activate all other representations in that memory. Therefore, satisfactory processing of a fragmented rape memory may require the repeated activation of each individual memory fragment.

In discussing the therapeutic process underlying exposure-based treatments for phobic anxiety, Lang (1977) coined the term "emotional processing" to refer to the mechanisms by which fear is extinguished. Expanding on this concept, Rachman (1980) noted that if an emotional experience is not "absorbed satisfactorily," PTSD-like symptoms occur. According to Rachman, the index of unsuccessful emotional processing is "the persistence or return of intrusive signs of emotional activity, such as obsessions, nightmares, pressured talk, phobias, inappropriate expressions of emotions" (p. 51). In an attempt to explicate the mechanisms through which emotional processing is accomplished, Foa and Kozak (1986) suggested that two conditions are necessary for fear reduction. First, the fear memory must be activated. Second, corrective information must be provided to include elements that are "incompatible with some of those that exist in the fear structure so that a new memory can be formed. This new information, which is at once cognitive and affective, has to be integrated into the evoked information structure for an emotional change to occur" (p. 22). The incorporation of this new information results in a reduction in fear responses (i.e., habituation) and in changes in meaning representations. We propose that changes in the meaning of the memory result in a more organized memory record. Until such organization occurs, the trauma representations remain in working memory, continuing to prime threat schemas and consequently reinforcing the perception that the entire world is dangerous and that the self is incompetent. Thus, the process of organizing the trauma memory, changing its meaning, and bringing it into fit with existing schemas is what characterizes successful posttrauma resolution.

Posttrauma Processing

The distinction among pretrauma factors, memory records of the trauma itself, and posttrauma processing is not without problems. In particular, the boundary between the memory of the trauma itself and posttrauma processing of the memory is often blurred. This is especially true when the traumatic event extends over a period of time. For example, a rape victim who was held by her assailant for hours after the completion of the rape, under the threat of being raped again, is likely to begin processing the first rape while still in the traumatic situation. Notwithstanding this limitation, we suggest that this distinction has heuristic value in understanding the etiology of PTSD.

Foa et al. (1989) suggested that traumatic events are, by nature, threatening and of monumental significance, and therefore the resulting memory will include intense fear responses. Other strong emotions, such as guilt, anger, shame, and disgust, are also represented in the memory record of the trauma (Kilpatrick et al. 1992). Foa et al. (1989) suggested that the strong emotions represented in the rape memory structure are highly aversive and, therefore, promote both cognitive and behavioral avoidance.

The conflict inherent between the victim's need to bring the trauma memories into agreement with preexisting schemas and the desire to avoid the pain evoked by remembering the trauma is a source of persistent tension. This conflict is manifested in the alternation between intrusive, reexperiencing symptoms and avoidance, numbing symptoms that has been viewed as the hallmark of PTSD by several authors (Foa et al. 1992; Horowitz 1986; van der Kolk 1987). How can this alternation be explained? Because the trauma records are distinct from other memories, they are primed by numerous internal and external cues and repeatedly enter working memory. Their presence in working memory, marked by reexperiencing symptoms, is necessary for successful integration of the trauma memory. However, remembering the trauma causes the victim marked distress. Avoidance strategies are then called into play to reduce this distress. Although successful in producing relief by temporarily removing the trauma records from working memory, avoidance strategies also prevent the emotional processing of the trauma. Paradoxically then, avoidance strategies that are intended to reduce distress serve to maintain PTSD symptoms that cause emotional distress.

When the victim is able to identify the cues that activate the rape memory, she mobilizes active strategies aimed at avoiding these cues. However, many unidentifiable cues also prime the trauma memory (Foa et al. 1989; Keane et al. 1985). The pervasiveness of the priming cues and the victim's failure to identify them preclude the success of effortful avoidance strategies and result in high tonic arousal (Blanchard et al. 1986). When active avoidance strategies fail to reduce distress, one way for the victim to gain relief is to "shut down the system." This shutting down is expressed in the numbing symptoms of PTSD.

Because the rape memory elicits intense distress, emotional processing may not take place even if the records remain in working memory for a prolonged period. The same anxiety-related mechanisms that interfere with the successful organization of information during the trauma may also hinder posttrauma processing. With time, though, most rape victims are able to organize the trauma memories and integrate them with existing schemas. Once this processing occurs, the trauma representations cease to reside in working memory, freeing resource capacity for the processing of information unrelated to the trauma. The victim can then view the rape as a distinct event rather than as representing the world as a whole and can begin to discriminate between safety and danger. She can also view her responses to the rape as appropriate reactions to a highly stressful event rather than as a sign of general incompetence. Successful emotional processing will result in flexible schemas that represent the world as sometimes safe and sometimes dangerous and the individual as sometimes competent and other times not.

As suggested earlier, when a trauma is incongruent with existing safety schemas or when it is consistent with existing danger schemas, victims are likely to experience severe posttrauma symptoms. However, we predict that following the rape the "invulnerable" victim will feel that "the world is a different place and I am a different person." In contrast, the "vulnerable" victim will express the feeling that "I always knew that the world was dangerous and that I was incompetent, but now I know that there is definitely no hope." The persistence of PTSD symptoms is recorded in memory and interpreted as further evidence of the victim's incompetence. This process is reflected in expressions such as, "I should have been able to put the rape behind me and feel better by now." As more time elapses, the association of the PTSD symptoms to the rape becomes less apparent to the victim, and these symptoms cease to "make sense." The absence of a coherent "story" to account for the symptoms further contributes to the victim's perception of herself as an inadequate coper. Thus, the failure emotionally to process the traumatic memory initiates a vicious cycle that perpetuates the PTSD symptoms.

DEVELOPMENT OF PTSD: EMPIRICAL STUDIES

Here we examine studies that investigated predictors of PTSD following rape and discuss the results within the theoretical framework proposed above. Accordingly, predicting variables are grouped into three clusters: predispositional factors (e.g., prior psychiatric difficulties), memory records of the trauma (e.g., severity of assault), and memory records of posttrauma processing (e.g., social support).

Predispositional Characteristics and PTSD

Demographic characteristics. Although few studies have examined the relation of demographic characteristics to the development of PTSD, several have related such variables to general postrape psychopathology. Three studies found that victimization at a younger age produced fewer difficulties than at an older age (Atkeson et al. 1982; McCahill et al. 1979; Ruch and Chandler 1983), and three studies reported no age effect on postrape reactions (Becker et al. 1982; Kilpatrick et al. 1985; Ruch and Leon 1983). Studies on the effect of marital status on postrape psychopathology are also equivocal. Two studies reported that married victims exhibited more postrape difficulties than did unmarried victims (McCahill et al. 1979; Ruch and Chandler 1983). No such relationship emerged in four other studies (Kilpatrick et al. 1985, 1989, 1992; Ruch and Leon 1983). Conflicting results also arise from studies on the effect of race on postrape difficulties. Four studies reported no racial difference in psychopathology (Burnam et al. 1988; Kilpatrick et al. 1985; Morelli 1981; Ruch and Leon 1983), but one study found that nonwhite victims experienced more difficulties than white victims (Ruch and Chandler 1983). Two studies found that victims with low socioeconomic status experienced more postrape problems than victims with high socioeconomic status (Atkeson et al. 1982; Burgess and Holmstrom 1978), and two studies found no relationship between socioeconomic status variables and PTSD (Kilpatrick et al. 1989, 1992).

In summary, the search for demographic predictors for rape-related psychopathology has not been fruitful. Indeed, the theoretical model that we have proposed does not predict a direct causal relationship between variables such as victim's age, race, or marital status and posttrauma psychopathology. Rather, such variables may influence pretrauma schemas, which, as discussed above, will influence emotional processing. For example, schemas of extreme invulnerability and extreme vulnerability may be present both in younger and older victims or in individuals with high or low socioeconomic status. Consequently, PTSD may be equally prevalent in different demographic groups. Similarly, the effect of marital status on postrape difficulties is likely to depend on whether the spouse serves as a source of social support or as a source for additional stress (Steketee and Foa 1987).

Previctimization adjustment. Several retrospective studies found that adjustment in rape victims after the assault was related to their psychological functioning prior to the rape. One good predictor of the severity of depression and anxiety 1 year after the rape was the degree to which the victim experienced psychological problems before the assault (Atkeson et al. 1982; Calhoun and Atkeson 1982). Similarly, the presence of a previous psychiatric history was related to poorer postrape adjustment (Burgess and Holmstrom 1978; Frank and Anderson 1987; Frank et al. 1981). Consistent with these results, our prospective study revealed a positive relationship between the severity of PTSD and previous psychiatric problems (Riggs et al., unpublished manuscript, 1992). Another measure of pretrauma maladjustment, a history of substance abuse, was also found to predict the presence of psychological symptoms following a rape (Burgess and Holmstrom 1978; Miller et al. 1982; Ruch and Leon 1983).

The consistent finding that pretrauma psychological problems predict posttrauma psychopathology appears incompatible with Janoff-Bulman's (1989) hypothesis that individuals who perceive the world as safe and themselves as invulnerable will be at high risk for posttrauma psychopathology; it is unlikely that victims who, prior to the trauma, had psychological problems held assumptions that the world was safe and that they were invulnerable. The positive relationship between pretrauma and posttrauma psychopathology supports our hypothesis that a trauma may activate an existing schema of danger and vulnerability, which, in turn, contributes to the development of posttrauma psychopathology.

Life stress. Burgess and Holmstrom (1978) reported that chronic stress prior to the rape appeared to increase difficulties following the assault, whereas transient acute stresses had little impact on postrape adjustment. Two studies suggested a curvilinear relation between general life stress and postrape adjustment. Victims who had experienced moderate pretrauma life stress appeared to fare better than those with either high or low levels of stress (Ruch and Leon 1983; Ruch et al. 1980). The curvilinear relationship suggested by these studies is consistent with our hypothesis that both victims with a sense of invulnerability (low stress) and those with a sense of high vulnerability (high stress) are at risk for chronic PTSD.

Previous victimization. Several studies found that rape victims with a history of victimization experienced more general psychopathology following the assault than those without such a history (Kramer and Green 1991; Roth et al. 1990; Ruch and Leon 1983). Burgess and Holmstrom (1978) reported that 86% of victims without a history of victimization were recovered when assessed 4–6 years later in contrast to only 47% of rape victims with such a history. Similarly, Resick (1987) demonstrated that rape victims with a history of criminal victimization or domestic violence experienced more severe postrape reactions than victims without such a history. A positive relationship between PTSD severity and a childhood victimization history was also found by Riggs et al. (unpublished manuscript, 1992).

How does a history of victimization exacerbate current PTSD symptoms? We propose that having been a victim of trauma led to the development of schemas of the world as dangerous and the self as vulnerable. The current victimization is congruent with these schemas and thus serves to prime them and bring them into active memory. The activation of these schemas, in turn, results in anxiety and feelings of inadequacy that lead to chronic PTSD. If schemas of the world and the self mediate the effect of previous victimization, we hypothesize that victimization during childhood is more likely to lead to postrape PTSD than is previous adult victimization, because early trauma should lead to stronger, more readily accessible, maladaptive schemas than trauma later in life.

Another potential mechanism underlying the relation between previous victimization and PTSD is the degree to which the victim uses dissociation as a coping style, thereby hindering emotional processing and increasing psychopathology. Support for this hypothesis comes from animal studies in which previous experience with inescapable shock hastened the production of opioid-mediated analgesia to later inescapable shock (Foa et al. 1992). In humans, we found that assault victims with a history of victimization dissociated more shortly after the trauma than those without such a history (Dancu et al. 1991). Several authors suggested that the process of assimilating trauma-related information is required for posttrauma recovery (e.g., Foa et al. 1989; Horowitz 1986). It follows that individuals who cope with traumatic experiences through dissociation will be more likely to develop chronic psychopathology. Support for this interpretation is derived from the finding that assault victims with PTSD dissociated more than those without PTSD (Dancu et al., unpublished manuscript, 1992). Obviously, a causal relationship between dissociation and PTSD cannot be ascertained from correlational data. It is entirely possible that the inability to process the trauma successfully and the consequent PTSD symptoms may foster dissociation rather than being caused by it.

Memory Records of the Rape and PTSD

A second factor that may affect the development of PTSD following a trauma is what was encoded in memory during the traumatic episode. As noted earlier, the trauma memory records seem typically disorganized and are characterized by extreme emotions, such as anxiety and dread, which may hinder emotional processing. Studies examining variables associated with the traumatic episode are discussed below.

Relationship between victim and perpetrator. Several studies have examined the relationship between postrape symptom severity and the victim's relationship to the perpetrator. The results of these studies are equivocal: six found no differences between the symptoms of victims assaulted by strangers and those assaulted by acquaintances (Frank et al. 1980; Girelli et al. 1986; Kilpatrick et al. 1987; Koss et al. 1988; Riggs et al., unpublished manuscript, 1992; Sales et al. 1984); two reported that rapes by strangers led to more anxiety and depression (Ellis et al. 1981; McCahill et al. 1979); and one found that victims who knew their assailants experienced greater difficulties than those raped by strangers (Scheppele and Bart 1983).

The mismatch hypothesis (e.g., Janoff-Bulman 1989) would predict that assaults by an acquaintance would be more incongruent with existing schemas and, therefore, would lead to more severe psychopathology. The empirical findings do not support this prediction. At least two factors may account for this discrepancy. First, most studies contrasted known versus unknown perpetrators. Perhaps the quality of the relationship between the victim and the assailant, rather than simply knowing or not knowing the perpetrator, is the critical factor. Thus, an assault by a friend may indeed violate expectations for love and consideration, but a rape perpetrated by a stranger may not differ from a rape by a man known only in passing. Second, rape by a stranger may be more brutal than rape by an acquaintance and therefore lead to more severe reactions. Indeed, rapes by strangers were found to involve more perpetrators, more threats of bodily harm, more physical assault, and more frequent use of a weapon than rapes by acquaintances (Koss et al. 1988). How, then, does the brutality of the assault affect posttrauma psychopathology?

Brutality of the assault. Studies that used indices of overall brutality or severity of the assault revealed that more brutal assaults led to more severe psychopathology (Cluss et al. 1983; Ellis et al. 1981; McCahill et al. 1979; Norris and Feldman-Summers 1981; Resick 1986). In contrast, attempts to relate specific aspects of the rape experience to the presence of PTSD and other psychiatric symptoms yielded an ambiguous picture. Injury (Kilpatrick et al. 1989; Sales et al. 1984) and duration of the assault (Riggs et al., unpublished manuscript, 1992) were positively associated with the severity of PTSD, but several studies have failed to find significant relationships between postrape symptoms and other rape characteristics, such as the presence of a weapon, location of the assault, and number of assailants (Atkeson et al. 1982; Becker et al. 1982; Frank et al. 1980; Kilpatrick et al. 1985; McCahill et al. 1979; Resick 1988; Ruch and Chandler 1983). Using path analytic techniques, we found that the effects of assault brutality were mediated by cognitive factors, such as perception of life-threat (Riggs et al., unpublished manuscript, 1992).

Perception of life-threat. Several studies have reported that psychological symptoms following rape are related to the victim's perception of life-threat during the assault (Ellis et al. 1981; McCahill et al. 1979; Sales et al. 1984). Moreover, Girelli et al. (1986) reported that perceived life-threat during the assault was a better predictor of postrape psychopathology than measures of objective assault severity. Two studies have examined the relation of perceived life-threat during a rape to PTSD. Rape victims who felt that their lives were in danger during the assault were almost 2.5 times as likely to develop PTSD as victims who did not perceive a threat to their lives (Kilpatrick et al. 1989). Similarly, the perception of life-threat was found to mediate the effects of the actual assault severity on postrape PTSD severity (Riggs et al., unpublished manuscript, 1992).

By what mechanisms do brutality and perception of life-threat affect posttrauma psychopathology? Clearly, assaults that are brutal and life threatening would be expected to elicit higher anxiety than less violent ones. Earlier, we discussed several mechanisms through which intense anxiety may disrupt information processing. We suggest that those mechanisms account for the positive relationship between assault severity and postrape symptoms.

It is important to note that the degree to which victims perceived a trauma as life threatening can be measured only retrospectively. Thus, it is unknown whether this perception is recorded during the rape itself or whether it develops during posttrauma processing. Indeed, alteration of memories by subsequent information is a well-established phenomenon (e.g., Loftus and Loftus 1980). An example of such a change in perception of threat was provided by a rape victim who appeared to recover satisfactorily, until she learned that her assailant had killed several other victims. This new information resulted in her reappraising the risk during her own rape, and consequently she developed PTSD symptoms (D. G. Kilpatrick, personal communication, October 1987). This example is particularly illustrative of the potency of the cognitive evaluation of danger.

Posttrauma Processing and PTSD

Earlier, we proposed that the victim's perceptions about herself and about the world influence the development of chronic PTSD. Schematic changes have not been directly studied. However, existing studies reviewed below support the hypothesized differences in the schemas of rape victims with and without PTSD.

Reactions immediately after the rape. We hypothesized that the presence of posttrauma symptoms will be perceived by the victim as a sign of incompetence and her inability to cope and that this perception will, in turn, exacerbate posttrauma symptoms. Several studies found that intense emotional reactions immediately after the trauma were related to the presence of chronic PTSD. In a retrospective study, Kilpatrick et al. (1985) reported that a victim's perception of her initial postrape distress predicted maladjustment 9 years after the assault. In our study, the severity of PTSD 2–4 weeks after the rape was significantly higher in victims diagnosed with PTSD 3 months later than in victims without PTSD. Initial anger, guilt, depression, anxiety, and rape-related fear were also higher in victims with persistent PTSD (Riggs et al., unpublished manuscript, 1992; Riggs et al. 1992; Rothbaum et al. 1992). Although these results are consistent with the hypothesis that a victim's perception of her postrape symptoms leads to chronic PTSD, it is possible that both intense immediate reactions to trauma and chronic PTSD are mediated by a third factor.

Additional, although indirect, evidence that the perception of the self as a poor coper mediates the chronicity of PTSD symptoms comes from the success of stress inoculation training, the teaching of coping skills, as a treatment for PTSD (Foa et al. 1991b; Resick and Schnicke, in press; Resick et al. 1988). Although self-schemas have not been assessed before and after treatment, victims spontaneously report that they feel more able to deal with stress, in general, and with trauma-related stress, in particular, after this treatment.

Trauma schema of PTSD victims. Information-processing theory would predict that a trauma is represented differently in the memory of victims with PTSD than in those without PTSD. It follows that trauma-related information will be processed differently by individuals with and without PTSD. Several studies support this prediction. Using a modified Stroop task, Cassiday et al. (in press) and Foa et al. (1991a) measured reaction time of rape victims to naming the colors in which rape-related and nonrape-related words were printed. Longer reaction times to trauma-related words, but not to other words, were found in victims with PTSD than in those without PTSD. The latter were no different for nonvictims. These results were interpreted as evidence for an attentional bias in PTSD victims toward trauma-related information. In addition, enhanced recall of combat-related words was found in combat veterans with PTSD as compared with those without PTSD (Zeitlin and McNally 1991). It appears, then, that PTSD victims allocate more attentional resources to trauma-related information and more readily retrieve such information than do victims without PTSD.

Effect of avoidance on persistence of other PTSD symptoms. As noted earlier, the tension between the victim's need to process the trauma and the tendency to avoid the distress associated with such processing characterizes most trauma victims. Avoidance may take the form of active attempts to suppress trauma-related thoughts or shun reminders of the trauma; it may also manifest as dissociation or emotional numbing. Although avoidance serves to decrease emotional distress, *excessive* avoidance may hinder emotional processing. It follows that the degree of avoidance symptoms would be positively related to reexperiencing and arousal symptoms. Data from our prospective study of rape and nonsexual assault victims support this view. Symptoms of active avoidance were correlated with arousal symptoms, whereas numbing symptoms were correlated with those of reexperiencing. Additional evidence in support of this hypothesis comes from the positive outcome of treatments that incorporate imaginal reliving of the trauma and direct confrontation with trauma reminders in reducing chronic PTSD (Foa et al. 1991b; Keane et al. 1989).

Controllability and "world dangerousness." We predicted that victims who perceive the world as generally dangerous are more likely to develop chronic PTSD than those who do not. It follows that the severity of PTSD will be positively associated with the victim's perception that she is unable to control the occurrence of negative events in her life. This prediction was partially supported by data from our study: positive correlations between perceived uncontrollability and measures of reexperiencing and arousal symptoms of PTSD emerged (Kushner et al. 1992). In interpreting these data, two caveats should be noted. First, correlations do not permit causal conclusions. As discussed earlier, it is possible that a victim's perception of her symptoms may lead to, rather than result from, the view that she cannot control her world or her emotional reactions. Second, the perception that the world is dangerous and uncontrollable may precede the trauma and influence both the severity of PTSD and posttrauma perceptions of uncontrollability.

Guilt and self-blame. Earlier, we suggested that immediate posttrauma symptoms contribute to the victim's perception of herself as an "inadequate coper," and that this perception will exacerbate the symptoms. Another aspect of negative self-schema is the victim's perception that she somehow brought the rape on herself, either by encouraging the rapist or by failing to halt the assault once it had begun. Such a perception may lead to feelings of guilt, or self-blame (Katz and Burt 1987). Riggs et al. (unpublished manuscript, 1992) found that guilt mediated the relationship between the brutality of the assault and the severity of PTSD symptoms. The effect of guilt on posttrauma psychopathology was also reported by Wyatt et al. (1990): rape victims who attributed their assault to internal factors (self-blame) experienced more negative reactions following the rape than did victims who made external attributions (other-blame).

Janoff-Bulman (1979) distinguished between characterological self-blame (i.e., attributing the cause of victimization to stable character traits) and behavioral self-blame (i.e., attributing the cause of the assault to specific behaviors that may be modified). She proposed that behavioral self-blame may serve to decrease the victim's perceived vulnerability and thus would have an adaptive function. Characterological self-blame, on the other hand, would reinforce the idea that future victimization is inevitable and would increase difficulties.

Two studies failed to support this hypothesis. Meyer and Taylor (1986) found that victims attributed the rape to one of three factors: poor judgment, societal factors, and victim type. Poor judgment was conceptualized as analogous to behavioral self-blame, and victim type was seen as analogous to characterological self-blame. Both poor judgment and victim type were associated with increased postrape depression. A more direct test of Janoff-Bulman's (1979) hypothesis was conducted by Frazier (1990). A strong association between characterological and behavioral self-blame was detected, and both were significantly related to postrape depression. Thus, it appears that negative self-schema, whether expressed as perceived failure to prevent the rape or as failure to cope with the sequelae of the trauma, may be a crucial factor in determining the persistence of PTSD.

Social support. The presence of social support may influence recovery following rape by impacting on the victim's schematic representations of the world and the self. Social support can influence a victim's world and self-schemas in three ways. First, the presence of a positive social environment may encourage the victim to talk about the traumatic experience, which would assist her in processing the trauma. Second, positive social interactions provide information that is inconsistent with the view that the world is indiscriminately dangerous, thus resulting in a more flexible schema. Third, the presence of social support may validate the victim's posttrauma symptoms, thus counteracting the perception that the symptoms represent inadequate coping.

Evidence for the positive effect of social support on posttrauma recovery comes from several studies (e.g., Burgess and Holmstrom 1978; Ellis et al. 1981; Norris and Feldman-Summers 1981; Sales et al. 1984). Burgess and Holmstrom (1978) and Ruch and Chandler (1983) found that rape victims with supportive relationships recovered more quickly following the assault than did victims without a support system. Similarly, rape victims with supportive husbands were less depressed, anxious, and fearful 4 weeks after the assault than were victims with nonsupportive husbands. Moreover, victims whose marital relationship deteriorated following the rape were more anxious and had lower self-esteem than victims whose marriages had been unsatisfactory prior to the assault (Moss et al. 1990).

Although the absence of social support may exacerbate PTSD symptoms, it is also likely that difficulties in social relationships are caused by posttrauma psychopathology (Becker et al. 1983; Resick et al. 1981).

Specifically, we predict that PTSD symptoms, such as detachment from others and emotional numbing, will interfere with the victim's social interactions. Indeed, immediate symptoms of PTSD were related to poor social adjustment, which was in turn related to the severity of PTSD later on (Riggs et al., unpublished manuscript, 1992). Thus, a vicious cycle may be operating to maintain PTSD symptoms: immediate symptom formation may reinforce maladjustive schemas, resulting in social alienation, which may further prevent successful emotional processing.

TREATMENT OF RAPE-RELATED PTSD

Because PTSD is a relatively new diagnostic category in the current nosological system, controlled studies of treatments for this disorder are scarce. In this review, we consider only group studies and case reports that included at least semistructured procedures for evaluating treatment outcome.

Crisis intervention and psychotherapy groups are the most commonly used interventions in rape crisis centers (Koss and Harvey 1987). Based on crisis theory (Burgess and Holmstrom 1976), these interventions involve information about postrape sequelae, active listening, and emotional support (Forman 1980). Treatment with dynamic psychotherapy often has been advocated as the final stage of crisis intervention (Burgess and Holmstrom 1974; Fox and Scherl 1972). However, controlled studies of these interventions are few. There are three reports of the effects of group psychotherapy for rape victims (Cryer and Beutler 1980; Perl et al. 1985; S. Roth, E. Dye, V. Leibowitz: "Group Therapy for Sexual Assault Victims," unpublished manuscript, 1991). All three studies indicated that treatment was somewhat effective in reducing postrape distress. However, the designs of the studies do not allow for unequivocal interpretation of the results.

Cognitive-behavior techniques have also been employed with rape victims. The placement of PTSD among the anxiety disorders led therapists to adopt treatment procedures that have been found effective in individuals with other anxiety disorders to the treatment of individuals with PTSD. Two major lines of thinking have been particularly influential in cognitive-behavior approaches to pathological anxiety. One is learning theory, which encompasses principles of both classical and operant conditioning; the other is the cognitive approach, which emphasizes the role of the interpretive meanings ascribed to events. Parallel to these two conceptual approaches, two types of treatments have been developed to ameliorate anxiety disorders. The first are exposure-based procedures during which patients are repeatedly confronted with the feared memory or situation until anxiety decreases. The second are anxiety management techniques in which patients are taught a variety of skills to manage anxiety.

The efficacy of cognitive-behavior treatments for postrape sequelae has been studied since the late 1970s with an emphasis on ameliorating anxiety and depression. Thus, early studies used measures of anxiety and depression to evaluate treatment outcome and did not assess PTSD symptoms. Strategies that have been used to address the psychiatric symptoms experienced by rape victims include exposure techniques, such as systematic desensitization (Frank et al. 1988) and flooding (Foa et al. 1991b) on the one hand, and cognitive techniques, such as cognitive restructuring (Frank et al. 1988) and stress inoculation training (Foa et al. 1991b; Resick et al. 1988; Veronen and Kilpatrick 1983) on the other hand.

The employment of exposure techniques with trauma victims consists of engaging the patient in the trauma memories with the intent of habituating intense fear responses to trauma reminders. With one exception (Becker and Abel 1981), systematic desensitization (imaginal exposure paired with muscle relaxation) with rape victims was found effective in reducing their fear and depression and in improving social adjustment (Frank and Stewart 1983; Frank et al. 1988; Turner 1979; Wolff 1977). In one study, flooding (prolonged exposure to highly feared stimuli) was also found to reduce assault-related symptoms (Haynes and Mooney 1975). As with the case of group psychotherapy studies, caution must be used when interpreting these results because none of the studies included control groups.

Whereas exposure techniques are designed to promote permanent habituation of anxiety, stress inoculation training and other cognitive techniques are designed to manage anxiety when it occurs by teaching patients skills to control their anxiety. Veronen and Kilpatrick (1983) adapted stress inoculation training (Meichenbaum 1974) for rape victims. The treatment program included a variety of cognitive-behavior techniques, such as muscle relaxation, controlled breathing, role playing, thought stopping, and guided self-dialogue. In several case studies (Kilpatrick and Amick 1985; Kilpatrick et al. 1982; Pearson et al. 1983) and one uncontrolled study (Veronen and Kilpatrick 1983), stress inoculation training was effective in reducing rape-related fear, anxiety, and depression in rape victims.

Three studies have compared the efficacy of different treatments for rape-related symptoms. Frank et al. (1988) examined data from several studies in which patients received either cognitive restructuring or systematic desensitization. No differences between the two treatments emerged. The absence of random assignment to treatments, the lack of a control group, and the failure to exclude recent victims (many of whom would be expected to improve with the passage of time) render these results uninterpretable.

Resick et al. (1988) compared stress inoculation training, assertion training, and supportive psychotherapy to a waiting-list control group. They found that rape victims in all three treatments experienced a greater decrease in symptoms, particularly fear and anxiety, than the waiting-list group. Although Resick et al. (1988) did not assess PTSD symptoms directly, they did administer the Impact of Event Scale (IES) (Horowitz et al. 1979), a measure of intrusion and avoidance symptoms. Rape victims in the three treatment groups evidenced a reduction in IES scores between pretreatment and posttreatment that was maintained at 6-month follow-up. All three treatments were equally effective in reducing postrape symptoms. One possible reason for the absence of differences among the treatments was that exposure to rape-related material was included in all three.

Foa et al. (1991b) conducted a controlled investigation of short-term (5 weeks) treatments for rape-related PTSD. They randomly assigned rape victims who met PTSD criteria to one of four treatment conditions: stress inoculation training, prolonged exposure, supportive counseling, or a waiting-list control group. There was no overlap in the procedures used in the three active treatments. In addition to assessing generalized fear, anxiety, and depression, Foa et al. (in press) assessed PTSD symptoms directly using the PTSD Symptom Scale.

All groups improved during the study on self-report measures of anxiety and depression as well as on the measure of PTSD symptoms. However, victims who were treated with stress inoculation training or prolonged exposure showed greater reduction in PTSD symptoms than those treated with supportive counseling or those on the waiting list. When specific clusters of PTSD symptoms (intrusion, avoidance, arousal) were examined, the results suggested that all treatments reduced arousal symptoms, but only stress inoculation training and prolonged exposure reduced avoidance and intrusion symptoms. Although stress inoculation training and prolonged exposure groups did not differ significantly from one another at posttreatment, mean symptom scores on most measures of psychopathology were lower following stress inoculation training than prolonged exposure. Treatment groups differed with regard to the percentage of victims who continued to meet PTSD criteria at the end of treatment. Of the stress inoculation training group, 50% no longer met criteria for PTSD; 40% of those treated with prolonged exposure also no longer met PTSD criteria. In contrast, 90% of the supportive counseling group and all of victims on the waiting list still had PTSD at the posttreatment assessment.

At a 3-month follow-up, patients in all three treatments remained improved. Although the groups did not differ significantly at follow-up, the mean scores following prolonged exposure were the lowest. The reversal in the pattern of mean scores for stress inoculation training and prolonged exposure from posttreatment to follow-up may imply that 3 months after treatment patients who received stress inoculation training ceased to use the skills they acquired. On the other hand, patients who repeatedly relived trauma memories during prolonged exposure may have remained somewhat distressed at the end of treatment, but exposure produced the expected organization of the rape memory, resulting in continued improvement. Currently we are examining the relative efficacy of stress inoculation training, prolonged exposure, and their combination. Preliminary analyses suggest that the combined treatment is more effective than either component alone. More than 80% of patients treated with the combined treatment did not meet PTSD criteria at the end of treatment.

Earlier we discussed the hypothesized relationship of chronic PTSD to the fragmented, disorganized nature of trauma memories and the perception of the world as indiscriminately dangerous and the self as an inadequate coper. If true, then treatments should be directed toward both organizing the memory and correcting the maladaptive schemas. How can the efficacy of stress inoculation training and prolonged exposure be understood within this framework?

Foa and Kozak (1986) proposed that the mechanisms underlying exposure-based treatments include habituation of emotional responses and correction of mistaken beliefs about the feared stimuli. We propose that repeated reliving of the rape memories during treatment with prolonged exposure decreases the anxiety associated with these memories (via habituation) and thus enables reevaluation of the meaning representations in the memory. The repeated reliving generates a more organized memory record that can be more readily integrated with existing schemas. Indeed, clinical observations suggest that, during prolonged exposure, the narratives of the traumatic experiences become more coherent, irrelevant details drop out, and verbal expressions of shock and incomprehension are replaced by expressions of realization, plans, and intents. Although prolonged exposure does not directly address the victim's world and self-schemas, once the trauma memory is emotionally processed, the victim is able to view the rape as a distinct event rather than representing the world as a whole and thus is able to discriminate between danger and safety. Moreover, the successful processing of the traumatic memories leads to a reduction in PTSD symptoms, particularly those of intrusion and avoidance, which, in turn, results in the victim's perception of herself as an adequate, rather than inadequate, coper. Indirectly, exposure treatments may also foster positive social interactions: if the victim no longer perceives the world as indiscriminately dangerous and herself as an inadequate coper, then she will more readily seek social support.

Stress inoculation training techniques seem to impact more directly on the self-schema of the victims, but do not address the trauma memory structure. By teaching the victim techniques for coping with stress and anxiety, such as relaxation and positive self-talk, these treatments foster a self-image of a successful coper. Stress inoculation training may impact indirectly in two ways on the victim's perception of the world. First, the increased perception of control may allow the victim to tolerate the experience of the trauma memories for longer periods of time, which may serve as self-directed prolonged exposure. Second, the perception of oneself as able to cope with stress reduces the negative valence of potential future threats: if the victim perceives herself as an adequate coper, she will expect to be able to avert potential dangers. Again, these schematic changes are likely to facilitate positive social interactions, which, in turn, will strengthen the functional schemas.

In summary, we suggest that prolonged exposure directly addresses the organization of the trauma memory and the resulting change in the world schema. Stress inoculation training, on the other hand, directly impacts on self-schema. It is, therefore, not surprising that a combination of the two treatments would prove more effective than either procedure alone in reducing PTSD symptoms. We predict that any treatment that directly or indirectly alters the victim's schemas of self and world will help to ameliorate symptoms of PTSD. Indeed, the effectiveness of treatments, such as supportive counseling focusing on problem solving (Foa et al. 1991b; Resick et al. 1988), may be due to changes they produced in the victim's self-schema.

CONCLUSION

In this chapter, we reviewed the literature on the prevalence, correlates, and treatment of postrape psychopathology with an emphasis on PTSD symptoms. Because of the high prevalence of rape in the United States and the high rate of PTSD among rape victims, it is important, both theoretically and practically, to identify factors that contribute to the development of chronic rape-related PTSD. To this end, we have proposed a theoretical model based on an information-processing approach to account for the psychological processes that lead to PTSD. We suggested that the predictors of PTSD are organized into three factors: pretrauma schemas, memory records of the trauma itself, and posttrauma processing of these memories and of posttrauma experiences. We proposed that PTSD is likely to occur when preexisting schemas of the victim interact negatively with memory records of the trauma and with the processing of these memories. Specifically, we predicted that PTSD is likely to develop when a trauma is inconsistent with a victim's pretrauma schemas of the world as safe and herself as invulnerable, or when the trauma primes existing schemas of the world as dangerous and the self as vulnerable. The literature about correlates of rape-related PTSD and its treatment appears consistent with hypotheses derived from the proposed model.

We believe that the theoretical model outlined above will prove to be a heuristic framework for organizing the results of existing studies about PTSD following rape and other traumata as well as for generating hypotheses about the etiology and maintenance of PTSD that will guide future research. In this chapter we have begun this process by delineating specific hypotheses that will direct our future research. One obstacle to adopting this model is the scarcity of reliable and valid instruments for assessing schemas and schematic changes. Strategies that have been employed to fill this gap include the development of self-report instruments that tap into schema-related concepts (Janoff-Bulman 1989; Resick et al. 1991), and the coding of schema categories evident in victim's accounts of their traumatic experiences (Roth and Newman 1991). A third strategy has been the adaptation of paradigms from cognitive psychology, such as priming paradigms, to the study of PTSD. An example of this strategy was the use of a sentence completion task to examine the schemas of panic disorder patients (Clark et al. 1988).

REFERENCES

Alba JW, Hasher L: Is memory schematic? Psychol Bull 93:203–231, 1983

American Psychiatric Association: Diagnostic and Statistical Manual of Mental Disorders, 3rd Edition. Washington, DC, American Psychiatric Association, 1980

American Psychiatric Association: Diagnostic and Statistical Manual of Mental Disorders, 3rd Edition, Revised. Washington, DC, American Psychiatric Association, 1987

Anderson JR, Bower GH: Human Associative Memory. Washington, DC, VH Winston, 1973

Atkeson B, Calhoun K, Resick P, et al: Victims of rape: repeated assessment of depressive symptoms. J Consult Clin Psychol 50:96–102, 1982

Bartlett FC: Remembering: A Study in Experimental and Social Psychology. Cambridge, England, Cambridge University Press, 1932

Beck AT, Emery G: Anxiety Disorders and Phobias: A Cognitive Perspective. New York, Basic Books, 1985

Becker JV, Abel GG: Behavioral treatment of victims of sexual assault, in Handbook of Clinical Behavior Therapy. Edited by Turner SM, Calhoun KS, Adams HE. New York, Wiley, 1981, pp 347–379

Becker JV, Skinner LJ, Abel GG, et al: The incidence and types of sexual dysfunctions in rape and incest victims. J Sex Marital Ther 8:65–74, 1982

Becker JV, Skinner LJ, Abel GG: Sequelae of sexual assault: the survivors perspective, in Sexual Aggression: Current Perspectives in Treatment. Edited by Stuart IR, Greer JG. New York, Van Nostrand Reinhold, 1983

Blanchard EB, Kolb LC, Gerardi RJ, et al: Cardiac response to relevant stimuli as an adjunctive tool for diagnosing post-traumatic stress disorder in Vietnam veterans. Behavior Therapy 17:592–606, 1986

Bower GH: Mood and memory. Am Psychol 36:129–148, 1981

Bowlby J: Attachment and Loss, Vol 1: Attachment. London, Hogarth, 1969

Bownes IT, Gorman EC, Sayers A: Assault characteristics and posttraumatic stress disorder in rape victims. Acta Psychiatr Scand 83:27–30, 1991

Burgess AW, Holmstrom LL: The rape trauma syndrome. Am J Psychiatry 131:981–986, 1974

Burgess AW, Holmstrom LL: Coping behavior of the rape victim. Am J Psychiatry 133:413–418, 1976

Burgess AW, Holmstrom LL: Recovery from rape and prior life stress. Res Nurs Health 1:165–174, 1978

Burnam MA, Stein JA, Golding JM, et al: Sexual assault and mental disorders in community populations. J Consult Clin Psychol 56:843–850, 1988

Burt MR, Katz BL: Rape, robbery, and burglary: responses to actual and feared criminal victimization, with special focus on women and the elderly. Victimology: An International Journal 10:325–358, 1985

Calhoun KS, Atkeson BM: Rape induced depression: normative data (Grant MH29750). Report submitted to National Institute of Mental Health, 1982

Calhoun KS, Atkeson BM, Resick PA: A longitudinal examination of fear reactions in victims of rape. Journal of Counseling Psychology 29:655–661, 1982

Cassiday KL, McNally RJ, Zeitlin SB: Cognitive processing of trauma cues in rape victims with post traumatic stress disorder. Cognitive Therapy and Research (in press)

Clark DM, Salkovskis PM, Gelder M, et al: Tests of a cognitive theory of panic, in Panic and Phobias: Treatments and Variables Affecting Course and Outcome. Edited by Hand I, Wittchen H. Berlin, Springer-Verlag, 1988, pp 149–158

Cluss PA, Boughton J, Frank LE, et al: The rape victims: psychological correlates of participation in the legal process. Criminal Justice and Behavior 10:342–357, 1983

Cryer L, Beutler L: Group therapy: an alternative treatment approach for rape victims. J Sex Marital Ther 6:40–46, 1980

Dancu CV, Riggs DS, Shoyer BG, et al: Dissociative symptoms among female crime victims: effects of childhood abuse. Paper presented at the seventh annual convention of the International Society for Traumatic Stress Studies, Washington, DC, October 1991

Ellis EM, Atkeson BM, Calhoun KS: An assessment of long-term reaction to rape. J Abnorm Psychol 90:263–266, 1981

Epstein S: The self concept: a review and a proposal of an integrated theory of personality, in Personality: Basic Issues and Current Research. Edited by Staub E. Englewood Cliffs, NJ, Prentice-Hall, 1980

Eysenck M: Attention and Arousal Equals Cognition and Performance. New York, Springer-Verlag, 1982

Eysenck MW, Keane MT: Cognitive Psychology: A Student's Handbook. London, Lawrence Erlbaum, 1990

Eysenck MW, MacLeod C, Mathews A: Cognitive functioning and anxiety. Psychol Res 49:189–195, 1987

Fiske ST, Taylor SE: Social Cognition. Reading, MA, Addison-Wesley, 1984

Foa EB, Kozak MJ: Emotional processing of fear: exposure to corrective information. Psychol Bull 99:20–35, 1986

Foa EB, Steketee G, Rothbaum BO: Behavioral/cognitive conceptualization of post-traumatic stress disorder. Behavior Therapy 20:155–176, 1989

Foa EB, Feske U, Murdock TB, et al: Processing of threat-related information in rape victims. J Abnorm Psychol 100:156–162, 1991a

Foa EB, Rothbaum BO, Riggs D, et al: Treatment of post-traumatic stress disorder in rape victims. J Consult Clin Psychol 59:715–723, 1991b

Foa EB, Zinbarg R, Rothbaum BO: Uncontrollability and unpredictability in post traumatic stress disorder. Psychol Bull 112:218–238, 1992

Foa EB, Riggs DS, Dancu CV, et al: Validity and reliability of a brief instrument for assessing posttraumatic stress disorder. Journal of Traumatic Stress (in press)

Forman BD: Cognitive modification of obsessive thinking in a rape victim: a preliminary study. Psychol Rep 47:819–822, 1980

Fox SS, Scherl DJ: Crisis intervention with victims of rape. Social Work 17:37–42, 1972

Foy DW, Resnick HS, Sipprelle RC, et al: Premilitary, military, and post-military factors in the development of combat-related posttraumatic stress disorder. Behavior Therapist 10:3–9, 1987

Frank E, Anderson BP: Psychiatric disorders in rape victims: past history and current symptomatology. Compr Psychiatry 28:77–82, 1987

Frank E, Stewart BD: Physical aggression: treating the victims, in Behavior Modification With Women. Edited by Bleckman EA. New York, Guilford, 1983, pp 245–272

Frank E, Stewart BD: Depressive symptoms in rape victims: a revisit. J Affect Disord 7:77–85, 1984

Frank E, Turner SM, Duffy B: Depressive symptoms in rape victims. J Affective Disord 1:269–277, 1979

Frank E, Turner SM, Stewart B: Initial response to rape: the impact of factors within the rape situation. Journal of Behavioral Assessment 62:39–53, 1980

Frank E, Turner SM, Stewart BD, et al: Past psychiatric symptoms and the response of sexual assault. Compr Psychiatry 22:479–487, 1981

Frank E, Anderson B, Stewart BD, et al: Efficacy of cognitive behavior therapy and systematic desensitization in the treatment of rape trauma. Behavior Therapy 19:403–420, 1988

Frazier PA: Victim attributions and post-rape trauma. J Consult Clin Psychol 59:298–304, 1990

Girelli SA, Resick PA, Marhoefer-Dvorak S, et al: Subjective distress and violence during rape: their effects on long term fear. Violence and Victims 1:35–45, 1986

Green BL, Wilson JP, Lindy JD: Conceptualizing post-traumatic stress disorder: a psychosocial framework, in Trauma and Its Wake. Edited by Figley C. New York, Brunner/Mazel, 1985, pp 53–69

Haynes SN, Mooney DK: Nightmares: etiological, theoretical, and behavioral treatment considerations. Psychological Record 25:225–236, 1975

Holmes MR, St. Lawrence JS: Treatment of rape-induced trauma: proposed behavioral conceptualization and review of the literature. Clinical Psychology Review 3:417–433, 1983

Horowitz MJ: Stress-Response Syndromes, 2nd Edition. Northvale, NJ, Jason Aronson, 1986

Horowitz MJ, Wilner N, Alvarez W: Impact of Event Scale: a measure of subjective distress. Psychosom Med 41:207–218, 1979

Janoff-Bulman R: Characterological versus behavioral self-blame: inquiries into depression and rape. J Pers Soc Psychol 37:1789–1809, 1979

Janoff-Bulman R: Assumptive worlds and the stress of traumatic events: applications of the schema construct. Social Cognition 7:113–136, 1989

Katz BL, Burt MR: Self-blame: help or hindrance in recovery from rape? in Rape and Sexual Assault, Vol 2. Edited by Burgess A. New York, Garland, 1987

Keane TM, Zimmering RT, Caddell JM: A behavioral formulation of post-traumatic stress disorder in Vietnam veterans. Behavior Therapist 8:9–12, 1985

Keane TM, Fairbank JA, Caddell JM, et al: Implosive (flooding) therapy reduces symptoms of PTSD in Vietnam combat veterans. Behavior Therapy 20:245–260, 1989

Kilpatrick DG, Amick AE: Rape trauma, in Behavior Therapy Casebook. Edited by Hersen M, Last CG. New York, Springer, 1985, pp 86–103

Kilpatrick DG, Veronen LJ: Treatment of fear and anxiety in victims of rape (Grant R01 MH29602, final report). Rockville, MD, National Institute of Mental Health, 1984

Kilpatrick DG, Veronen LJ, Resick PA: The aftermath of rape: recent empirical findings. Am J Orthopsychiatry 49:658–659, 1979

Kilpatrick DG, Veronen LJ, Resick PA: Psychological sequelae to rape: assessment and treatment strategies, in Behavioral Medicine: Assessment and Treatment Strategies. Edited by Dolays DM, Meredith RL. New York, Plenum, 1982, pp 473–497

Kilpatrick DG, Veronen LJ, Best CL: Factors predicting psychological distress among rape victims, in Trauma and Its Wake. Edited by Figley CR. New York, Brunner/Mazel, 1985, pp 113–141

Kilpatrick DG, Saunders BE, Veronen LJ, et al: Criminal victimization: lifetime prevalence, reporting to police, and psychological impact. Crime and Delinquency 33:479–489, 1987

Kilpatrick DG, Best CL, Saunders BE, et al: Rape in marriage and dating relationships: how bad is it for mental health? Ann N Y Acad Sci 528:335–344, 1988

Kilpatrick DG, Saunders BE, Amick-McMullan A, et al: Victim and crime factors associated with the development of crime-related post-traumatic stress disorder. Behavior Therapy 20:199–214, 1989

Kilpatrick DG, Resnick HS, Freedy JR: Post-traumatic stress disorder field trial report: a comprehensive review of the initial results. Paper presented at the annual meeting of the American Psychiatric Association, Washington, DC, May 1992

Koss MP, Harvey MR: The Rape Victim: Clinical and Community Approaches to Treatment. Lexington, MA, Stephen Greene Press, 1987

Koss MP, Gidycz CA, Wisniewski N: The scope of rape: incidence and prevalence of sexual aggression and victimization in a national sample of higher education students. J Consult Clin Psychol 55:162–170, 1987

Koss MP, Dinero TE, Seibel C, et al: Stranger, acquaintance and date rape: is there a difference in the victim's experience. Psychology of Women Quarterly 12:1–24, 1988

Kramer T, Green BL: Posttraumatic stress disorder as an early response to sexual assault. Journal of Interpersonal Violence 6:160–173, 1991

Kushner MG, Riggs DS, Foa EB, et al: Perceived controllability and the development of post traumatic stress disorder in crime victims. Behav Res Ther 31:105–110, 1992

Lang PJ: Imagery in therapy: an information processing analysis of fear. Behavior Therapy 8:862–886, 1977

Law Enforcement Assistance Administration: Criminal victimization surveys in 8 American cities (Publ No SD-NCS-C-5). Washington, DC, U.S. Department of Education, 1975

Loftus EF, Loftus GR: On the permanence of stored information in the human brain. Am Psychol 35:409–420, 1980

MacLeod C, Mathews A, Tata P: Attentional bias in emotional disorders. J Abnorm Psychol 95:15–20, 1986

Mandler JM, Goodman MS: On the psychological validity of the story structure. Journal of Verbal Learning and Verbal Behavior 21:507–523, 1982

Masserman JH: Behavior and Neurosis: An Experimental Psychoanalytic Approach to Psychobiologic Principles. Chicago, IL, University of Chicago Press, 1943

Mathews A, MacLeod C: Discrimination of threat cues without awareness in anxiety states. J Abnorm Psychol 95:131–138, 1986

McCahill TW, Meyer LC, Fishman AM: The Aftermath of Rape. Lexington, MA, DC Heath, 1979

McCann IL, Pearlman LA: Psychological Trauma and the Adult Survivor: Theory, Therapy, and Transformation. New York, Brunner/Mazel, 1990

Meichenbaum D: Cognitive Behavior Modification. Morristown, NJ, General Learning Press, 1974

Meyer C, Taylor S: Adjustment to rape. J Pers Soc Psychol 50:1226–1234, 1986

Miller WR, Williams M, Bernstein MH: The effects of rape on marital and sexual adjustment. American Journal of Family Therapy 10:51–58, 1982

Morelli PH: Comparison of the psychological recovery of black and white victims of rape. Paper presented at the meeting of the Association of Women in Psychology, Boston, MA, March 1981

Moss M, Frank E, Anderson B: The effects of marital status and partner support on rape trauma. Am J Orthopsychiatry 60:379–391, 1990

Nadelson CC, Notman MT, Zackson H, et al: A follow-up study of rape victims. Am J Psychiatry 139:1266–1270, 1982

National Victim Center and Crime Victims Research and Treatment Center: Rape in America: a report to the nation (Research Report #1992-1). Washington, DC, National Victims Center and Crime Victims Research and Treatment Center, 1992

Neisser U: Cognition and Reality: Principles and Implications of Cognitive Psychology. San Francisco, CA, WH Freeman, 1976

Nisbett RE, Ross L: Human Interference: Strategies and Shortcomings of Social Judgement. Englewood Cliffs, NJ, Prentice-Hall, 1980

Norris J, Feldman-Summers S: Factors related to the psychological impacts of rape on the victim. J Abnorm Psychol 90:562–567, 1981

Pearson MA, Poquette BM, Wasden RE: Stress inoculation and the treatment of post-rape trauma: a case report. Behavior Therapist 6:58–59, 1983

Perl M, Westin AB, Peterson LG: The female rape survivor: time-limited group therapy with female/male co-therapists. Journal of Psychosomatic Obstetrics and Gynecology 4:197–205, 1985

Perloff L: Perception of vulnerability to victimization. Journal of Social Issues 39:41–61, 1983

Piaget J: Psychology and Epistemology: Toward a Theory of Knowledge. New York, Viking, 1971

Rachman S: Emotional processing. Behav Res Ther 18:51–60, 1980

Rescorla RA: Variations in the effectiveness of reinforcement and nonreinforcement following prior inhibitory conditioning. Learning and Motivation 2:113–123, 1971

Resick PA: Reactions of female and male victims of rape or robbery (Grant R01-MH37296, final report). Rockville, MD, National Institute of Mental Health, 1986

Resick P: Reactions of female and male victims of rape or robbery (Grant MH37296, final report). Washington, DC, National Institute of Justice, 1987

Resick PA: Reactions of female and male victims of rape or robbery (NIJ Grant 85-IJ-CV-0042, final report). Washington, DC, National Institute of Justice, 1988

Resick PA: Victims of sexual assault, in Victims of Crime: Problems, Policies, and Programs. Edited by Lurigio AJ, Skogan WG, Davis RC. Newbury Park, CA, Sage, 1990, pp 69–86

Resick PA, Schnicke MK: Cognitive Processing Therapy for Sexual Assault Survivors: A Therapist Manual. Newbury Park, CA, Sage (in press)

Resick PA, Calhoun AS, Atkeson BM, et al: Social adjustment in victims of sexual assault. J Consult Clin Psychol 49:705–712, 1981

Resick PA, Jordan CG, Girelli SA, et al: A comparative outcome study of behavioral group therapy for sexual assault victims. Behavior Therapy 19:385–401, 1988

Resick PA, Schnicke MK, Markway G: Relationship between cognitive content and post-traumatic stress disorder. Paper presented at the Association for Advancement of Behavior Therapy, New York, November 1991

Riggs DS, Dancu CV, Gershuny BS, et al: Anger and post traumatic stress disorder in female crime victims. Journal of Traumatic Stress 5:613–625, 1992

Roth S, Newman E: The process of coping with sexual trauma. Journal of Traumatic Stress 4:279–299, 1991

Roth S, Wayland K, Woolsey M: Victimization history and victim-assailant relationships as factors in recovery from sexual assault. Journal of Traumatic Stress 3:169–180, 1990

Rothbaum BO, Foa EB, Riggs DS, et al: A prospective examination of post-traumatic-stress disorder in rape victims. Journal of Traumatic Stress 5:455–475, 1992

Ruch LO, Chandler SM: Sexual assault trauma during the acute phase: an exploratory model and multivariate analysis. J Health Soc Behav 24:184–185, 1983

Ruch LO, Leon JJ: Sexual assault trauma and trauma change. Women Health 8:5–21, 1983

Ruch LO, Chandler SM, Harter RA: Life change and rape impact. J Health Soc Behav 21:248–260, 1980

Sales E, Baum M, Shore B: Victim readjustment following assault. Journal of Social Issues 40:17–36, 1984

Scheppele KL, Bart PB: Through women's eyes: defining danger in the wake of sexual assault. Journal of Social Issues 39:63–81, 1983

Steketee G, Foa EB: Rape victims: post-traumatic stress responses and their treatment. Journal of Anxiety Disorders 1:69–86, 1987

Turner SM: Systematic desensitization of fears and anxiety in rape victims. Paper presented at the Association for the Advancement of Behavior Therapy, San Francisco, CA, 1979

van der Kolk BA: Psychological Trauma. Washington, DC, American Psychiatric Press, 1987

Veronen LJ, Kilpatrick DG: Stress management for rape victims, in Stress Reduction and Prevention. Edited by Meichenbaum D, Jaremko ME. New York, Plenum, 1983, pp 341–374

Wolff R: Systematic desensitization and negative practice to alter the aftereffects of a rape attempt. J Behav Ther Exp Psychiatry 8:423–425, 1977

Wyatt GE, Notgrass GM, Newcomb M: Internal and external mediators of women's rape experiences. Psychology of Women Quarterly 14:153–176, 1990

Zeitlin SB, McNally RJ: Implicit and explicit memory biases for threat in post-traumatic stress disorder. Behav Res Ther 29:451–457, 1991

Afterword

by Robert S. Pynoos, M.D. M.P.H., Editor

Humanity has always been plagued by natural calamities and has perpetrated the most egregious violent harm on itself. Over the course of history, the capacity of human beings to endure and rebound has been evident. Yet the accumulating knowledge about posttraumatic stress reactions indicates that trauma can exact an enormous toll on individuals in terms of private suffering and functional impairment. Trauma may also have a transgenerational legacy in that these disturbances may influence future generations, perhaps through effects on parental character and competence. In addition, traumatic events may also have social and political consequences, extending to alterations of the structure and vital functions of neighborhoods, communities, nations, and the world at large.

These chapters illustrate two current trends: the use of more refined delineation of traumatic exposures and their association with posttraumatic stress symptoms, and an enriched understanding of the interaction of trauma and development throughout the life cycle. As a result, we may gain a better appreciation of the traumatic roots in adolescence or young adulthood of significant historical, political philosophies and assumptions about the social contract. Nowhere is this better illustrated than in the impact of torture and the threat of decapitation on the mind of Machiavelli (de Grazia 1989). Within 9 months of his release from incarceration, Machiavelli enunciated in *The Prince* a set of political principles that has established a place in the proliferation of violence in human affairs (Pynoos 1992).

One difficulty surrounding the diagnosis of posttraumatic stress disorder (PTSD) has been classifying these reactions within a traditional spectrum of normality and pathology. A sociobiological perspective raises the question of the utility to the individual as well as the group of such intense, complex, and often enduring biological, mental, behavioral, and cultural responses as described in the preceding chapters. As Bremner et al. describe in Chapter 3, these biological systems not only govern the immediate response to extreme danger, but also provide for memory processing that permits an extended period of reappraisal. It is as if the individual can neither afford to overassign too many dangers as potentially catastrophic that are not, nor fail to classify correctly those that are.

Traumatized individuals often endure continued vigilance and reactivity to reminders out of proportion to current danger and at great personal cost. However, often enough their prosocial actions to prevent future occurrences may benefit the group or social system. The victim of an airplane disaster may suffer from living in the immediacy of that catastrophe for a prolonged period of time, but his or her persistent efforts to ensure changes in Federal Aviation Administration policy may improve the standards of aviation safety from which we all benefit.

It has been the veterans of the Vietnam War who brought renewed attention in the United States to the psychological insults of war and who, through their perseverance, helped to create a national research and clinical agenda, reflected in the establishment of the Veterans Administration National Center for Posttraumatic Stress Disorders. An unforeseen outcome of the Vietnam PTSD research has been that the methodologies, neurobiological discoveries, and clinical insights have acted as catalysts to improve scientific and clinical approaches to childhood trauma. The ensuing enriched understanding is beginning to return full circle to increase our understanding of the interplay of child and adult trauma, including how the reverberations of childhood trauma may compromise adult recovery. The establishment of the Violence and Traumatic Stress Branch of the National Institute of Mental Health highlights the importance to society of this area of study and represents a commitment to a research and clinical agenda of the highest scientific quality and value.

As these chapters indicate, the field of traumatic stress has become increasingly complex within a relatively short period of time. It is incorporating knowledge from a variety of disciplines, including more sophisticated models from the fields of neurobiology, memory and learning, and child and adult development. The expanded knowledge about traumatic stress is also challenging these fields to take into account the profound effects of traumatic exposures in constructing more comprehensive explanatory models.

It is hard to imagine another field of psychiatry that brings together in such intimacy instantaneous, dramatic biological changes and intense, ongoing mental activities. New investigations into the biology of traumatic stress may uncover biological responses closely associated with specific traumatic features, which may also serve as strong predictors of severity and course. The biological consequences may include not only a propensity for acute reactivity but also slow biological recovery to later traumatic reminders or subsequent stresses. The fact that these biological systems also enhance and extend a period of cognitive reappraisal implies the importance of mechanisms of mental modification in mediating the stress response, not only acutely, but over time.

The inclusion of PTSD in DSM-III (American Psychiatric Association 1980) has led to a decade of research, principally aimed at examining the disorder and mediating variables. There are already signs that this next decade will see increased attention to the refinement and integration of treatment techniques and to comparative studies of treatment efficacy. Because early intervention may prove most efficacious, there will be important public health and ethical issues regarding the allocation of mental health resources for the provision of clinical care. By giving scientific voice to the legacy of trauma, researchers and clinicians in the field of traumatic stress may also help to make prevention more of a societal concern.

REFERENCES

American Psychiatric Association: Diagnostic and Statistical Manual of Mental Disorder, 3rd Edition. Washington, DC, American Psychiatric Association, 1980
de Grazia S: Machiavelli in Hell. Princeton, NJ, Princeton University Press, 1989
Machiavelli N: The Prince. Translated by Bull G. London, Penguin Group, 1961
Pynoos R: Violence, personality, and post-traumatic stress disorder: developmental and political perspectives, in The Mosaic of Contemporary Psychiatry in Perspective. Edited by Kales A, Pierce CM, Greenblatt M. New York, Springer-Verlag, 1992, pp 53–65

Contributors

J. Douglas Bremner, M.D.
Assistant Professor, Department of Psychiatry, Yale University School of Medicine, New Haven, CT

Dennis S. Charney, M.D.
Professor, Department of Psychiatry, Yale University School of Medicine, New Haven, CT; and Chief of Psychiatry Service, West Haven Veterans Administration Medical Center, West Haven, CT

Jonathan Davidson, M.D.
Associate Professor, Psychiatry and Director, Anxiety and Traumatic Stress Program, Duke University Medical Center, Durham, NC

Michael Davis, Ph.D.
Professor, Department of Psychiatry, Yale University School of Medicine, New Haven, CT

Edna B. Foa, Ph.D.
Director, Center for the Treatment and Study of Anxiety; and Professor of Psychiatry, Medical College of Pennsylvania, Philadelphia, PA

David Foy, Ph.D.
Professor of Psychology, Graduate School of Education in Psychology, Pepperdine University, Culver City, CA

Matthew J. Friedman, M.D., Ph.D.
Executive Director, National Center for Post-Traumatic Stress Disorder, Veterans Administration Medical and Regional Office Center, White River Junction, VT

Bruce Kagan, M.D., Ph.D.
Assistant Professor of Psychiatry and Biobehavioral Sciences, University of California-Los Angeles, Los Angeles, CA; and Chief, Molecular Neurophysiology Laboratory, West Los Angeles Veterans Administration Medical Center, Los Angeles, CA

John H. Krystal, M.D.
Assistant Professor, Department of Psychiatry, Yale University School of Medicine, New Haven, CT

Charles R. Marmar, M.D.
Associate Professor of Psychiatry, University of California-San Francisco, San Francisco, CA; and Director, Posttraumatic Stress Disorder Program, San Francisco Veterans Administration Medical Center, San Francisco, CA

Anthony J. Marsella, Ph.D.
Professor, Department of Psychology, University of Hawaii, Honolulu, HI

Robert S. Pynoos, M.D., M.P.H.
Associate Professor, Department of Psychiatry and Biobehavioral Sciences, University of California-Los Angeles, Los Angeles, CA; and Director, Trauma Psychiatry Services, University of California-Los Angeles, Los Angeles, CA

David S. Riggs, Ph.D.
Staff Psychologist, National Center for Posttraumatic Stress Disorder, Boston Veterans Administration Medical Center, Boston, MA

Steven M. Southwick, M.D.
Associate Professor, Department of Psychiatry, Yale University School of Medicine, New Haven, CT

E. Huland Spain, Ph.D.
Health Research Scientist, Matsunaga Research Project, National Center for PTSD, Department of Veteran Affairs, Honolulu, HI

About The Sidran Foundation

The Sidran Foundation, Inc. is a national non-profit organization devoted to education, advocacy, and research on behalf of people with psychiatric disabilities, including individuals who have experienced mental health problems as a result of catastrophic trauma.

Currently available from the Sidran Press, the foundation's publishing division, is *Multiple Personality Disorder from the Inside Out* (1991), Cohen, Giller, and Lynn W., editors. In this acclaimed book, 146 people who have MPD, and their significant others, reveal the complex issues of diagnosis, therapy, and maintaining personal relationships. *Dissociative Disorders: A Clinical Review*, edited by David Spiegel, M.D., is a state-of-the-art review of the field of dissociative disorders, encompassing: definitions of terms, epidemiology (studies of incidence and distribution), etiology (studies of cause), the courses of the disorders, and treatment approaches. Also available is *The Way of the Journal: A Journal Therapy Workbook for Healing*, by Kathleen Adams, M.A., a therapist who teaches the use of reflective writing as a therapeutic process for trauma survivors. *My Mom Is Different*, by Deborah Sessions, an illustrated book for children, is an ideal vehicle with which to introduce the concept of multiplicity to the young children of newly-diagnosed parents. The Sidran Press also makes available two general informational brochures—*Multiple Personality and Dissociation* and *Traumatic Memories*—for patients, family members, and the lay public. Single copies of these brochures are available at no charge; packages of 50 brochures each may be ordered for a small fee. Forthcoming titles include *PTSD: Survivors' Views of Combat Trauma* and *Knowing the Ropes: Advocating Effectively for Consumers of Psychiatric Services*.

The foundation provides information for consumers, families, and professionals and maintains lists of therapists, support networks, publications, and other resources in the area of trauma-induced emotional disabilities. *The Sidran Foundation Bookshelf*, a direct-mail book and tape distribution service, offers a carefully selected, annotated list of print and audio-visual materials about traumatic abuse and dissociation.

For further information, or for a *Sidran Foundation Bookshelf* catalog, contact:

    The Sidran Foundation and Press
    2328 W. Joppa Road, Suite 15
    Lutherville, MD 21093
    (410) 825-8888 phone; (410) 337-0747 fax